Real Lives, Celebrity Stories

Real Lives, Celebrity Stories

Narratives of Ordinary and Extraordinary People across Media

Edited by

Bronwen Thomas and Julia Round

B L O O M S B U R Y

NEW YORK · LONDON · NEW DELHI · SYDNEY

Bloomsbury Academic

An imprint of Bloomsbury Publishing Inc

1385 Broadway   50 Bedford Square
New York   London
NY 10018   WC1B 3DP
USA   UK

www.bloomsbury.com

Bloomsbury is a registered trade mark of Bloomsbury Publishing Plc

First published 2014

© Bronwen Thomas and Julia Round, 2014

Library of Congress Cataloging-in-Publication Data
A catalog record for this book is available from the Library of Congress

ISBN: HB: 978-1-4411-0238-6
ePDF: 978-1-4411-4618-2
ePub: 978-1-4411-9715-3

Typeset by Integra Software Service Pvt. Ltd.
Printed and bound in the United States of America

Contents

Introduction

Bronwen Thomas and Julia Round
Bournemouth University, UK

While it has long been recognized that narrativizing or storying the self has become a major preoccupation of contemporary culture, very little attention has been paid thus far to the precise forms these narratives take, or to considering their impact *across* media. Most studies of the representation of "real lives" or "celebrity culture" tend to be media-specific, for example focusing on the Hollywood star system, or the emergence and prevalence of reality TV. Moreover, few studies to date look at real people in the media and celebrities alongside one another, when as this volume demonstrates, they are increasingly interconnected and interdependent.

This volume adopts a new approach, offering case studies from across a wide range of media, and drawing on narrative and linguistic theory, as well as on theories and models derived from media, film, and cultural studies. The volume also includes reflections from researchers working directly with real-life stories (Lambrou) and from practitioners whose job it is to script, direct, and produce the "real" (Batty). Some of the chapters (e.g., Batty, Bradley, and Kimber) deal with how the presentation of the self depends on the repetition of narrative structures that come to seem natural or obvious to us, whereas other chapters (Lambrou, Pearson, and Bronwen Thomas) explore how audiences and "ordinary people" respond to, are affected by, but also help co-create the stories they encounter. The volume also addresses the responsibilities that come with storytelling in the context of representing "real lives," and the ethical and political issues resulting from the attempt to impose structure, perspective, and meaning on events and individuals that may defy comprehension (see, e.g., Lambrou and Kimber). The chapters in this volume also consider the transformative potential of narrative, helping foreground and celebrate the everyday and the quotidian (Bradley, Round, and Grennan), and to provide individuals with a language or "script" that helps them deal with the new and the perplexing (Sue Thomas, Batty).

One of the objectives of the volume is to try and dispel the sense of mutual suspicion that still divides narrative theory from media and cultural studies. Narrative theorists often accuse media and cultural studies of "text blindness" (Hauksen 2004), eschewing any kind of textual analysis or attention to form, and also refusing to make any kind of evaluative judgment about aesthetic value. Meanwhile, media theorists are rightly critical of classical narratology and its formalist preoccupation with "text." In this context, postclassical narratology has shown a willingness to engage with narrative affect and emotion, drawing on work in the cognitive sciences to explore how theory of mind can help us move from text to storyworld (Herman 2002) and from close reading to understanding narrative as an intersubjective experience (Herman 2003, Palmer 2004). Moreover, the influence of linguistics and stylistics has seen a shift toward approaching narrative as situated discourse, resulting in far greater attention being paid to the social and cultural contexts in which narratives are found.

The impact of new media and digital technologies has contributed significantly to overcoming many critical and conceptual divisions, and to eroding the notion of fixed boundaries between disciplines, but also between fundamental categories such as fiction/nonfiction, author/reader, and self/other. Excited by the possibilities that digital technologies have presented for storytelling, postclassical narratology (e.g., Ryan 2004) has revisited its structuralist roots to argue that it is uniquely placed to explore narrative structures across media, and to demonstrate how narrativization is embedded even in the most seemingly factual of discourses. Contemporary narrative theory also increasingly responds to the affordances of emerging new media, particularly as a means of gaining greater awareness and understanding of the role of the reader/audiences, and of accessing narratives that once would only have been available orally to a small or restricted group of people. Transmedia storytelling offers audiences the opportunity to engage with a text in various forms according to their own preferences. The text(s) thus becomes a unique experience that varies from person to person, demonstrating the importance of considering narrative structure alongside audience demand and response. In grander terms, the move from localized storytelling to broadcasting back to narrowcasting demonstrates the mobility and multiplicity of today's audience(s) and their effect on the texts they consume; these are considerations that this collection aims to incorporate into its discussion.

The medium of the text is also increasingly a consideration, regarding audience, structure, and content. In this regard, new media have taken traditional means of representation in exciting directions. The possibilities for representing the self visually have long been a subject of fascination in multiple genres of high and low art. From the self-portrait to the *mise en scène*, visual means of representing experience have problematized and interrogated the notion of one's self and one's story. The use of iconic celebrity images in high art (such as the work of Andy Warhol) or the appearance of celebrity figures in comics (see, e.g., Shirley 2005) can take multiple forms, from the subversive to the idealized, and a divide between person and persona is often exploited. Conversely, the rise of autobiography in visual narratives such as comics has demonstrated that a fascination with telling one's own story and engaging with issues of the "everyday" crosses media and genre. Originally a staple of British and American underground "comix", autobiography has risen to become a central theme in these countries' mainstream comics today. Some of the earliest comics criticism (Eisner 1985, McCloud 1993) discusses the impact of caricature and recognition on reader identity. Film adaptations of titles such as *Persepolis* (2007) or *American Splendor* (2003) have further extended the reach of diverse visual methods of storying the self within a wider cross-feed of ideas across media, including fine art and performance spaces.

Both "old" and "new" media present us with endless tales of "People Like Us" and the fantasy that sharing your story with millions of others can be rewarding and transformative, bringing instant celebrity and validation. Contemporary representations of reality such as those that have come to define MTV perform an important function, especially for young Millennials, providing them with a kind of "identity workbook" (Klein 2013) through which they may generate and negotiate their sense of their place in the world. The digital revolution has prompted much theorizing about the ways in which identity and a sense of self are created through narrative, and the extent to which new media forms may allow individuals to play out versions of themselves, to create a "second self" (Turkle 2005) and gain a sense of empowerment. However, there has also been condemnation and criticism of the potential for exploitation that these seeming freedoms may bring, creating a "freakshow" (Dovey 2000) mentality in which often vulnerable individuals may be encouraged to expose themselves to ridicule.

The impact of digital technologies and the rise of reality TV have also led theorists to revisit and question the idea of celebrity itself. Instant and "micro" celebrities have emerged from social media, whereas "structured reality" shows and celebrity magazines and online gossip sites help stimulate interest in the "behind the scenes" lives and lifestyles of these individuals. This has led to increasing discussion surrounding the notion of privacy in the public sphere, and to concerns about the extent to which turning every aspect of a person's life into a story is either healthy or desirable. Richard Dyer's work on celebrity culture brings together a range of critical approaches to explore the ways in which "star" personas are constructed, and reflects upon the consequences of these processes for audiences and fans (1980, 2004). It has subsequently been suggested, for example by Turner (2004), that much of the current fascination with celebrity compensates for the loss of community and religion in contemporary society, leading to a reliance on parasocial relationships with screen personalities, and to the idea that the self can be manufactured and optimized through mediation. Turner identifies a "demotic turn" (82) in contemporary culture in which the explosion of the ordinary across our screens offers validation and a comforting sense of ritual that not only reflects but also constructs how we come to conceive of the everyday and the real.

However, many theorists also recognize that the attitudes of audiences and fans may be less than reverential at times, as they may take pleasure in seeing their icons caught unawares and seeing the extraordinary reduced to the level of the ordinary (Ellis 2007). Indeed, they may even participate in activities that both celebrate and mock the objects of their devotion and affection. Spoof accounts for celebrities on Twitter and My Space amongst others provide a means for fans to play with and contest the onscreen or "official" versions of these people that we are offered by publicists and the like, whereas fanfiction and fanvids often go further, creating alternate universes in which the age, class, sexuality, and even ethnicity of the subjects can be reimagined in potentially subversive ways. Meanwhile, digital natives and the YouTube generation may be forgiven for taking for granted the ability to customize and personalize content online, and for instinctively viewing with suspicion narratives that present themselves as authentic or true.

Of course, any discussion of how the notion of identity has shifted from something that is fixed or continuous to something that is radically unstable, fluid, and performed must be informed by postmodern and gender theories. Many of the chapters in the volume make reference to the debates and discussions arising out of this, and recognize that the kinds of personal narratives we find across contemporary cultural forms may be fragmented and highly self-reflexive. The postmodern and poststructuralist turn that underpins much of contemporary culture is epitomized by the way we storify ourselves. Jean Baudrillard's (1981) work on the simulacra seems applicable here, and telling "my story" can perhaps be viewed as a process of reproduction that may reflect or pervert reality, or even create or simulate an entirely new reality. The creation of a simulated self (or the "self-as-brand") that replaces the "real" is of course most apparent in celebrity culture but such synecdoche is practiced too in everyday life. A move away from essentialist definitions underpins much contemporary cultural theory, for example as can be seen in Judith Butler's (1990, 1993) work on gender performativity, which suggests that the gendered self is little more than a collection of performances and that identity becomes fragmented, mobile, and performed. The consequences for personal understanding and identity politics are extreme, and such issues seem especially pertinent for reality TV and transformative narratives. The self becomes a site of ideological struggle whose performance enacts and creates identity. This philosophical argument can also be found in other contemporary cultural theories, such as Julia Kristeva's (1982) discussion of abjection as taking place at the border of the self. Kristeva argues that abject imagery discomfits by transgressing and disrupting boundaries between the subject and the object, and confronting us with this knowledge and the potential for collapse. Narrative in this context becomes a safety net, a strategy for constructing and cohering identity around events, ideologies, and social practices.

In the opening section of the volume, "Stories We Live By," the chapters consider how familiar story structures and metaphors help us navigate new narratives and genres. Sue Thomas focuses on how metaphors of cyberspace have evolved to both shape and respond to our relationship with and experience of the virtual. This approach serves to expose how subtle shifts have occurred in the ways in which language helps us to imagine and communicate the sense of identity, space, and place that we discover online. Finding that many of these metaphors derive from nature, Sue Thomas argues that they are becoming increasingly spiritual and esoteric as we move beyond wires and move many of our activities into the mysterious and yet-to-be-defined realm of the "cloud."

Craig Batty argues for the importance of the character journey in understanding factual programs. Analyzing a range of examples taken from reality TV, he demonstrates how important the affective dimension is to understanding the narrative structure of factual shows and why they attract such engaged and devoted audiences. Batty argues that both practitioners and theorists can learn a great deal from recognizing the centrality of the character journey, and from recognizing that it functions as much more than a structuring mechanism.

Narrative at its most basic is often defined as a movement from one state of affairs to another, resulting in a transformation for the central character, which also often brings about change in the world he or she inhabits. In the second section of the volume, the chapters focus on contemporary variants of these transformative narratives. Peri Bradley's discussion of transformative TV considers the ideologies inflicted upon and represented by the body in shows such as *Supersize vs Superskinny*. Through a close reading of the codes used to construct the contestants, alongside discussion of the social and ideological context, Bradley argues that audiences and contestants are directed toward a reading of transgressive bodies as disobedient and that their reclamation by society is an act with ideological and political consequences.

Simon Grennan's chapter then considers three participatory works of art with a social message. Grennan argues that, although these works come from diverse artistic precedents, the shared discourse they exist within means that they rely upon similar assumptions about the audience and the self regarding the narrativizing of "real life" as art. Using Goffman's (1959) theories of self-enactment, Grennan suggests that their shared discursive methodology allows these artworks to not only represent but also reenact the matrix of both social constraint and self-constraint and opportunities that we live within.

Julia Round's chapter draws on adaptation theory to explore the ways in which the life of comics artist Harvey Pekar, told over four decades in *American Splendor*, has subsequently been retold and reimagined across media in ways that extend and transform the *American Splendor* story for new audiences. Round applies Labov and Waletsky's (1967) model of narrative to show how the comic book adapts the everyday experiences of "our man" into a familiar narrative shape: providing narrative distance and objectifying the self while simultaneously subverting the visual style of traditional comics. She then explores how the movie based on the comics plays with convention and mixes media to perpetuate this problematizing of the act of documenting the life, and examines how Harvey himself reflected on the movie experience in a subsequent collection of comics. Round argues that the *American Splendor* story told across media presents us with the need to develop a richer notion of intertextuality, which is multidirectional and allows for an ongoing interaction between the subject and the audience.

In the third section of the volume, the chapters focus on the politics and ethics of representing the "real." In addition to exploring issues of reliability and authenticity in representing real lives or real events, all three chapters also consider how the affective responses of those exposed to the storifying of the real may have profound and ongoing implications.

Marina Lambrou's chapter reflects on her experiences of conducting ethnographic research involving the personal narratives of survivors and those affected by the terrorist attacks in New York and London. She documents the process by which the research was conducted, and the impact that working with these narratives had; not just on those who told their stories, but also on the researcher who experienced first hand their re-living of their traumas. For those involved in working with real people and their stories, the chapter provides an instructive insight into the rewards and the challenges of this kind of work.

Darren Lilleker analyzes the rhetoric used in Barack Obama's autobiographies with reference to their differing intentions and audience. Lilleker discusses the ways in which Obama storifies his individual experiences into the universal sphere, relating these to political metanarratives and identifying a range of different narrative approaches (e.g., event-driven, explanatory, and so forth) that are used to do this. He argues that the Obama "brand" hinges on an implied authenticity driven by the structuring of his arguments around events, which are then explained and evaluated to reach a teleological loaded conclusion: that Obama's personal narratives could be about any black man (and perhaps even any man), which makes them integral in connecting broad and diverse sections of the American society to his vision of a new politics.

Shaun Kimber's chapter offers a comparative analysis of four realist films based on the Henry Lee Lucas story. Kimber situates these films in their historical and cultural context and reflects upon the differences between the narratives with respect to the critical theory that defines the serial killer and the uses of this figure in terms of genre, historical context, and cultural concerns. The rise of the serial killer as a celebrity figure (individualized, notorious, even glamorized) can be seen in both news and entertainment media today and Kimber's chapter engages with this development through close reading of the variations between these four versions of the same story.

In the concluding section of the volume, the attention turns to celebrities and their lives and afterlives as told through official and unofficial, individual and collective accounts. Both chapters in this section also explore the ways in which fan communities construct their own narratives of celebrity lives, often explicitly contesting official versions, and subverting official sources to explore and document their responses and memories.

Bronwen Thomas's chapter reflects upon the strategies used by fans in Real Person Fanfiction, situating this practice within key debates surrounding authenticity, celebrity, and the dominant ideologies of sexuality and discourse. Thomas challenges condemnatory and derogatory attitudes toward such fiction and instead approaches these texts as part of a situated critical practice. She demonstrates the joy of metafictional play as a key aspect of fandom, using close readings of RPF taken from *Torchwood* and *The Social Network* to demonstrate that such narratives frequently display a high level of reflexivity and critical thought.

Roberta Pearson's chapter explores the posthumous remembering of Frank Sinatra across a wide range of discourses, taking in family histories, official and unofficial commemorations in various locations claiming some kind of connection to Sinatra, tourist sites, walks, and even commemorative stamps. Her focus is primarily on what she calls "commodified public memory"— sanctioned forms that may exploit the commercial exploitation of Sinatra's memory, but which are contested and fought over constantly. Pearson argues that celebrity studies and the emerging field of memory studies may fruitfully learn from one another in confronting the complex questions raised when it comes to trying to document and seek out connections between public and private, individual and collective memories of well-known and well-loved personalities such as Sinatra.

This collection brings together diverse critical approaches and primary material in order to interrogate the multiple and variable methods used to narrativize life. By reflecting upon audiences, narrative strategies, and engaging in close analysis of the characteristics of the resulting texts, it suggests that stories of both real and celebrity lives share many of the same motivations, methods, and results when it comes to their creation, sustenance, and reception.

References

Baudrillard, Jean. 1994 [1981]. *Simulacra and Simulacrum*. Trans. Sheila Glaser. Ann Arbor, MI: University of Michigan Press.

Butler, Judith. 1990. *Gender Trouble*. London: Routledge.

Butler, Judith. 1993. *Bodies that Matter*. London: Routledge.

Dovey, Jon. 2000. *Freakshow: First Person Media and Factual Television*. London: Pluto Press.

Dyer, Richard. 1980. *Stars*. London: BFI.

Dyer, Richard. 2004. *Heavenly Bodies*. London: BFI.

Eisner, Will. 1985. *Comics and Sequential Art*. Tamarac, FL: Poorhouse Press.

Ellis, John. 2007. "Stars as a Cinematic Phenomenon." In *Stardom and Celebrity: A Reader*, edited by Sean Redmond and Su Holmes, 90–97. London: Sage.

Goffman, Erving. 1959. *The Presentation of Self in Everyday Life*. New York: Anchor Books.

Hauksen, Liv. 2004. "Coda: Textual Theory and Blind Spots in Media Studies." In *Narrative Across Media: The Languages of Storytelling*, edited by Marie-Laure Ryan, 391–402. Lincoln: University of Nebraska Press.

Herman, David. 2002. *Story Logic: Problems and Possibilities of Narrative*. Lincoln: University of Nebraska Press.

Herman, David. (ed.) 2003. *Narrative Theory and the Cognitive Sciences*. Stanford: CSLI Publications.

Klein, Amanda Ann. 2013. MTV reality programming and the labor of identity construction. http://www.cstonline.tv/mtv [accessed May 10, 2013]

Kristeva, Julia. 1982. *Powers of Horror*. New York: Columbia University Press

Labov, William, and Joshua Waletzky. 1967. "Narrative analysis: Oral versions of personal experience." In *Essays on the Verbal and Visual Arts*, edited by J. Helm, 12–44. Seattle: University of Washington Press.

McCloud, Scott. 1993. *Understanding Comics*. New York: Paradox Press.

Palmer, Alan. 2004. *Fictional Minds*. Lincoln: University of Nebraska Press.

Ryan, Marie-Laure. (ed.) 2004. *Narrative Across Media*. Lincoln: University of Nebraska Press.

Shirley, Ian. 2005. *Can Rock and Roll Save the World?* London: SAF Publishing.

Turkle, Sherry. 2005. *The Second Self: Computers and the Human Spirit*. Cambridge, MA: MIT Press.

Turner, Graeme. 2004. *Understanding Celebrity*. London: Sage.

Part 1

Stories We Live By

1

Storying Cyberspace: Narratives and Metaphors

Sue Thomas
Independent Researcher

Introduction

Cyberspace has given rise to many new terms. A surprising number of them, such as "information superhighway" and "surfing the internet," are rooted in real-world metaphors that have been re-purposed for the digital. This practice seems to have evolved from the imperative to make sense of the new and highly abstract experience of being online by seeking comparable experiences in the physical world. This chapter tracks the history of the cyberspace metaphor and considers its impact on the narrative of our lives online.

It is useful to begin with a clarification of the meaning of the term *cyberspace* itself, especially since it had two different beginnings. The word was first coined by science fiction writer William Gibson in a 1982 short story "Burning Chrome," then later popularized in his debut novel, *Neuromancer*, published 2 years later. The story goes that his imagination was fired by the existence of the internet even though he had not yet accessed it. The internet had come into being in 1969 when two computers on the West Coast of the USA—one in Los Angeles and the other in Menlo Park, near San Francisco—were connected to form what was then called the Arpanet. By the time Gibson heard about it, the network had spread beyond the United States but was still mostly used only by the military and some university-based scientists. In 1994, however, the World Wide Web was launched by Tim Berners-Lee and suddenly an obscure technical facility was transformed into the virtual space familiar to us today. So, the concept of "cyberspace" began as an element in a science fiction tale but its use became more widespread when John Perry Barlow, a lyricist for the Grateful Dead and early internet enthusiast, adopted it to make a conceptual connection between Gibson's imaginary place and the "real" space of the online world. It is not known when Barlow first began using it in this way, but it was certainly widely accepted by 1996 when he responded to the proposed Telecommunications Reform Act by authoring "A Declaration of the Independence of Cyberspace" in which he outlined the ephemeral nature of this new environment: "Cyberspace consists of transactions, relationships, and thought itself, arrayed like a standing wave in the web of our communications. Ours is a world that is both everywhere and nowhere, but it is not where bodies live" (Barlow 1996). The document made the case that the new terrain operated beyond traditional law: "Your legal concepts of property, expression, identity, movement, and context do not apply to us. They are all based on matter, and there is no matter here" (Barlow 1996).

Metaphors

Barlow's sentiments typify the way that many internet users have used metaphors to make sense of the abstract space of the internet. According to Stanford psychologist Lera Boroditsky, the job of the metaphor is "to provide relational structure to an abstract domain by importing it (by analogy) from a more concrete domain" (Boroditsky 2000: 3) and there is certainly no domain more abstract than cyberspace. The work of George Lakoff and Mark Johnson provides a useful tool with which to examine this process. In 1980 they concluded that "Since much of our social reality is understood in metaphorical terms, and since our conception of the physical world is partly metaphorical, metaphor plays a very significant role in determining what is real for us" (Lakoff and Johnson 1980: 146). "Many of our activities are metaphorical in nature," they wrote, explaining that

> The metaphorical concepts that characterize those activities structure our present reality. New metaphors have the power to create a new reality. This can begin to happen when we start to comprehend our experience in terms of a metaphor, and it becomes a deeper reality when we begin to act in terms of it.
>
> Lakoff and Johnson 1980: 146

Similarly, in cyberspace our logical selves may not see what happens in cyberspace as "real," but the way we receive it subconsciously can lead us to interact with it as if it were "real." In the virtual realm, not only do metaphors play a significant role in determining what is real for us, but they also determine how the ephemeral unreal can be shaped into the real. To examine how this works in practice, let us look at four kinds of metaphors, which, according to Lakoff and Johnson, lie at the heart of the process. They are described as structural, orientational, ontological, and container, and examples of each can also be found in the discourse of cyberspace.

Structural metaphors occur where one concept is metaphorically structured in terms of another. The authors provide the example of the metaphor that "ARGUMENT IS WAR" (Lakoff and Johnson 1980: 14) based on the notion that popular discourse about argument uses the vocabulary of war. For example, in an argument one might "attack a position" or "gain ground." We know that an argument is not the same thing as a war, but we may understand the process of an argument through terms normally used for the process of a war. An example of a structural metaphor related to cyberspace might be "cyberspace is an ocean in which one can surf, dive, or be immersed."

Orientational metaphors take structural metaphors a step ahead. Rather than structure one concept in terms of another, they organize whole systems of concepts in relation to one another. Generally, orientational metaphors tend to be spatial in nature, using concepts like up-down, in-out, front-back, on-off, and deep-shallow. The authors explain that "these spatial orientations arise from the fact that we have bodies of the sort we have and that they function as they do in our physical environment" (Lakoff and Johnson 1980: 14). They give the example of HAPPY IS UP; SAD IS DOWN, for example "I'm feeling *up*. You're in *high* spirits. He's really *low* these days. I *fell* into a depression." Such metaphorical orientations are not arbitrary, say Lakoff and Johnson, because

> They have a basis in our physical and cultural experience. Though the polar oppositions up-down, in-out etc., are physical in nature, the orientational metaphors based on them can vary from culture to culture. For example, in some cultures the future is in front of us, whereas in others it is in back.
>
> Lakoff and Johnson 1980: 14

Orientational metaphors are crucial in determining the landscape of cyberspace. Obvious examples are logging on and off the internet, going in and out of chatrooms, and searching inside files. They help us understand where we are, but ontological metaphors clarify our relationship with those surroundings: "When things are not clearly discrete or bounded, we still categorise them as such, e.g., mountains, street corners, hedges, etc. Such ways of viewing physical phenomena are needed to satisfy certain purposes that we have: locating mountains, meeting at street corners, trimming hedges" (Lakoff and Johnson 1980: 23).

Another way to put this might be that in order to *use* the world as we experience it, we need to have a sense of it as a collection of bounded objects that "make physical phenomena discrete just as we are: entities bounded by a surface" (Lakoff and Johnson 1980: 25). However, ontological metaphors can only serve a limited range of purposes because "merely viewing a nonphysical thing as an entity or substance does not allow us to comprehend very much about it" (Lakoff and Johnson 1980: 27). Lakoff and Johnson illustrate their point with the example THE MIND IS AN ENTITY, which might be expressed, they propose, as THE MIND IS A MACHINE:

> *We're still trying to grind out the solution to this equation.*
> *My mind just isn't operating today.*
> *Boy, the wheels are turning now!*
> *I'm a little rusty today*
>
> Lakoff and Johnson 1980: 27

Cyberspace is itself an ontological metaphor because the term "space" assumes a physical location, giving rise to remarks like, "I spend too much time in cyberspace."

Once we accept that cyberspace is a place, we can populate it with container metaphors. We ourselves are containers, with an inside and an outside, and we are able to move in and out of other containers. Where there are no clear boundaries, we define them so that we can quantify their size or the amount of substance they contain. Lakoff and Johnson give the example of a tub of water: "When you get into the tub, you get into the water. Both the tub and the water are viewed as containers, but of different sorts. The tub is a CONTAINER OBJECT, while the water is a CONTAINER SUBSTANCE" (Lakoff and Johnson 1980: 30). If this is so, an internet chatroom might be seen as a container; however, is it a container object or a container substance? Most likely, it is a container substance and the hardware that enables it—the routers, servers, cables, etc.—form the container object. However, unlike the bathtub, which is clearly visible and tangible, the infrastructure of the internet is increasingly hidden. Indeed, we are more likely to describe it as the *cloud*, another container substance metaphor, rather than confront the technicalities of the networked objects that serve it.

So where exactly is the chatroom and what happens if I go "into" it? Of course, there is no "room" and I have not physically "entered" anything, but a metaphor that allows me to imagine I am moving through space while sitting at my computer helps me make the cognitive adjustment necessary for "meeting" my colleague via the network. Once it is established that we are together in something mutually understood as a "room," other constructions can quickly follow so that soon there is a sense of a "door" through which we may enter and leave, and perhaps even virtual "furniture" where we can sit down and make ourselves comfortable, as we do in the virtual world of Second Life. Soon, there is a shared space with a strong sense of the physical and appropriate conventions of behavior will soon follow, all generated from the mutual agreement that, for our purposes, this real-time sequence of programing code might be called a "room."

Since the publication of *Metaphors We Live By*, a number of theorists have built on Lakoff and Johnson's work, now widely called conceptual metaphor theory, or, in some cases, sought to dispute it. For example, context-limited simulation theory is based on a perceptual simulation model of language use and interpretation developed by Barsalou (1999), which focuses on the neural system and upon nuances of expression, perception, and feeling. This approach is especially useful for the interpretation of feelings and situations that are complex, difficult to express, and perhaps in a state of flux (Ritchie 2006). A discourse dynamics framework is underpinned by two principles about language, thought and culture—their inseparable inter-connectedness and their dynamic nature. This approach, drawn largely from research by Lynne Cameron (2006), recognizes that complex dynamic systems such as language and culture operate on multiple scales and levels, from the millisecond to millennia, and from the individual to the international, and provides a framework with which to map different types of metaphor phenomena. Vyvyan Evans (2006) contributes another theory, that of Lexical Concepts and Cognitive Models, which models the nature of conventional meaning associated with words and seeks to understand the ways in which words combine to produce utterances. Metaphor provides resonance within that process as a way to express communicative intentions. Gerard Steen (2008) calls for a three-dimensional model of metaphor that contests Lakoff and Johnson's proposal that most metaphors are produced metaphorically, that is, by a cross-domain mapping involving some form of comparison, by asking an important question: is metaphor produced or received as *deliberately* metaphorical, or not? He argues that it is likely that most deliberate metaphor is processed metaphorically (by comparison) as opposed to non-deliberate metaphor, which is processed by categorization.

Although we may not see what happens in cyberspace as "real," the way we use metaphors to think about it can make it real because "similarities based on conventional metaphors are ... *real in our culture*, since conventional metaphors partly define what we find real" (Lakoff and Johnson 1980: 153). And in relation to cyberspace "Since much of our social reality is understood in metaphorical terms, and since our conception of the physical world is partly metaphorical, metaphor plays a very significant role in determining what is real for us" (Lakoff and Johnson 1980: 146). Approaching the notion of metaphor from another direction, new media critic N. Katherine Hayles reminds us in *Writing Machines* that traditionally metaphor has been defined as a verbal figure, but when used via symbol-processing machines such as computers "the transfer takes place not between one word and another but rather between a symbol (more properly, a network of symbols) and material apparatus" (Hayles 2002: 22). To account for this process she proposes the term material metaphor, "a term that foregrounds the traffic between words and physical artefacts" (Hayles 2002: 22). Hayles' main concern is with the book and so she uses the notion of material metaphor to discuss the impact of digital texts upon the metaphoric network of reading and writing, but it can also be applied to many of the activities we undertake in cyberspace as we seek to comprehend its relationship to physicality. The term "surfing the internet," for example, is common amongst web users around the world irrespective of whether they themselves have ever surfed, and indeed its origin is claimed by a land-locked librarian from the town of Syracuse, New York.

Surfing the internet

In 1990, Jean Armour Polly was working at the Liverpool Public Library near Syracuse when she was asked to write an article explaining the internet to readers of the Wilson Library Bulletin. The journal had sensed an upswell of interest in the topic, and Polly's reputation as a technological innovator within the library service made her the obvious choice to write it. She decided to start with an account of a typical trip around the internet:

> Today I'll travel to Minnesota, Texas, California, Cleveland, New Zealand, Sweden, and England. I'm not frantically packing, and I won't pick up any frequent flyer mileage. In fact, I'm sipping cocoa at my Macintosh. My trips will be electronic, using the computer on my desk, communications software, a modem, and a standard phone line. [...] I'll be using the Internet, the global network of computers and their interconnections, which lets me skip like a stone across oceans and continents and control computers at remote sites.
>
> Polly 1993

She was keen to find the right title for the piece, something appropriate for an activity that was still so new there was no single term to describe it:

> In casting about for a title for the article, I weighed many possible metaphors. I wanted something that expressed the fun I had using the Internet, as well as hit on the skill, and yes, endurance necessary to use it well. I also needed something that would evoke a sense of randomness, chaos, and even danger. I wanted something fishy, net-like, nautical.
>
> Polly 1990

At that moment her gaze fell on the mouse-mat she was using. It was a gift from Steve Cisler, leader of the Apple Library User's Group in Cupertino, California, and the organizer of an online discussion group about libraries and computers where Polly was a moderator. She had no connections with surfer culture and was not even a keen swimmer, but the metaphor came to her as a form of cultural flotsam and she was inspired to grab it. Later, she wrote of the mouse-mat "It pictured a surfer on a big wave. 'Information Surfer' it said. 'Eureka,' I said, and had my metaphor" (Polly 1990). Her article, "Surfing the Internet," was published in print in June 1992 and that December she made it available online, where it was downloaded over 500 times in the first 14 hours.

Information superhighway

The early 1990s was a period of rapid growth for the internet and it became clear even before the World Wide Web became widely available in 1994 that issues of governance, commerce, and law were becoming pressing. But how could governments legislate for a nonexistent space?

The search for suitable metaphors became urgent. Then in December 1993, 9 months after "Surfing the Internet" was published, the then US Vice-President Al Gore gave an address to the National Press Club in which he provided the influential journalists collected there with a term that would come to dominate writing and discourse about the internet for several years to follow. Explaining new legislation to open up opportunities for the telecommunications industries, Gore drew a picture of the time when transport networks were vitally important for commerce. But today, he continued, "commerce rolls not just on asphalt highways but along *information highways*" (Gore 1993). Knowingly or not, in using the term "information highway" he was echoing a very similar phrase,

"Electronic Super Highway," which had been coined by experimental video artist Nam June Paik 20 years earlier in 1974. Paik was born in Seoul in 1932 and moved to New York in 1964.

In 1974, the Rockefeller Foundation hired him to provide a vision document for its Art Program. The result, inspired by both the interstate system and the then infant internet, predicted that

> The building of new Electronic Super Highways will become an even huger enterprise. Assuming we connect New York with Los Angeles by means of an electronic telecommunication network that operates in strong transmission ranges, as well as with continental satellites, wave guides, bundled coaxial cable, and later also via laser beam fiber optics the expenditure would be about the same as for a moon landing, except that the benefits in term (*sic*) of by-products would be greater.
>
> Paik 1974

In the same document, the artist also coined the term "broadband communication network."

Very few people today credit a Korean video artist with the origination of one of the most powerful internet metaphors. Most imagine that it first appeared in Al Gore's speech but in fact neither was the sole originator. Rather, the term is a fusion of the two: Paik's "Electronic Super Highway" with Gore's "Information Highway," producing "Information Superhighway." Until his death in 2006, Nam June Paik forcefully defended his origination of the term but his idea had come too early for mass adoption, whereas Gore had given his speech just at a time when opinion-makers were looking for a foundational story for the internet. In a period when the uncertain phenomenon of the internet seemed to threaten many established business practices, it was frequently interpreted as a rough and unnavigable wilderness. Al Gore offered a guiding hand. Americans were well-accustomed to pioneer imagery; they knew exactly what it meant to cut new routes across hostile territory, and they knew all about cars and trucks. When Gore proclaimed that soon there would be not just narrow paths leading into the darkness, but entire highways through the internet, he offered some urgently needed reassurance:

> Today, commerce rolls not just on asphalt highways but along information highways... These are highways carrying information rather than people or goods. And I'm not talking about just one eight-lane turnpike. I mean a collection of Interstates and feeder roads made up of different materials in the

same way that roads can be concrete or macadam—or gravel. Some highways will be made up of fiber optics. Others will be built out of coaxial or wireless. But—a key point—they must be and will be two way roads.

Gore 1993

His vision was to create a high-speed network to connect every home and every business, and the main imperative for his talk was the need to "unscramble the legal, regulatory and financial problems that have thus far threatened our ability to complete such a network" (Gore 1993). But he also added a warning:

> If we allow the information superhighway to bypass the less fortunate sectors of our society—even for an interim period—we will find that the information rich will get richer while the information poor get poorer with no guarantee that everyone will be on the network at some future date.

Gore 1993

This vision powerfully connected with his audience. Chris Anderson would later write in *The Economist*: "ubiquitous, open networking seems as fundamental to civilisation's needs in the first half of the 21st century as ubiquitous, open roads did in the first half of the 20th" (Anderson 1995).

The growing interest in cyberspace metaphors was driven by the need to understand and quantify the impact of new technologies upon society, culture and politics, linguistics and philosophy, literature, music and art, business, economics, and law; the growing numbers of interface designers, a new profession, were anxious for advice on how to create the most effective user experience; marketers wanted to know how to promote and sell goods and services online, and educationalists and trainers were keen to understand the most appropriate pedagogy for the wired learner. As Al Gore had demonstrated, the right metaphor could be a powerful commercial and political tool at a time when public understanding of the internet was very limited. Not everyone, however, agreed with the mechanistic notion of the superhighway. In 1994 libertarian Esther Dyson wrote:

> The fashion right now, one I follow, is to think of the Internet as a living environment, a place for societies, communities, and institutions to grow—rather than as something to be constructed, a superhighway for example. That leads to appropriate metaphors, looking at the Net as something to be cultivated and nurtured rather than built or engineered. The guiding metaphor is evolution.

Dyson Release 2.0 1997

However, while politicians, corporations, and educators sought to identify the right metaphors for their own agendas, ordinary internet users were developing their own interpretations of cyberspace.

Cyberspace metaphors

In 1998, interface researchers Maglio and Matlock (1998: 1) argued that the particular language people use when talking about web activities "is metaphorical and is motivated by basic image schemata which emerge from embodied experience." They found differences between experienced and inexperienced web users in the way they talked about their web actions, but their data showed that "even novice web users conceive of themselves as actively moving on the web under their own steam" (Maglio and Matlock 1998: 8). They decided that not only do we use spatial metaphors to describe our experience, but that their power lies in the fact that "people *naturally use spatial metaphors*—that they cannot help but use them" (Maglio and Matlock 1998: 8).

Earlier, in 1995, Ruth Palmquist, a librarian at the University of Austin, Texas, had conducted a study of 100 articles published that year. She wanted to identify a set of metaphors that might successfully convey to the novice user the purposes and activities possible on the internet and World Wide Web. Palmquist outlines her method in detail in her paper and I will not include it all here, but below is a brief insight into the process she used. To help her judge the utility of metaphors in this context, she looked to the work of researchers Madsen and Butler. According to Madsen, she reported, a good metaphor is one that has the following characteristics: (1) Richness of structure, providing a variety of associations to other ideas or concepts. (2) Applicability of structure, ensuring the metaphor is appropriate and not misleading. For example, a common early habit of indicating that a word processor is like a typewriter led to various misconceptions. (3) Suitability of metaphor to an intended audience (this is especially relevant in a multicultural multinational context). (4) Well understood literal meaning for the same intended audience. Palmquist notes here that "the frequency of occurrence of related notions like 'road signs', 'road kill', 'toll booths', 'mapping', 'pathways', 'pot-holes' etc. was extremely large," providing a graphic example of the way Gore's speech about the information superhighway 2 years earlier had impacted popular consciousness (Palmquist 1996). Butler's 1986 study provided her with a different set of criteria, in this case to be used for the evaluation of the metaphor in technical information materials. She cites a selection of his basic classifications: (1) Place or location, via naming, such as "windows," "trash can," "folders"; (2) Actions, via activities, such as "surfing," "weaving"; (3) Qualities, especially anthropomorphic qualities, such as "dreams," "fear and loathing"; (4) Modeling metaphors, which stress a combination of two or more of the above, such as "marketplace," "library." As a result of her research, Palmquist categorized her own set of internet metaphors as follows:

- Travel/Explore
- Fire or Water
- Commerce/Politics
- Animals
- Anthropomorphic
- Communication
- Tools/Machines/Process
- Other

She concluded at the time of the sample (1995) that there were two distinctly different relationships to be modeled between human and computer. The first was based on metaphors related to specific software functions such as trash can, file folder, etc. The second she described as a newer type of relationship—"that of the computer as an access route to a broader environment of information sources and services" (Palmquist 1996). She does not appear to note that the first set of metaphors apply to both offline and online machines, whereas the second generally only applies to networked machines. She does, however, point to the "surprisingly large" number—43 percent—of references that could be classed as anthropomorphic, while reporting that 25 percent of the metaphors gathered "defied classification and were assigned to the inevitable Other category" (Palmquist 1996).

Librarian Lee Ratzan examined the results of studies by Palmquist and others, and concluded that their greatest weakness was that "they could not or did not reveal why users described the internet as they did" (Ratzan 2000). He wanted to know how users describe the online environment, and why they describe it that way. He created an online questionnaire and used the first 350 responses as the basis for his analysis. There is no information on the socio-economic-professional backgrounds of the target participant group or how he distributed invitations to take part. Interestingly, he notes that in his findings "the phrase 'information superhighway' which appeared often in the mass media has not had a deep penetration into the user cognitive image." His paper reporting on the results of the study was published in 2000 but he does not provide the year of the survey. However, it seems safe to assume it was probably 1999, demonstrating that either the meme was losing potency by then, or perhaps had been transformed into a different but related concept. He does note, however, that females were more likely than males to use both highway metaphors of some type and that the same was also true with regard to frontier metaphors. He also notes that

> Metaphors from novices often bear a sense of confusion, complexity or frustration while experts are much more anchored in reality. One may speculate that the former is an expression of the novelty of the Web experience. This explanation is appealing but is not consistent with the fact intangible metaphysical metaphors were used solely by Experts and never by Novices. This might be indicative of a cognitive paradigm change and a function of the amorphous nature of the Web.
>
> Ratzan 2000

The survey asked participants to select a skill level from Novice, Intermediate, Advanced, and Expert. Results showed that of the 182 female and 167 male participants, men tended to consider themselves as high-skilled users (56 men and 22 women rated themselves as Expert) whereas women tended to perceive themselves as lesser-skilled users (9 men and 19 women rated themselves as Novice). When asked to complete the sentence "The internet is a ... " novices used terms such as "bottomless pit," "maze," "snaggled skein of yarn," "wide endless road," "big bookstore," and "locked library." Some Experts, on the other hand, proposed "chameleon," "community," "idea processor," "haven for free speech," "bookstore with a switchboard," and "huge library." The Experts also contributed terms that Ratzan categorizes as "metaphysical," such as "new dimension," "void of omnipotence," "cooperative chaos," "fractal," and "world that exists in consciousness." He concluded that metaphor images seem to change as skill level develops, and noted that "Novices tended to use finite, tangible, delimited, closed, delineated metaphors while Experts tended to use more metaphysical, intangible, open metaphors" (Ratzan 2000).

In 2002, Cohen and Blavin analyzed the evolution of internet metaphors in relation to law, pointing out that "When courts encounter new technologies not yet anticipated by the law, their reliance on analogical reasoning plays a profoundly important role in the application of proper legal rules" and cautioning that "By failing to adopt appropriate metaphors in regulating new technologies, courts risk creating bad law" (Cohen and Blavin 2002: 268). They discussed three main inferences that had been the subject of legal deliberations: the information superhighway, cyberspace, and the internet as "real" space. In the early years, the majority of internet use was in the United States, and many of the lawsuits discussed in relation to the information superhighway related to interstate trading and issues of federal versus state law. There was often a struggle to understand the implications of new kinds of computer features, for example metatags: "Use of the highway billboard metaphor is not the best analogy to a metatag on the internet. The harm caused by a misleading billboard on a highway is difficult to correct. In contrast, ... resuming one's search for the correct website is relatively simple" (*Bihari v. Gross*, 119 F. Supp. 2d 309, 319–321 (S. D. N. Y. 2000), cited by Cohen and Blavin 2002: 274). The eventual conclusion was that the information superhighway is *not* like a regular highway, its links are *not* like road signs, and its structure is *not* like a mere conduit but instead embodies several destinations, each with its own content. The concept of "cyberspace" caused a different set of difficulties because it suggested not that internet space was like something else, but that it was another kind of geographic space, unique and distinct. This idea was reinforced by John Perry Barlow (1993), who proposed that the electronic frontier resembles the nineteenth-century American West in its natural preference for social devices that emerge from its conditions rather than those that are imposed from the outside. Until the West was fully settled and "civilized" in this century, order was established according to an unwritten Code of the West, which had the fluidity of common law rather than the rigidity of statutes. Ethics were more important than rules. Understandings were preferred over laws, which were, in any event, largely unenforceable (Cohen and Blavin 2002). However, say Cohen and Blavin (in sharp contrast to the utopian vision expressed by Barlow et al.), an increasing number of commentators have argued that the internet "is not a mysterious place hermetically sealed from the real world" (280) and "Unlike a 'brick and mortar outlet' with a specific geographic locale, and unlike the voluntary physical mailing of material from one geographic location to another, the uncontroverted facts indicate that the Web is not geographically constrained" (Third Circuit, cited by Cohen and Blavin 2002: 279).

If the internet is seen as real space, different conditions apply; it can be zoned, subject to trespass, and divided up into holdings similar to real property. In *Reno v. ACLU* in 1997, Justice O'Connor had anticipated this development when she announced that "[c]yberspace undeniably reflects some form of geography" (cited by Cohen and Blavin 2002: 283). In his 1999 book *Code and other Laws of Cyberspace*, Lawrence Lessig fought back with the argument that the internet is an artificial environment architectured from code and that there is nothing inherent about it that makes it a space divorced from traditional territorial boundaries, human values, or government control. This interpretation was widely taken up and used in the courts. Cohen and Blavin concluded that "many courts no longer view the internet as a 'borderless frontier' intrinsically disconnected from territorial boundaries. Rather, they have at least begun to investigate whether the ever-advancing architecture of the internet is indeed capable of being accurately linked to real space" (Cohen and Blavin 2002: 284).

However, what happens when the internet can be carried around, and accessed not from a desktop or laptop computer but from a small pocket-sized machine? In 2007 researchers from Nokia, one of the world's leading mobile telephony companies, and Adaptive Path, a leading human–computer interaction company, explored ways in which some common internet metaphors might transfer to the mobile phone experience (Isomursu et al. 2007). Working with users in the United States, Europe, and Hong Kong, they found that certain common internet memes had no resonance in the mobile environment: *(1) The Ocean: Surfing, Scuba Diving, and Snorkeling.* The researchers report that this metaphor "proves challenging on a mobile device because the form, environmental factors, and visual cues do not combine to create a context that facilitates exploration." Problems occur when the expectations of "ocean" and "surfing" metaphors from the PC internet experience collide with the mobile internet context, as illustrated by one interviewee who said "It's called surfing for a reason, because it's like a flow. It's following a wave of information. If you can't click on links, you can't surf. You can't follow that wave." *(2) Campfire, Watering Hole, and Cave.* This set of metaphors refers to the ways in which the internet allows users to metaphorically sit around the campfire, watering hole, or cave, and share stories. Above all, there is a focus on both community and privacy. The researchers report that mobile internet telephony allows the user to access news and forums connected to his or her home base(s) wherever it/they might be, thus providing the campfire experience. They also make the important point that

> More than the cave being a specific site in the web, it seems that for many the experience of browsing the web by oneself provides the metaphorical cave where the user can escape from the surrounding world. Again, mobile internet expands this concept further: mobile devices can provide the cave where the user can isolate herself even in a rush-hour train.

(3) Walled Garden. Rather like a "gated community," this term has twin resonances of safety and threat, depending on which side of the wall you are. General consensus seems to be that users who choose to set their preferences to create a walled garden around their internet experience, whether on mobile or computer, may be driven by their own fear or insecurity. More important are the constraints created by mobile providers for regulatory reasons, such as in Hong Kong where high charges keep users inside a walled garden controlled by the provider. Users were not at all happy with this experience and strongly disliked any limits to their internet access. *(4) Mystery and Magic.* Although there is a complex history of magic and mystery related to the internet, in this study the category has a very specific meaning related to the difficulty of understanding mobile internet tariffs and allowances, which results in users often feeling out of control of their bills in a similar way to their discomfort about being trapped in a constrained user environment. But the researchers also report a positive sense of magic and mystery amongst users when shown new and unfamiliar mobile features such as "portkeys," which connect the physical world with the virtual: "For example, touching an ordinary looking picture frame with a picture of a grandson with a mobile phone may initiate a call to the grandson." *(5) The Information Superhighway.* Although this metaphor may be generally considered to be outdated, in mobile telephony it remains the principal mode because "Mobile use of the internet is more like following a straight path. One focuses on the straight road ahead with a specific destination in mind and may not even notice possible side roads" (Isomursu et al. 2007: 262–264).

The linearity of mobile technology in 2007 proved to be its most negative feature, and one that persists even today in most smartphone interfaces; but it is interesting to note that although this "single view" is unappealing to users more accustomed to the Windows environment, the idea of the phone user retreating to her private "cave" in a crowded place is an appealing one, which can be widely substantiated by general observation.

Over a 3-month period in 2008, technical communications researcher Rebecca Johnston collected editorials with the term "internet" in the title. Her sources were all US-based and produced by staff writers, expert guests, or letters to the editor. They discussed a range of topics such as social and economic issues, politics, gambling, censorship, voting, community, and the role of the internet itself. Her results showed a prevalence of metaphors for physical space, physical speed, salvation, and destruction. Many of these were related to natural forces: "Multiple metaphors compared the internet to nature, usually comparing the internet to phenomenon that caused death and destruction in nature. In these articles, web sites were flooded, experienced a wave of hits, eroded revenue, acted like fast-flowing waters, and had comments poured on them" (Johnston 2009).

Johnston's findings contrast with the many positive water metaphors that have evolved around internet experience, but she makes the point raised by Lakoff and Johnson that conflicting metaphors fit coherently into a larger social or cultural system. In a similar vein, geographer Stephen Graham, writing in 1998, refers us to Doreen Massey's 1993 suggestion that places need to be defined in relational terms too, as "articulated moments in networks of social relations and understandings" rather than as "areas with boundaries around" (Massey 1993: 66), and cautions against the dangers of adopting "simplistic concepts of space and place" (Graham 1998: 181) in relation to information technology. "We need to reject the extremely resilient 'Euclidean' notions, still implicitly underlying many treatments of the geographies of information technology, that treat spaces and places simply as bounded areas embedded within some wider, objective framework of time-space" (Graham 1998: 181). One way to do this is to eschew the command-and-control approach of deliberately designing metaphors intended to shape the way we think about the internet, and to look instead at the evolving metaphors to be found in the everyday discourse of users in many cultures and many countries.

For example, in 1996, telecommunications expert Harmeet Sawhney wrote a paper about what he saw as the central questions relating to the information superhighway. At that time it was assumed that there would be much more control over the evolution of the internet than has actually happened. To that end, Sawhney was anxious to clarify the nature of the beast, pointing out that the trial and error method of choosing metaphors was no longer appropriate "because we are no longer in the discovery mode. Instead, we should very carefully choose one metaphor which will help us make wise decisions regarding the socio-cultural issues raised by the new technologies" (Sawhney 1996: 305). As an example, he told the story of how Lord Reith, the visionary behind the BBC, was a proponent of the idea that broadcasting should be the servant of culture, with the result that historically the commercial aspects of broadcasting have been subordinated to the cultural ones. By the same light, he said, some have called "for the creation of 'public lanes' on the information superhighway" (305) to ensure that the internet was not overwhelmed by commercial interests. He made it clear that it was vital to strike a balance between the utilitarian and aesthetic aspects of the technological world we design and create. [] The obvious starting point would be to do away with old mechanistic metaphors and adopt more organic ones which forefront the impact of technological development on us as thinking and feeling human beings. For example, we can think about the telecommunications infrastructure as an environment rather than a highway.

Sawhney 1996: 306

This change, he felt, would have the effect of engaging our imaginations in a way that is very different from information superhighway. "The involvement would be more immediate and personal. The most important question would be '*How do we wish to live*?' (Giedion 1967: xxxiv; emphasis in original) rather than 'What are the data transfer speeds?'" (Sawhney 1996: 307) At the same time, Sawhney pointed out that whichever metaphor might be chosen, it may not last for long: "Even though we have no choice but to use metaphors based on the past to understand the future, we have to realise that these metaphors may have to be abandoned as the future reveals itself" (Sawhney 1996: 300). Indeed, Microsoft founder Bill Gates does just this in his 1995 book *The Road Ahead*, where he discounts the highway metaphor in the opening pages and then spends the whole book using it, presumably for the familiar ease of his readers. He downgrades the metaphor instead to "a lot of country lanes," and then later describes it as a marketplace destined to become "the world's central department store" (Gates 1995: 6).

Geographer Martin Dodge classifies internet metaphors into three main categories. First, metaphors of invisibility, which he subdivides into the following: (1) materially unseen; (2) transparent in use; (3) disappearance by social naturalization; and (4) occlusion through institutional normalization. There is a tendency to think of the internet as invisible, but doing so leaves the door open to fudging issues of infrastructure, ownership, and responsibility. Second, the usual linguistic spatial metaphors such as the superhighway, frontier, and other mostly transport-oriented metaphors, and third, visual metaphors for internet infrastructure. He identified four groups of images of the internet. The most common visual analogy to explain the internet as a spatially extensive infrastructure is a physical network of wires—not a web, which would be too conformist in shape. Then there is the global view, with network arcs or data flows shown encircling the world, followed by machinic portrayals—the world in miniature inside the machine. Last, he lists abstract visions that are often of an organic nature: "These metaphors draw on naturalistic iconography of organic structures (fractal branching of trees and leaves, structured lattices and webs, the fine filigree patterning of brains or veins) and emergence aesthetics redolent of meteorology and astronomy (cloud patterns, glowing gas nebulas and star clusters)" (Dodge 2008: 135).

All the metaphors discussed above have their roots in Western culture, but in 2002 Dinesh S. Katre drew upon a leading example of Indian saint literature, *Dnyaneshwari*, for metaphors to be used in the design of a range of interface agents (Katre n.d.). Proposing that metaphoric expressions in prevailing artforms should be studied for their appropriate application in software interface design in order to help humanize the interface, he outlines several examples from *Dnyaneshwari*. Here is the example of the river:

> The river represents the subject of knowledge and the banks of the river are like the division of opinions and viewpoints. There is night of ignorance. There is a pair of birds, which is separated on the banks of river. It is unable to see each other due to darkness. The pair of birds represents the spiritual knowledge and the devotee who is in search of it. They both are able to meet when the sun rises.
>
> Katre n.d.

The primary objective of Saint Dnyaneshwari was to use metaphors to present spiritual knowledge to laymen in the most simplified manner. Katre proposes building scenarios using linked metaphors drawn from the literature. This may, perhaps, only communicate a complete meaning to those already familiar with *Dnyaneshwari* but that need not be a reason not to use it where appropriate.

Conclusion

For some, the growth of mobile wireless internet and the increasing ubiquity of the cloud mean that the notion of cyberspace is in decline. For writer Alex Soojung-Kim Pang, for example, the concept has already passed away. Riffing on the title of Lakoff and Johnson's book, he says,

> Cyberspace is a "metaphor we live by," born two decades ago at the intersection of computers, networks, ideas, and experience. It has reflected our experiences with information technology, and also shaped the way we think about new technologies and the challenges they present. It had been a vivid and useful metaphor for decades; but in a rapidly-emerging world of mobile, always-on information devices (and eventually cybernetic implants, prosthetics, and

swarm intelligence), the rules that define the relationship between information, places, and daily life are going to be rewritten.

Pang 2010

Author James Bridle shares that view. "All our metaphors are broken," he writes.

> The network is not a space (notional, cyber or otherwise) and it's not time (while it is embedded in it at an odd angle) it is some other kind of dimension entirely. BUT meaning is emergent in the network, it is the apophatic silence at the heart of everything, that-which-can-be-pointed-to.

Bridle 2012a

Bridle has developed a school of thought around what he calls the "New Aesthetic," which is, he writes, "not a thing which can be done. It is a series of artefacts of the heterogeneous network, which recognises differences, the gaps in our overlapping but distant realities, ways of thinking about the future which are different from ideas which have gone before" (Bridle 2012b).

These tiny movements are, perhaps, the stories of digital life today. Maybe they are told in tiny 140-character slices where there is less room for metaphor. Perhaps they capture the placelessness of mobile media, such as the tale reported by Brunei journalist Azlan Othman in 2005 when he went to Bandar Seri Begawan to investigate accounts of digital hauntings in the form of encounters with ghostly mobile phones. Bandar Seri Begawan is the capital of the Sultanate of Brunei, set in a region of tropical rainforest just a bus ride from the border with Malaysia. The majority of Bruneians are ethnic Malays whose culture features a rich tradition of ghosts and flying vampires, known as "Pontianak" in Malay, which inhabit not just traditional locations such as banyan trees and unoccupied houses but also modern buildings and highways. The best-known Malaysian spirit encounter, for example, is a much-distributed photograph of an unknown ghostly woman with long hair seated on a balcony behind a man posing for the picture (Othman 2005). Recently, however, the focus has shifted away from photography and toward mobile media. Othman heard about hi-tech spirits causing mobile phones to ring when no incoming call is received, and about night-shift security personnel hearing phones ringing in uninhabited jungle areas along the border. It was widely believed in the region that phones could be connected to the spirit world and activated, perhaps, by the transmission of "scary encounters sent over the phone for the brave to view"—such as the photograph of the ghostly woman on the balcony. In the end he found no evidence of these manifestations and concluded that the mobiles probably belonged to smugglers, but the story reminds us that, unlike the 1990s when it was easy to visualize the boundaries between online and offline, today the lines are much more blurred. As we drift wirelessly in the cloud, it is perhaps not surprising that, for some, the prevalent metaphors are not of pioneers battling in frontier wildernesses, but of disembodied spirits haunting the digital ether.

References

Anderson, Chris. 1995. "A survey of the internet: The accidental superhighway—Like a flock of birds." *The Economist.* http://www.temple.edu/lawschool/dpost/accidentalsuperhighway.htm [accessed August 11, 2008].

Barlow, John Perry. 1993. "The economy of ideas." *Wired.* http://www.wired.com/wired/archive/2.03/economy.ideas_pr.html [accessed August 1, 2012].

Barlow, John Perry. 1996. *A Declaration of the Independence of Cyberspace.* February 8, http://homes.eff.org/~barlow/Declaration-Final.html [accessed April 20, 2008].

Barsalou, L. 1999. "Perceptual symbol systems." *Behavioral and Brain Sciences 22*: 577–609.

Boroditsky, Lera. 2000. "Metaphoric structuring: Understanding time through spatial metaphors." *Cognition 75*: 1–28.

Bridle, James. 2012a. "#sxaesthetic." *booktwo.org.* March 15, http://booktwo.org/notebook/sxaesthetic/ [accessed August 30, 2012].

Bridle, James. 2012b. "About." *The New Aesthetic.* http://new-aesthetic.tumblr.com/about [accessed August 30, 2012].

Cameron, Lynne. 2006. "A discourse dynamics framework for metaphor." *Metaphor Analysis Project.* http://creet.open.ac.uk/projects/metaphor-analysis/theories.cfm?paper=ddfm [accessed August 28, 2009].

Cohen, I.G. and J.H. Blavin. 2002. "Gore, Gibson and Goldsmith: The evolution of internet metaphors in law and commentary." *Harvard Journal of Law and Technology 16, no.1*: 265-285

Dodge, Martin. 2008. *Imagining Internet Infrastructures: Spatial Metaphors.* http://personalpages.manchester.ac.uk/staff/m.dodge/thesis/chap_4.pdf [accessed August 1, 2012].

Dyson, Esther. 1997. *Release 2.0.*

Evans, Vyvyan. 2006. "Lexical concepts and cognitive models theory and metaphor." *Metaphor Analysis Project.* http://creet.open.ac.uk/projects/metaphor-analysis/theories.cfm?paper=lccm [accessed August 28, 2009].

Gates, Bill. 1995. *The Road Ahead.* London: Viking.

Gibson, William. 1982. *Neuromancer.* London: Gollancz.

Gore, Al. 1993. "Gore's remarks on the NII." December 21, http://www.ibiblio.org/nii/goremarks.html [accessed August 14, 2008].

Graham, Stephen. 1998. "The end of geography or the explosion of place? Conceptualising space, place and information technology." *Progress in Human Geography 22, no.2*: 165–185.

Hayles, N. Katherine. 2002. *Writing Machines*. Cambridge: MIT.

Isomursu, Pekka, Rachel Hinman, Minna Isomursu, and Mirjana Spasojevic. 2007. "Metaphors for the mobile internet." *Knowledge, Technology & Policy 20, no. 4*: 259–268.

Johnston, Rebecca. 2009. "Salvation or destruction—metaphors of the internet." *First Monday, 14*, April 4–6, http://www.uic.edu/htbin/cgiwrap/bin/ojs/index.php/fm/article/viewArticle/2370/2158.

Katre, Dinesh S. "Unconventional inspirations for creating software interface metaphors." *C-DAC*. http://www.cdac.in/html/pdf/icmd-metaphors-final.pdf [accessed September 2, 2012].

Lakoff, George and Johnson. 1980. *Metaphors We Live By*. Chicago: University of Chicago Press.

Maglio, Paul P. and Teenie Matlock. 1998. *Metaphors We Surf the Web By*. http://www.ischool.utexas.edu/~i385e/readings/Maglio1998.pdf [accessed July 4, 2012].

Massey, Doreen. 1993. "Power-geometry and a progressive sense of place." In *Mapping the Futures: Local Cultures, Global Change*, edited by John Bird, Barry Curtis, Tim Putnam, and Lisa Tickner, 59–69. London: Routledge.

Othman, Azlan. 2005. "Ghostly "Mobile" Claims." *BrunDirect.com*. May 15, http://www.brudirect.com/DailyInfo/News/Archive/May05/150505/nite02.htm [accessed February 28, 2011].

Paik, Nam June. 1974. "Media planning for the postindustrial society—The 21st century is now only 26 years away." *Media Art Net*. http://www.medienkunstnetz.de/source-text/33/ [accessed January 24, 2011].

Palmquist, Ruth A. 1996. "The search for an internet metaphor: A comparison of literatures." *ASIS 1996 Annual Conference Proceedings*. http://www.asis.org/annual-96/ElectronicProceedings/palmquist.html [accessed August 5, 2008].

Pang, Alex Soojung-Kim. 2010. *The End of Cyberspace*. http://www.endofcyberspace.com/ [accessed September 2, 2012].

Polly, Jean Armour. 1990. "Birth of a metaphor." *Netmom*. http://www.netmom.com/about-net-mom/26-surfing-the-internet.html [accessed October 29, 2010].

Polly, Jean Armour. 1993. *Surfing the INTERNET: An Introduction Version 2.0.3*. May 15, http://web.urz.uni-heidelberg.de/Netzdienste/internet/what/polly.html [accessed September 16, 2012].

Polly, Jean Armour. 2008. "Who invented surfing the internet?" *Netmom*. http://www.netmom.com/about-net-mom/23-who-invented-surfing-the-internet.html [accessed November 2010].

Polly, Jean Armour. 2010. Interview by Sue Thomas. *Interview*, November 2.

Ratzan, Lee. 2000. "Making sense of the web: A metaphorical approach." *Information Research*. http://InformationR.net/ir/6-1/paper85.html accessed 14/8/05 [accessed August 14, 2005].

Ritchie, David. 2006. "Context-limited simulation theory of metaphor." *Metaphor Analysis Project*. http://creet.open.ac.uk/projects/metaphor-analysis/theories. cfm?paper=cls [accessed August 28, 2009].

Sawhney, Harmeet. 1996. "Information superhighway: Metaphors as midwives". *Media, Culture & Society 18, no. 2*: 291–314.

Steen, Gerard. 2008. "The paradox of metaphor: Why we need a three-dimensional model of metaphor, metaphor and symbol". *Metaphor and Symbol 23*, no. 4: 213–241.

2

Me and You and Everyone We Know: The Centrality of Character in Understanding Media Texts

Craig Batty

RMIT University, Australia

Introduction

Excitement grows in the children as their mother returns home. They squeal with excitement as they see her walking up the garden path toward the house. They push open the fly screen and run to her with hugs and kisses. But instead of embracing them with love and affection, their mother sweeps them aside and screams out, "It was so dark-sided!"

She cries as she walks over to the couch and begins to scream out allegations of religious heresy: that "she" is dark-sided too, and has dabbled in "dark-sided stuff." Her confused husband and children try to console her, but she does not relent. Her eyes bulge: she is angry and feels betrayed. She heaves herself up and screams out, "This is my house. I want no money. I want nothing. I want my God and I want my family." She proceeds to rip up what looks like an envelope of money, calling it tainted and against her beliefs. She calls herself the "God Warrior" and turns on the camera crew, screaming at them to get out of her house. She rips off her cardigan and begins her rampage, making more threats to the crew: "Get the hell out of my house, in Jesus' name I pray."

She is inconsolable, even with her beloved family. She screams at everyone for partaking in tarot cards, astrology, and witch books. She is aggressive to the cameraperson, making further threats. She proclaims, "Every dark-sided person get out of my house. If you believe in Jesus you can stay here." She then flies off the handle again, criticizing everything that "she" and her family believe in.

This sounds like it could be fiction: a scene from a film, perhaps, or even a comedy sketch. But it is real; or, more accurately, it really happened. This is in fact what happened when Marguerite Perrin, "God Warrior" contestant from the 2005 season premiere of *Trading Spouses*, an American format very similar to the popular *Wife Swap*, returned home. It was Perrin's reaction to spending 2 weeks with the Flisher family, "she" being their "New Age Humanist" mother, Jeanne. Discussions of staging and editing aside, the point is that these events happened. Perrin's volatile reaction to having experienced the "dark side" clearly provided a strong hook to the season premiere, and instantaneously created a character that audiences could talk about, laugh about, and mock. The number of postings of this scene on YouTube, including various parodies, is a testament to this.

However, what was it that made this such a spectacular start to the new season of *Trading Spouses*, and a cultural event? The answer lies in Perrin herself, the primary participant of the show. Arguably, though, calling her a *participant* is not enough: Marguerite Perrin is a *character*. She is a character that audiences were attracted to so much that not only did they watch the show, they re-watched it, blogged about it, and created parodies of it. Perrin bears all the traits of a fictional protagonist to draw in her audience: a complex backstory, a unique persona, a strong voice, and alarming actions.

It is through such characters that we experience media. It is through their perspective, point of view, and narrative drive—through agency—that audiences are able to follow what is happening. Not only that, it is through characters that we understand media. We make sense of what is happening on both a plot and a thematic level. Through character reflection and emotional arcs, we are able to *feel* what the narrative is trying to suggest; we are offered a way of reading the text. As Watson suggests, "by our stories, as it were, shall we be known; and sometimes such stories have the power of myths to leave all facts—and often reality—behind" (cited by Batty and Cain 2010: 13). In other words, whatever type of media text we are engaging with, we are experiencing someone's story: ours (personal essay or video diary), theirs (Facebook page or newspaper article), even something's (a car or a washing machine advertisement). Noteworthy here is Watson's suggestion that it is not what exists that interests us, but what is meant. It is the underlying mythical quality of a text that is truly appealing—the meaning that lurks beneath. As Cunningham concurs, "Myth is not concerned with facts, but with patterns and analogies that reveal our human situation" (2008: 57). Arguably, then, we do not care about "surface level" components of a narrative in and of themselves; rather, we care about what they are telling us, the "subtextual level" that meaning and understanding bestow.

In previous works, notably *Movies that Move Us: Screenwriting and the Power of the Protagonist's Journey* (Batty 2011), I argued that screenplays are composed of two interwoven yet distinctive narrative threads: the physical journey and the emotional journey. Together, they allow meaning to be made: the physical plotting of a character's journey in order to tease out his or her emotional journey and, by association, the theme. The backbone to this argument was character: without a character we have no story because we have nobody to guide us through the narrative, and to care about. This may sound simple, but it is a fundamental component of making media work. If we understand that audiences need characters—rely on them, in fact—then not only can we deconstruct texts through using this lens, we can also create and develop texts. Whether we are academics or practitioners is unimportant; what *is* important is that we acknowledge the development processes that shape a text to become appealing to an audience.

For the purposes of this chapter, then, these development processes involve the definition and creation of character. To go back to Watson, we are not concerned here with "facts" or "participants": we are concerned with "myths" and "characters." It is my contention that we need to step away from notions of truth and authenticity when examining media texts, and instead embrace notions of fictionality and characterization. This then gives us the lens through which to understand exactly how media texts have been constructed in order to convey the intentions of their creators, which then provides options for deeper theorization and critique. Characterization can be understood in various ways, from the person presenting to the expert advising to the participant featured (Batty and Cain 2010: 10), but this understanding can only be achieved by a sincere acknowledgment of the importance that character plays in a media text. Marguerite Perrin is a clear case in point.

Understanding character and structure

Murray Smith's work on the importance of character in film is useful for the broader context of characters in media texts. He writes that, "Characters are central to the rhetorical and aesthetic effects of narrative texts" (1995: 4), reinforcing the idea that besides adding individual visual and aural texture to the text in question (the aesthetic), they are fundamental in making the intention known (the rhetoric). In other words, characters are used to populate a narrative and make it feel credible, as well as to guide us through the narrative so as to elicit meaning. Their effectiveness affords their affectiveness. Smith denounces research that has devalued the role of character, instead celebrating the role that it plays in the creation of audience experience: "Even if we acknowledge the massive determining power of material and ideological structures, our immediate experience of the social world is through agency—agents filling the roles assigned to them by these structures" (1995: 18). To relate back to Watson and Cunningham's ideas, Smith sees the character-as-agent as generating the "transparent myth" of film (1995: 45), or character as a "surface" component in the narrative that makes meaning ("subsurface") possible. The name of his model to deconstruct the character-as-agent, the *structure of sympathy*, is a nice reminder that the way an audience interacts with and understands a narrative— sympathy/empathy—is through a structured character journey. As he writes:

> We watch a film, and find ourselves becoming attached to a particular character or characters on the basis of values or qualities roughly congruent with those we possess, or those that we wish to possess, and experience vicariously the emotional experiences of the character: we identify with the character.
>
> 1995: 2

To take this notion of an audience being guided through the narrative of a text by character, Hockley's (2007) work is also useful. He sees the emotional connection between character and audience as one rooted in psychological attachment, suggesting that a way of interpreting the narrative space of film— and, as I would argue, any media text—is "as an expression of the inner state of the central identification figure" (2007: 43): the main character/protagonist. Furthermore, how the character is played out in the text helps generate the desired meaning. As with Smith's argument, audience attachment (sympathy/ empathy) is "structured" through the character and his or her activity within the text. In the case of film, Hockley's focus, this activity is dominated by action: "inner psychological concerns and attitudes take on a visual form within the film—story space becomes psychological space, if you will" (2007: 43). It is this notion of psychological space, a space in which both character and audience connect, "speak," and meld, that is of major interest here.

In simple terms, we can understand the audience–character connection and how it develops through the structure of the text as pertaining to *narrative pleasure*: "a mechanism by which audiences judge the success of a [...] text, seeking to find plot points and dramatic junctures which adhere not only to their expectations, but their ability to understand the story told" (Batty and Waldeback 2008: 149). Narrative pleasure is thus elicited through understanding the intention of the story, through understanding what the text is really about. As reflective beings, we want more than mere facts: we need to know what they mean, and why they are being given to us. In a news report, for example, we do not care about how much the price of petrol has increased over the past twelve months: we care about how it has affected us, and our ability to pay for it. In a television cookery show, we do not care about what makes the perfect lamb casserole: we care about how someone goes about making it perfect, and what it might do for his or her (or our) self-esteem. Narrative pleasure, then, posits not that we must enjoy the story being told or the theme being explored, but that we understand what is being told or explored through the craft of structuring meaning. We take pleasure in the narrative because we understand what it is trying to achieve; and, because we need someone or something to guide us through the narrative—a central identification figure—we psychologically connect to the character as a way of rendering meaning possible. Arguably, because character provides a way of navigating our way through and understanding structure, character *is* structure. The two are interlocked in a relationship whereby physical action influences emotional development, and emotional development influences physical action, where meaning is created through the structuring of a character arc/journey. As screenwriting author and story consultant Robert McKee tells us:

> Structure and character are interlocked. The event structure of a story is created out of the choices that characters make under pressure and the actions they choose to take, while characters are the creatures who are revealed and changed by how they choose to act under pressure. If you change one, you change the other.
>
> 1999: 106

This may sound "very Hollywood," but in fact this is the point. The argument I am trying to make is that understanding character from a fictional point of view, which may very well be Hollywood in nature, helps us understand how media texts have been created, and thus the intentions of their creators. Regardless of the scale to which they appear, the core elements of all stories involving one or more characters are an established situation, a threat to that situation, the movement into a new situation, dealing with the new situation, and coming away from the new situation with lessons learned that can be applied (or denied) in the original situation. This works for high-concept films, reality TV, novels, feature articles, radio advertisements—and much more.

Fusing fact with fiction

Derek Paget is well known for his work on the drama documentary (or documentary drama) genre, which refers to films or television dramas whose content is derived from real people and/or events. His work is a useful reference point here because of the genre's focus on fusing fact with fiction. As a definition, Paget posits that the drama documentary "uses the sequence of events from a real historical occurrence or situation and the identities of the protagonists to underpin a film [or television] script intended to provoke debate about the significance of the events/occurrence" (1998: 82). What is interesting about this definition is the use of the word "underpin," which suggests that rather than it being *about* the person and/or event, it is in fact about something else. It has some other purpose: to provoke debate. The factual elements of the text are thus merely a way of enabling understanding to emerge, a way of structuring meaning. Paget's view that the real situation is used to "provoke debate" places the idea of subject matter in a somewhat vulnerable position, where it can be manipulated to achieve the needs of the creator. In this way, and to go back to the core argument of the chapter, the fictional processes involved in creating a story based on real people and/or events enable the filling of what Beattie calls an "information gap," whereby fictionalization "provides a way of invoking psychological or emotional motivations capable of rendering human actions intelligible" (2004: 153). This information gap, then, can be equated to understanding, where fictionalization provides a way of bestowing meaning to mere facts. To reiterate, this clearly suggests some degree of audience manipulation, which although leaving a text open to critique, is arguably essential in its creation. The staple of such factual-oriented texts is not telling us *what* happened and *how*, but *why*. As Sophie Meyrick, an Australia-based TV producer whose recent work has included series-producing *Grand Designs Australia*, revealed:

> There is no doubt that Australian broadcasters are interested in character-led programming at the moment, especially the ABC and SBS. Character-based shows are thriving on pay television: *Pawn Stars, Storage Wars, American Pickers,* and so forth [and the] tendency at the moment is to explore topics

through an individual's experience of it. So, for example, *Grand Designs* and *Grand Designs Australia* are not shows about building houses, they are about the owners' experience of it. The construction of the house provides the backdrop for the personal journey.

Meyrick 2013

What is important to understand is how such ideas of fictionalization are applied in practice. Although we can speculate on what these processes mean, it is arguably more interesting to understand how these processes take place, and/or how they might take place in the future by other practitioners. Considering the work of writers like Paget and Beattie, I developed in an earlier publication a model that can be used to understand the practice of fictionalization (Batty 2007: 5–6). Coming specifically from a screenwriting perspective, though entirely applicable to other media texts, the intention was to sketch out a framework for understanding and shaping a narrative structure that would generate meaning (the information gap) about a real person and/or event. Similar to Smith's structure of sympathy, it was broad yet designed to prise open a text in order to examine the creative elements that had gone into it. Thus, four areas of consideration—framing, focus, selection, and resolution—were proposed as ways of examining how "audience identification, emotional attachment and narrative pleasure" (2007: 5) could be generated and structured into a narrative with the intention of eliciting meaning. As with this chapter, the lens through which the framework was modeled was character: how the central identification figure and supporting cast were "tools" used by the screenwriter to tell their story. As Hutzler tells us, "You can only reach the universal through the personal" (2005: 8), indicating that only through character can we achieve meaning. For Paget, also, "People sometimes want to ratify emotionally what they may already have understood intellectually. The camera's promise of complete seeing can only ever achieve completion if our emotions are stirred dramatically as well as our understanding increased intellectually" (2004: 207). Whichever way we look at it, we need characters to guide us through the text and help us understand the situations presented.

It is here that I want to focus on a particular form of media to provide material for the remainder of the chapter: factual television. Broadcasters today prefer to refer to "reality television" as "factual television" because it can include so many different varieties: factual entertainment, observational documentary, constructed documentary, drama documentary, and so forth (Meyrick 2013). Within this "meta" form, I will refer specifically to factual entertainment. This "micro" form will be useful for the arguments being made not just because of how it purposely mixes reality with fiction, but how it blatantly mixes real people and real situations with entertainment and audience allure. In this form, as we will see, although the spine of each series relates to a particular reality (a household, a workplace, a leisure outlet), there are clear conflict- and character transformation-driven structures at play. Reality thus becomes a framing device for something more interesting and meaningful for an audience: character development.

The participant as character

Recalling the 2004 "Merlin incident" from the Australian *Big Brother*, where, upon eviction, contestant Merlin Luck wore a sign declaring "Free Th [sic] Refugees," refused to speak to the interviewer, and sat with gaffer tape over his mouth, Cuthbertson reminds us that even when attempts are made to provoke political debate, audiences quickly revert to reacting to the participant—or character—making the debate (2005: 76). What this suggests is that when watching factual entertainment series, we are in fact watching nothing more than drama, with its required cast of characters who will undoubtedly react under pressure to situations they are likely to be unfamiliar with. When a dozen strangers are grouped in a house and given tasks to complete, for example, obvious conflict is on the horizon. Furthermore, when these strangers have been chosen carefully to create as much dramatic tension as possible, all having their own backstory, personality, and beliefs, then they are no longer strangers: they are characters, cast in what is hoped to be a dynamic unfolding drama. In short, participants become characters: no longer faceless figures of reality, but important components of a narrative who will bring meaning to the text.

If we think back to the early days of factual entertainment, most notably championed in the United Kingdom, and the BBC in particular (Lewis 2008: 72), characters like Maureen Rees (*Driving School*), Eileen Downey (*Hotel*), and Jeremy Spake (*Airport*) entered our living rooms—and our lives—on a weekly basis, guiding us through their numerous work- and life-related trials and tribulations. And what is important to reinforce here is that they were characters, not participants. They were not the learner driver, the hotel manager, or the airport worker: they were the silly-but-lovable Welsh woman who did not deserve to be on the road, the hard-faced "snobby" control freak, and the ever-so camp, married Aeroflot employee who spoke fluent Russian and rolled his eyes a lot. The situations we saw them in were important, but only because they provided a framework in which they could react. Key to their characterization, too, was the act of reflection they would partake in, signposting to us clearly that they were not mere participants but characters who were learning valuable life lessons along their journey. More recent shows like *Wife Swap, Supernanny*, and *Holiday Showdown* embrace this act of reflection even more obviously—both within the situation by the characters themselves, and outside of the situation by the presenter—positing that the essence of the narratives presented is not action and event, but character transformation and growth: a more devoted wife, a kinder parent, a more generous father, and so forth.

Kristyn Gorton's work is useful to discuss here because of her interest in the emotional aspect of television. For her, television is all about "feeling," and in fact can be a marker for what makes a television text good or not so good, in the sense of how much we feel about the characters in their situations (2006: 72–77). With regard to factual entertainment, she cites Annette Hill's discussion of *Wife Swap*: "When viewers witness the 'ordinary' 'drive of life' in reality programs, they are immersed in the experience of watching and also reflecting on how this relates to them, storing information and ideas, collecting generic material along the way" (2009: 100). There is a relationship, then, between the audience and the characters they are watching, as noted by Hockley (2007). Gorton goes on to ask her own questions of how emotion in factual entertainment is "fashioned by producers to elicit a response from the audience" (2009: 100)—in other words, taking the practitioner's view about how these series are put together. According to television commissioning editor Ralph Lee, series such as *Wife Swap*, *Supernanny*, and *That'll Teach 'Em* are "heavily interventionalist" (cited by De Jong 2008: 170), meaning they are tightly constructed, highly formatted, and narratively restrictive. The use of emotion in these series, then, permeates the on-screen actualities taking place and provides a way of collapsing boundaries—class, gender, race, and so forth—between participants and their audiences, in order to generate a shared feeling (Gorton 2009: 100). In other words, the interventionalist strategy is one of structuring emotion, or, what we might call *emotioneering*. Furthermore,

> while superficially operating as light entertainment, many reality or lifestyle programmes such as *Wife Swap* [...] seek legitimacy through a suggestion that they play a deeper pedagogic role: they invite us, the audience, to reflect on our intimate feelings and relationships through an empathetic engagement with the participants.
>
> 2009: 100

The word "legitimacy" is an interesting choice here, alluding to the notion of such series seeking judgment as "successful" or "authentic" from its audience through, I would argue, its emotional appeal. In this way, and thinking specifically from a practitioner's point of view, only through careful emotioneering will factual entertainment series be completely understood by their core audiences. It is through the emotions of their participants—or, through character journeys— that series such as *Wife Swap, Supernanny*, and *That'll Teach 'Em* elicit meaning and therefore generate audience appeal.

To further this idea of the character journey, which I alluded to at the start of this chapter, let us consider the development of characters through these television series. As with fictional dramas, characters are not static: they undertake a series of activities (plot, physical journey) and through doing so, undergo a character arc (story, emotional journey). As Gorton identifies:

> One of the catchy aspects of programmes such as *Wife Swap* is the notion that distances and differences can be overcome through emotional exposure. That a simple case of walking in another's shoes could lead to self-transformation, self-actualisation and community.
>
> 2009: 101

As with drama, the character journey is based on the premise that someone ventures into an unknown world and experiences something new: or to use Gorton's words, walks in another's shoes. From doing this, life lessons are learnt, new knowledge is acquired, and fresh understanding is brought back to the original world. As with series such as *Wife Swap*, this is made apparent through the character returning to his or her home and family before a reflective de-brief takes place. In addition, it is specifically through this act of reflection that the character's transformation is made blatant: how he or she feels they have grown from their experiences.

Even shows at the lifestyle end of the spectrum, such as *Location, Location, Location, Property Ladder*, and *Grand Designs*, are essentially more about character journeys than they are bricks and mortar. Questions like, "Will they find a new home in Devon?" and, "Will the custom-made German windows ever arrive?" are structurally important, yet somewhat sidelined by more important character development questions like, "Will they ever get over the trauma of the move?" and, "Will they eventually find happiness?" In this way, the format of these shows can be seen to dictate the physical journey (moving house, converting a barn), whereas their participants dictate the emotional journey (overcoming personal obstacles, finding inner happiness). Participants thus become characters in a fictionalized narrative whose emotional impact is reliant on capturing—or staging—the right kind of footage for subsequent editing.

We can turn here to factual entertainment "guru" Robert Thirkell, who, from his long career developing a plethora of series, clearly understands the dramatic necessity of character transformation. He writes that "A subject on its own is not a potentially moving film: you need the story to have a chance" (2010: 6). In other words, a participant is boring: it is the participant's story, brought about by their transformational arc, that is interesting. Furthermore, "It needs to be a story that the people involved in really care about, and are hopefully passionate about too; it also helps if it is one that has an easily understandable challenge or quest" (2010: 6). Therefore, both those making the series and those consuming it need to care about the story; they need to feel emotionally connected to the transformations of the characters, which are carefully woven into an identifiable quest (the plot). To go back to an earlier point, intervening in the narrative in order to structure the character's emotional journey—emotioneering—leads to a greater sense of pleasure. This is why, as Ralph Lee posits:

> Transformation is what drives a lot of those documentaries […] they're about feeling that you've watched someone's life transformed. It's sort of powerful and empowering for the viewers that they feel that kind of privilege of seeing someone's life transform.
>
> cited by De Jong 2008: 170

To reinforce this sense of character transformation, and to go back to an earlier point, casting is clearly important. Characters are not only apparent as themselves, but against others, through contrast and context. As Holmes and Jermyn argue in yet another discussion of *Wife Swap*—a discussion that could just as easily be applied to *Come Dine With Me, Trading Spaces*, and *Holiday Showdown*—program makers clearly draw together juxtaposing couples or families in order to heighten the dramatic tension of the swap, and with "class frequently the crux of the contrast" (2008: 237). Class is perhaps an easy choice of contrast for the program maker in that there are so many easily identifiable markers of difference, such as appearance (body and apparel), attitude (beliefs and cultural understanding), and lifestyle (consumer choice and market ability). For Holmes and Jermyn, it is the use of *mise-en-scène* in the opening sequence of episodes that clearly and quickly establishes such class divides: "whether the camera is examining frozen beef burgers or apparently pretentious chandeliers, we are invited to judge these clues as markers of (class) taste" (2008: 237).

Conflicting characters may be put together purposely for dramatic potential, such as the careful decision-making that goes into casting series such as *Big Brother, Holiday Showdown, Supernanny*, and *Faking It*. As Meyrick explains: "Most of the time you're looking for characters who will go through a personal transformation, so finding people who will react to a situation that is a big contrast to their normal life is the way to go […] or else it won't work for the audience" (2013). Alternatively, conflicts may emerge over time and therefore require to be edited for dramatic effect, as with fly-on-the-wall series such as *Airline, Border Security, Club Reps*, and *Big Fat Gypsy Weddings*. As Meyrick points out:

> With shows like *Border Security* you have to find your characters in the field and that simply involves filming as many people as possible and in the edit choosing who stays and who goes. You always know though, when filming, who your best characters are. You get a feel for it.
>
> 2013

Either way, cast design is apparent: characters being used to challenge and present one another with obstacles, and through discussion—often heated—struggle for power and try to negotiate meaning. As an example of such cast design, Holmes and Jermyn point out not just the inherent differences between characters in *Wife Swap*, but their visual differences, too. From an episode in series two, they describe how "the now notorious 'benefits scrounger' Lizzie Bardsley swapped with aspirational working mum Emma. Lizzie's aggressive manner and unwieldy, obese body connote both working-class disorder and an unregulated femininity, especially when contrasted with Emma's petite, neat prettiness." (2008: 238)

To go back to Thirkell once more, and the production-based rhetoric of his writing, the fact of the matter is quite simple: we require characters who are in conflict. Without them, factual entertainment ceases to exist: "What all these [series] share are different mindsets banging into each other like tectonic plates that underlie a country colliding. If you can hit these fault lines you may be on to a winner." (2010: 5)

The presenter as character

Moving away from the participants themselves, we must consider the role that the presenter plays in the narrative's cast. The presenter is also a character, one who whether we see or not (narrator) has an important function in guiding how we understand both the situations taking place and those undertaking them. Again, this character—whether present or omniscient—is an integral agent of the series who allows us, if not forces us, to make meaning about what we see.

Arguably, presenters in the early days of factual entertainment were not so much seen as they were heard, narrators who guided us toward preferred meanings. Three examples are useful here. First, the narrator of BBC series *Airport* was well-known British actor John Nettles, who had already found fame with the drama series *Bergerac*, and who would go on to become synonymous with the internationally successful drama series *Midsomer Murders*. The choice of Nettles to narrate *Airport* was an interesting one because besides being well known, and therefore potentially able to attract bigger audiences (especially of a particular demographic), he is well known for having a unique voice. Nettles has a very calm, some would say charming, temperament, which makes his voice easily recognizable; it is associated with coolness, order, and trust—and, importantly, is very middle class. This was perhaps quite apt for *Airport*, a series that observed the often-frantic activities at one of the world's busiest airports, London Heathrow, and which, compared to its neighbors Gatwick and Stansted, appeals to a more middle-class, long-haul, and business traveler. The choice of Nettles, then, not only gave a well-known voice to the series, it gave it character, one that was in various ways complementary to the situations and people being observed.

Lakesiders, another BBC series that followed life at a large Essex shopping center, used actress Pauline Quirke as its narrator. This choice was also interesting for two reasons: first, because Quirke had become famous with the British sitcom *Birds of a Feather*, and was thus well known to the audience; and second, because of her cockney accent, which is synonymous with London and its outer boroughs (including Essex). Quirke's accent, along with her *Birds of a Feather* persona, made her an effective choice for *Lakesiders* because of her connotations of being "down-to-earth," "brassy," and someone who would take no nonsense. This was very much the *Lakesiders'* demographic, and as such gave the series a sense of character that was appealing to its target audience.

The third example is another BBC series, *Hotel*, which was narrated by actor Andrew Sachs. Sachs is best known for playing the role of Manuel in the British sitcom *Fawlty Towers*, which makes his role as narrator interesting because of his fictional link to hotels. *Fawlty Towers* was, of course, a calamity of an establishment, and although nothing so ridiculous happened at *Hotel's* Adelphi in Liverpool, his association with slapstick humor in a hotel setting certainly added a sense of character to the series. In all three examples, then, there is a clear correlation between series and narrator: the addition of an omniscient character who adds an extra level of story to the unfolding action.

More common in today's factual entertainment series is the presenter who is very much part of the action. This can vary, from the presenter as observer of action to the presenter as instigator of action, but in all its varieties the core function of this figure is that he or she is a character who brands the series, both for textual consumption (the series itself) and for extra-textual consumption (appearances, spin-offs, merchandise, and so forth). Tania Lewis writes about presenter and chef Jamie Oliver, whose career rocketed in a very short time from being a sous chef to an international campaigner for healthy eating. She notes: "Jamie represents a figure of mobility—appealing to both working class and aspirational viewers as well as middle class consumers, while also addressing a broader demographic in terms of youth and gender" (2008: 61). This is interesting from a character point of view because it reminds us that he embodies the "perfect" television presenter: one who appeals to a wide audience demographic, therefore attracting a multitude of audience types. This is useful for the broadcaster, of course, who is able to generate a greater amount of revenue from advertisers. Not only that, though, it means there is greater potential for the series to have a life beyond the screen, which was indeed the case with Oliver when he subsequently developed a range of high-quality kitchenware and a line in nutritious yet affordable meals for the "everyday" family.

The reason that all of this was possible, and why Oliver became so successful, was his character: not just his inherent character, but how he was sculpted into and branded as a specific type. He was no longer a young chef who cared about good food and healthy meals for children: he was Jamie Oliver. As Lewis writes, his persona was that of a "young, blonde, good-looking 'lad' who wears his hair a little long and is softly spoken, but who also self-consciously has a kind of performative cockney persona" (2008: 61). The suggestion of performativity is interesting here as it supports the idea of Oliver being sculpted into a character that audiences can—and want to—consume. Many television cookery series before Oliver's arrival were hosted by much more straight-laced, middle-class presenters (Loyd Grossman, Delia Smith, Jane Asher, and so forth) who, by and large, spoke in Received Pronunciation. What Oliver did was give cookery shows character, where even a simple element like accent, as noted with Pauline Quirke (above), can—and did—radically change the feel of a series, and open it up to new audiences (whilst, as Lewis maintains, still retaining some of the "traditional" audience types). It is interesting to note here how the success of Oliver paved the way for more cookery series "characters," including Nigella Lawson, James Martin, and The Hairy Bikers.

Kirstie Allsop and Phil Spencer are another interesting example of the sculpting and branding of presenters to give a series character. First appearing together on the Channel 4 show *Location, Location, Location* in 2000, they were an unlikely pair: a largely down-to-earth property developer who had made his money from hard work and risk and an upper middle-class interior designer and lifestyle expert whose father is a Baron and whose cousin is famous designer Cath Kidston. Early episodes revealed them to be unnatural presenters: they were awkward, clunky, and staid. They may have had the subject knowledge, but they were far from presenter material. However, what developed over subsequent years was a bigger focus on them as a presenting duo. Although their helping people to find new homes is still the central focus of the series, there is much greater emphasis—and awareness—of Allsop and Spencer (or Kirstie and Phil, as they are commonly known) from the point of view of their relationship with one another and with the home-seekers. This is played out on two levels: first of all, their on-screen bickering and banter (who knows best, who has the best eye for a bargain) and, second, their unofficial competition to be the one who actually finds the home-seekers their new home. In recent series, there is also an increased emphasis on Kirstie and Phil sitting together and reflecting on their experiences of working with the home-seekers. In many ways, then, as the Kirstie and Phil "brand" has developed over time, the series (and its spin-off, *Relocation, Relocation*) has become much more about them than it ever was. Now clearly defined characters, they attract audiences who want to see *them* at work each week, and at odds with one another; they want to see what happens in the world of Kirstie and Phil, not just where the Smiths or the Joneses will eventually find a three-bedroomed townhouse in a good school catchment area.

When considering the role of the presenter in factual entertainment, and especially the allure they have as a character in and of themselves, it is useful to turn to a fascinating study undertaken by French psychologists Beauvois et al. (2012). They were interested in exploring the obedience of a television audience to its game show host, thus making interesting assumptions about the creator–receiver relationship as alluded to through the discussion of character and audience here. Beauvois, Courbet, and Oberle "transposed Milgram's obedience-to-authority paradigm (Milgram 1963, 1974) to a TV game show setting where a female host (an accomplice of the experimenters) asked people to deliver (fake) electric shocks to other persons" (2012: 112). The intention was, quite simply, to discover "whether and when people would comply with, or resist, the televisual authority incarnated by the host of the game" (2012: 112). In setting up a fake game show with all its verisimilitudinous components (lighting, cameras, production personnel, and so forth), the psychologists rendered their experimental "field" as very plausible. Participants, recruited from the internet, were told that the "game show" was a pilot for a new TV concept, and that the creators were testing whether or not the game worked to their satisfaction. Beauvois, Courbet, and Oberle's interests were clearly in the psychological aspect of the experiment, as evidenced by the level of statistical detail in their article; nevertheless, their end of experiment summary is useful here. They write, for example, that "the hold that television has on people is such that, for persons on the stage of a TV game show, it represents an authority strong enough to make them commit clearly immoral or dangerous acts," and that "the only experimental condition that triggered significantly more disobedience (to extents like those found by Milgram) was the condition where the agent of authority went off stage" (2012: 118). In other words, the game show host possesses such power that he or she can radically alter the behavior of the participant or the audience. Or, simply, "We thus attributed obedience behaviors to the prescriptive power delegated to the host position" (2012: 118).

We might here consider famous game show hosts such the UK's Bruce Forsyth (*Bruce's Price is Right, Bruce Forsyth's Play Your Cards Right*) and Vernon Kay (*All Star Family Fortunes, Million Dollar Mind Game*), America's Bob Barker (*Truth or Consequences, The Price is Right*), and Australia's Larry Emdur (*The Price is Right, Wheel of Fortune*), not because they subject their contestants to electric shocks, but because they have become synonymous with the series they have presented: audiences have tuned in as much to see the host as they have to watch the show. As can be seen with the case of Bruce Forsyth, even series can come to be named after their bedazzling presenters: a true testament to their character appeal.

The expert as character

We might also consider the role of the expert in factual entertainment: the character who possesses knowledge that is central to the premise of the series, such as the fashion advisor, health expert, or lifestyle coach. As Lewis notes, the expert is sometimes embodied in the figure of the "celebrity intellectual," but what has more commonly developed is a trend that sees "fashion stylists, real estate experts, and home décor specialists jostling for screen time with the history boffins and other more traditional [...] experts" (2008: 72–73).

Powell and Prasad, in their article on the celebrity expert, are concerned with "how television, print, and advertising play a role in constructing media stars who transfer particular lifestyle knowledge through to the lived experience of ordinary people" (2010: 111), a figure they call the "cultural intermediary" (2010: 111). Although their article is more concerned with the cultural and political ramifications of the celebrity expert, it is useful in supporting this chapter's argument that it is through agents—celebrities—that we are able to make sense of the world we live in. In the United Kingdom, it is through Jamie Oliver we understand food; through Linda Barker we understand furniture; and through Colin McAllister and Justin Ryan we understand home decoration (2010: 111–113). Powell and Prasad use the Linda Barker (of *Changing Rooms* fame) DFS furniture campaign (2003–Present) to argue that it is through her status as a well-known and admired "celebrity"—a cultural intermediary—that she is able to not only validate shoppers' tastes but also endorse their lifestyle and, arguably, authenticate their existence (2010: 114). Images of Barker, in print, on television, and online, apparently help strengthen these marketing "claims," as does her all-important signature that appears on product packaging. I would like to suggest that this "extra textual" activity also helps validate the television series from which she became famous in the first instance: a two-way flow of celebrity "guarantee" that, when perpetuated long enough, in fact makes it difficult to discern where the cycle (celebrity, characterization, validation) began in the first place.

With a focus on lifestyle television series in particular, Lewis writes that because

all these shows are marked by a strongly instructional and educational focus, they draw upon a variety of types of "expert" knowledge, from the "commonsense" approach offered on the highly popular *Supernanny* to the more credentialed expertise featured on shows such as *Honey We're Killing the Kids*.

2008: 90

Arguably, the commercial or educational aim of the series will impact the choice of expert. For example, a series wishing to educate an audience about something politically important might use an expert with a high level of credence, such as a government official or an academic. A series wishing to attract high audience numbers and increase advertising revenue might, instead, use an expert with a strong character: someone recognizable and/or likeable who can be used to brand the series. An interesting case study in this regard is "Dr" Gillian McKeith, a nutrition expert who fronted the highly popular Channel 4 show *You Are What You Eat*. What is interesting about McKeith is her contested status as an expert and how a questioning of this led to the demise of the series—and McKeith herself.

McKeith's much-publicized credentials were an important factor in the show's initial success. High ratings were followed by numerous books, recipes, and a range of health products. However, these products were withdrawn from the market following a damning report from the Medicines and Healthcare products Regulatory Agency (MHRA), who was not convinced about their scientific "truth." Worse was still to come, however, when speculations began to circulate about McKeith's qualifications, specifically, if Dr McKeith did actually possess a Doctorate. Accusations that her "Dr" title was not real (Goldacre 2008), nor were her so-called qualifications from an accredited American college/university, resulted in McKeith quickly—and famously—abandoning the title. She publicly maintained her credentials, but was neither willing nor able to actually prove them. Subsequently known simply as Gillian McKeith, she quickly faded from the public limelight. What makes this an interesting case study from the point of view of character is that McKeith became so famous, so quickly. Lovingly known as the "poo lady" because of her infatuation with examining patients' feces, she became synonymous with the series and attracted many followers who, besides consuming her on television, consumed her books, her products, and the lifestyle that she "endorsed." She quickly shifted from protagonist to antagonist, though—from a "Dr" we could trust to a "quack" who had betrayed her loyal fan base. This shifting of allegiances does not just make sense from the perspective of the situation; it resembles, moreover, the fluctuating fidelity that audiences have with characters in television soap operas.

To continue this character saga, McKeith was quickly replaced by a new protagonist to the suite of healthy eating series: Dr Christian Jessen. What makes Jessen a successful replacement to McKeith is his legitimate status as a doctor, or, as he has become, a doctor-turned-celebrity. Fronting highly popular series such as *Embarrassing Bodies* and *Supersize vs Superskinny*, Jessen is understood in direct contrast to McKeith; he is her "better" replacement, and, arguably, he only "works" because professionally he is everything that McKeith is not. Jessen is openly gay, too, which arguably influences his public branding: he can be trusted, and unlike McKeith, has nothing to hide. If we consider dramatic notions of protagonism and antagonism, then we can note that as McKeith's credentials were publicly put into question, Jessen's popularity increased. Our trust in one character was lost, and so therefore projected and rebuilt in an alternative.

We might look to other "legitimate" factual entertainment series experts in our quest for understanding how audiences are drawn to characters, not mere participants. Examples include designer Kevin McCloud (*Grand Designs*), architect George Clark (*Build a New Life in the Country*), property developer Sarah Beeny (*Property Ladder*), and property expert Phil Spencer (*Location, Location, Location*). With these character experts, we are drawn to personalities, voices, and perspectives on a subject matter in an attempt to negotiate our way through a series, all the while not at the expense of credibility: these are legitimate characters who know what they are talking about. From the enigmatic connoisseur (McCloud), to the down-to-earth grafter (Clark), to the lovingly "told you so" mother (Beeny), these expert presenters promise to have been there, done that, and know how to pass on the advice to others. They represent the archetypal Hero who has returned from a successful adventure and assumed the role of Mentor for future Heroes-to-be.

Conclusion

I would like to conclude this chapter by speculating on the idea of story in a broad sense, and its relation to the world we live in. To start with, do we merely enjoy stories or do we *need* stories in order to live? How effective and affective are they? I would argue that as the boundaries between fact and fiction continue to blur, we are increasingly exposed to an overwhelming experience of story: stories told in everyday spaces and places, from cinema theaters and living rooms to buildings, shopping malls, clothing, and interior design. The world can be seen as one giant narrative where an inherent understanding of story structure and character emotion produces a clear and defined awareness of the self in relation to the rest of the world. In other words, I have undertaken this action therefore I feel this way; I dress like this so people are likely to see me as such; my house looks like this so the perception will be that I am like that, and so forth. Stories are inherent in everything we do, not just everything we see or read. From dressing in the morning to relaxing at night, from decorating a living room to cooking a meal, we play out small but important narratives that, when pieced together, tell the bigger narrative that is our life: small tales of a bigger story.

Factual entertainment series, then, do not merely represent but *promote* this fascination for what I would like to call a "storied world." By putting their characters (participants, presenters, experts) in situations designed to challenge them, physical struggle brings about emotional transformation, and with it, audience resonance. Meyrick is keen to point out that as a program maker, she is always honest with her subjects about what they are getting involved in. As she told me:

> I have never lied to anyone about what is going to happen to them, and if someone does, it is unethical. Of course people are often very confronted with seeing themselves in the completed show [… but] as a program maker, if you have no integrity then you would not be able to sleep at night. (2013)

Nevertheless, factual entertainment series transport us on journeys that require *characters* to elicit meaning. Through protagonism, antagonism, and emotional growth, we acquire narrative pleasure and narrative comprehension.

The centrality of character is applicable to any media text. Without them, we know nothing; or, perhaps more accurately, we understand nothing. Whether they are the participant in a factual entertainment series, the presenter of a television debate, or the expert giving advice in a magazine advertisement, it is through them that we understand what it being told—or sold—to us. We identify with them as characters because in addition to speaking our language (literally and metaphorically), they make facts—and feelings—intelligible. They represent me and you and everyone we know; and more than that, they embody our in-built system for turning information into intelligence and emotion. Their importance is so crucial that we need to pay attention not to what stories are being told, but *whose* stories are being told, and by *whom*. If we can accomplish this, we will be able to comprehend completely and truly what the media text is actually trying to say.

References

Batty, Craig. 2007. "Trust me… I'm a Screenwriter! Exploring Problems of Narrative Structure and Closure in Contemporary Film's Portrayal of 'The Real.'" In *Proceedings of the Documentary Tradition*, Dallas.

Batty, Craig. 2011. *Movies that Move Us: Screenwriting and the Power of the Protagonist's Journey*. Basingstoke: Palgrave Macmillan.

Batty, Craig and Sandra Cain. 2010. *Media Writing: A Practical Introduction*. Basingstoke: Palgrave Macmillan.

Batty, Craig and Zara Waldeback. 2008. *Writing for the Screen: Creative and Critical Approaches*. Basingstoke: Palgrave Macmillan.

Beattie, Keith. 2004. *Documentary Screens: Nonfiction Film and Television*. Basingstoke: Palgrave Macmillan.

Beauvois, Jean-Leon, Courbet, Didier, and Dominique Oberle. 2012. "The prescriptive power of the television host: A transposition of Milgram's obedience paradigm to the context of TV game show." *European Review of Applied Psychology* 62, no.3: 111–119.

Cunningham, Keith. 2008. *The Soul of Screenwriting: On Writing, Dramatic Truth, and Knowing Yourself*. New York: Continuum.

Cuthbertson, Ed. 2005. "Reality television: Popcorn for the hungry." *Screen Education* no. 39: 76–79.

De Jong, Wilma. 2008. "'The Idea That There's a "Truth" That You Discover is Like Chasing the End of a Rainbow': An interview with Ralph Lee." In *Rethinking Documentary: New Perspectives and Practices*, edited by Thomas Austin and Wilma De Jong, 167–171. Maidenhead: Open University Press.

Goldacre, Ben. 2008. *Bad Science*. London: Fourth Estate.

Gorton, Krisitn. 2006. "A sentimental journey: Television, meaning and emotion." *Journal of British Cinema and Television* 3, no.1: 72–81

Gorton, Kristin. 2009. *Media Audiences: Television, Meaning and Emotion*. Edinburgh: Edinburgh University Press.

Hockley, Luke. 2007. *Frames of Mind: A Post-Jungian Look at Cinema, Television and Technology*. Bristol: Intellect.

Holmes, Su and Deborah Jermyn. 2008. "'Ask the Fastidious Woman from Surbiton to Hand-Wash the Underpants of the Aging Oldham Skinhead . . .': Why not wife swap?" In *Rethinking Documentary: New Perspectives and Practices*, edited by Thomas Austin and Wilma De Jong, 232–245. Maidenhead: Open University Press.

Hutzler, Laurie. 2005. "Reaching worldwide audiences." *ScriptWriter Magazine* no.23: 6–8

Lewis, Tania. 2008. *Smart Living: Lifestyle Media and Popular Expertise*. New York: Peter Lang.

McKee, Robert. 1999. *Story: Substance, Structure, Style, and the Principles of Screenwriting*. London: Methuen.

Meyrick, Sophie. 2013. Interviewed by Craig Batty, March 8.

Paget, Derek. 1998. *No Other Way To Tell It: Dramadoc/Docudrama on Television*. Manchester: Manchester University Press.

Paget, Derek. 2004. "Codes and conventions of dramadoc and docudrama." In *The Television Studies Reader*, edited by Robert C. Allen and Annette Hill, 196–208. London: Routledge.

Powell, Helen and Sylvie Prasad. 2010. "'As Seen on TV': The celebrity expert: How taste is shaped by lifestyle media." *Cultural Politics* 6, no.1: 111–124

Smith, Murray. 1995. *Engaging Characters: Fiction, Emotion, and the Cinema*. Oxford: Oxford University Press.

Thirkell, Robert. 2010. *Conflict: An Insider's Guide to Storytelling in Factual/Reality TV and Film*. London: Methuen.

Part 2

Transforming the Ordinary/ Everyday

3

The Good, the Bad, and the Healthy: The Transforming Body and Narratives of Health and Beauty in Reality TV

Peri Bradley

Bournemouth University, UK

Introduction

The transforming body has recently emerged as a pivotal figure in contemporary culture and more specifically reality TV concerned with health. This transforming body as an "ethical" body will be explored in relation to recent reality TV texts, placing them in both historical and ideological contexts. At the center of this Foucauldian concept is the idea of what it is right to *be* rather than what it is right to *do*. Simply put, morality becomes a question of how you care for yourself rather than how you care for others. Moral fiber is literally equated with physical fiber where the flesh itself is taken as a measure of integrity. Morality and goodness are now measured by an ideal of physical health and fitness, rather than spiritual purity. This notion evokes Descartes' dualism, with the Cartesian split between the ethereal mind and the material body and the belief that all that is physical can be controlled. With contemporary technological advancements, there has developed a belief that by taking control of the actual material of the body itself each individual will become a unit of ethical behavior (attached to the body rather than to the mind) that will seep into the fabric of society itself.

The strand of the media that is most closely bound up with the notion of meta-narratives as it purports to deal with universal "truths" or authenticity is reality TV. It has many forms and many functions, all of which appear innocuous and harmless and created in the name of info or entertainment. However, an examination of the specific UK reality television program, *Supersize vs. Superskinny* (Remarkable Television, Channel 4, UK, 2007–Present), a program that deals with somatic issues of morality and ethics, reveals an underlying trend by the media to act in a prescriptively political manner that moves morality and ethics away from their former position as shared and socially cohesive values to that of individual and socially isolating projects, which are confined to and expressed by the body. This chapter is an attempt to demystify and clarify the purpose and consequences of these programs in their cultural and industrial context.

The high profile of the ethical body has been increasingly elevated by the rising number of reality TV programs, in both the United States and the United Kingdom, that use the transforming bodies of the participants as the foundation of their narrative structure. These programs tend to revolve around the capability of the technology of plastic surgery to transform the body, such as *Extreme Makeover* (Lighthearted Entertainment, New Screen Entertainment, Living TV 2002–2010), *The Swan* (Galen Productions, Living TV 2006–2009), and *Ten Years Younger* (Maverick Television, Channel 4, UK 2004–2009). These specific programs are concerned with glamorizing and perfecting the body to produce an ideal, a type of Vitruvian Man that ordinary people can aspire to. Simultaneously a strand of health programs also appeared, such as *The Biggest Loser* (NBC, 25/7 Productions, 2004–Present) and *Fat March USA* (Ricochet Television, ABC 2007) in the United States, and *You are What You Eat* (Celador Productions, Channel 4 2004–2006) and *Supersize vs. Superskinny* in the United Kingdom, which still have the transforming body at their core, but are less about representing the ideal body and more about representing an ideal society expressed and contained by the ethical body. Reality TV is acknowledged to be largely about spectacle, and a consideration of how this spectacle is employed and deployed in the program is also related to Foucault's clinical gaze. The clinical gaze derives from his text *The Birth of the Clinic* (1991) where he analyzes the institution of the Clinic itself and how medical discourse influences and manipulates the body. Foucault speculates that the formation of clinics and hospitals signaled an ordering and organization of the treatment of disease and the individual, and effectively became the responsibility of the state.

The forging of medicine to the nation and thereby the state places both the clinic and the doctor as political. The economics of a state are bound up with the well-being of its work force that are required to be healthy to be able to function in the workplace, earn money, and, more importantly, spend money. Without these basic strata of fiscal stability, the nation itself wanes and "sickens." Therefore the doctor (as an agent of the clinic and thereby the nation-state) operates in a political manner to ensure that even the lower echelons of society (the poor) remain healthy and able to perform their assigned role in the economic structure. This results in an obligation being placed upon the poor to demonstrate their gratitude in a way that the rich were and are not expected to. Thereby the poor became the object rather than the subject of the clinical gaze as their poverty rendered them powerless to resist the necessity of observed treatment. Foucault's study of the political significance of medicine and the clinic and its use of the poor is illuminating when applied to transformation texts of reality TV that base their content on modern-day medicine and its methods.

When analyzing these texts it becomes apparent that the contestants/subjects are selected from particular lower and disadvantaged social groups. It is very much a case that these people are unable to afford the treatment offered by the programs, such as personal trainers, dieticians, dentists, psychologists, and plastic surgeons, just as Foucault's poor of the seventeenth, eighteenth, and nineteenth centuries were unable to afford clinical treatment. The moral problem that he identifies is similar, in that the patient is identified as the object of the clinical gaze due to his/her lack of financial capability. In the case of reality TV, the subject comes under the voyeuristic gaze of the television audience and the clinical gaze of the doctor—both of which examine, diagnose, and judge. The patient becomes the spectacle. The audience are complicit in the exploitation of the patient and the immorality of exposing his/her body, his/her "disease," and its pathology in the name of "infotainment." This "immorality" is attached to the lack of "ethical" behavior with regard to the body, such as overeating, undereating, or unhealthy eating, which thereby renders the body at its furthest from the cultural and acceptable ideal. Therefore, there is a perception of physical traits that do not conform to the ideal, as part of a spectrum of disease that can be treated and controlled. This perception then places a responsibility on the patient to actively seek a "cure" by working to conform to normative images and therefore be able to function properly as part of society. This aspect, combined with the availability of a large and willing body of "patients" seeking that cure and who are unable to finance it, further facilitates the circulation of Foucault's "normative images of 'model man.'" Thereby the imperfect and extreme bodies of the "patients" are presented as a spectacle of transgression and abnormality that operates as a type of "freakshow," in direct contrast to the societal ideal of the "model man" that is exemplified in the media.

In *Supersize vs. Superskinny*, the abnormal bodies of the contestants are displayed as a spectacle (in a moment of contemplation of their faults) and are required to take part in the television equivalent of a trial of martyrdom, which has to be endured in order to emerge as a healed and whole ethical body. The basis of the program relies upon two participants who are chosen for their extreme bodies and their extreme diets. One of the participants is always morbidly obese and the other bordering on the anorexic. To understand completely how the program operates as both a narrative and an agent of governance, the meanings of the obese body and the underweight body must be considered in their historical, cultural, and political contexts. The obese body is most often critically engaged with from a feminist perspective, as in Orbach's *Fat is a Feminist Issue* (1998) and Bordo's *Unbearable Weight* (2003), but in order to contemporize the issue and examine it more relevantly for a global economy, the concept "globesity" (global obesity) will be employed. The term was originally coined by the World Health Organization (WHO) in 2001, although they initially identified the obesity epidemic in the 1990s, and reveals the regard of obesity as a pandemic: a disease where being fat is equated with being ill. Orbach's and Bordo's theories of how women's body weight is used to distract and displace their attention away from matters of power and empowerment onto the more trivial issues of appearance and the ideal focuses specifically on the cult of thinness as a tool of patriarchal control. However, studies of the "fat" body reveal it as an indicator of social and cultural shifts in perceptions of diet, social welfare, and income as well as ethics and morality that use medicine and science to validate their use as a tool of governance. This is not to disregard feminist issues embedded in concerns over weight, but it is hoped to extend and interrelate them more comprehensively to address the function and purpose of the body completely and how it is employed in a cultural and political sense.

The obese body and the anorexic body

The history of the scientific study of obesity can be charted from the ancient Greeks up to the twenty-first century. By observing the change in how it is regarded and how the obese body operates as a signifier of health, wealth, social position, and morality, it is possible to reveal the meaning attached to excessive and surplus fat in both a local and global context (macro and micro). As Sander Gilman (2010) explains, for the ancient world, obesity played a role as a case study for medicine and its systems. Particularly in Ancient Greece, management of the body, including its intake of food and consequent weight, was an integral part of a complex religious and holistic structure that connected the human to the divine through food and the humors. These humors incorporated blood, yellow bile, black bile, and phlegm, all of which had to be in balance to maintain good health. They were also key to body shape and type, with phlegm being associated with those who were pale, lazy, inert, cool, and of course fat. Gilman points out that Greek medicine was based in dietetics or as he puts it "eating as healing" (Gilman 2010: 23). There was a core belief held by Hippocrates and other esteemed Greek physicians that there was a causal relationship between food and health so that,

> Certain foods were not only healthful but curative, just as a surfeit of others were the cause of illness, and central among those illnesses was obesity ... fat and thin could be either "natural" antithesis or signs of illness in terms of the balance and unbalance of the humours. Thus, fat reflects the pathological state of the body caused by imbalance.
>
> Gilman 2010: 23

This can still be seen to be in operation today, perhaps to a greater extent as the public are constantly reminded of what constitutes a healthy diet and the improvements in both bodily function and social function that can be attained through eating the "right" foods. The correctness of these foods can be identified not only by their "good" nutritional value and lack of "bad" elements such as fats and sugar, but also by their hierarchical value within the class system that identifies organically grown or free-range products as better than those that are intensively or "factory" generated.

Moreover, these imposed value judgments have an ideological implication that environmentally responsible food that is better for the ecosystem is also better for the health of the nation and ultimately of the individual. This is proven by evidence provided by scientists and endorsed by governments in order to convince "customers" of the value of particular foods and instruct them in the correct or "ethical" way to shop. As discussed previously, this is not a case of ethics as part of a religious model of correct behavior but as a more current notion of ethics as attached to the body and its appearance of "goodness." Therefore, the behavior necessary to maintain the "good" or healthy and attractive body, such as the purchase of "healthy" food, can be considered ethical. Television as part of the media has had a role to play in the instruction of ethical shopping and cooking. Programs like *Jamie's School Dinners* (Fresh One Productions, Channel 4 2005) and *Jamie's Ministry of Food* (Fresh One Productions, Channel 4 2008) were specifically aimed at improving education in healthy eating across schools and the nation. Such programs actually challenged what state authorities endorsed or allowed at the time but the public support provoked by the call for change actually altered perceptions and policy. The impact these texts had on the nation's psyche and general eating patterns also implemented a shift in awareness and culpability within the food industry and for government attitudes. The food industry, including supermarkets and other retailers, is an integral part of the discourse of fault and responsibility surrounding the health of the nation and the obesity epidemic. In an attempt to identify the root cause, blame has been attributed variously to the food industry generating huge profits on snack and convenience foods; to government policy allowing and even encouraging them to do so; and to the personal responsibility of undisciplined individuals who are ignorant of the "proper" way of using snack food as part of a balanced diet (Blythman 2006). What becomes apparent from this discourse is the ideological basis that each aspect operates from. As Michael Gard and Jan Wright speculate,

> the dire predictions and sheer intensity of "obesity talk" has more to do with preconceived moral and ideological beliefs about fatness than a sober assessment of existing evidence…rather than a global health crisis or an "objective" scientific fact, the "obesity epidemic" can be seen as a complex pot-pourri of science, morality and ideological assumptions about people and their lives which has ethically questionable effects.
>
> Gard and Wright 2005: 3

This raises questions about the regard of obesity as a self-imposed disease that is required to go through the process of medicalization in order to be brought under control. When considering the medical construction of obesity in the twentieth century, Samantha Murray identifies a shift from the placement of the fat body as a "societal parasite" to "societal victim" (Murray 2008: 47). Thus, the individual responsibility for obesity diminishes as hereditary and psychological factors are acknowledged, transferring responsibility from "patients" to "societal institutions and cultural changes" (Murray 2008: 48) until gradually in the 1980s obesity was actually categorized as a disease. However, this was not a simple process but one that saw the treatment of obesity as a matter of self-awareness, self-discipline, and self-authorship rather than just individual blame. As Murray points out, this medicalization is a form of disciplinary medicine that supplies the "patients" with the knowledge and tools to manage and control their health and weight, thereby placing responsibility firmly back with the sufferers. As this has become part of a medical discourse that includes and expresses itself through public health campaigns and, most recently and abundantly, television texts, this can be seen as a development that "veils an institutional and systemic urging of behavioural imperatives in order to regulate and order society" (Murray 2008: 50). This "ordering" of society is clearly the same force of governance and governmentality that disperses the ideological influence of authority under the cover of instructional and supportive advice. This is reinforced by Murray's statement that,

> by presenting healthy "lifestyle models" modern medical discourse refrains from explicit and/or coercive interventions into the lives of subjects, yet simultaneously draws on the authority of the medical "voice" to govern citizens "at a distance" with the expectation that medicine's rendering of "health" is a "proper" and "moral" means of living an ethical life.
>
> Murray 2008: 50

Television texts involved in lifestyle and health instruction such as *Supersize vs. Superskinny* illustrate this model at work and conform to a familiar narrative structure. The badly behaved bodies of the inmates/contestants are initially put through a process of psychological and emotional deconstruction. Then, after several stages designed to promote self-awareness of their "disease" (obesity or borderline anorexia), they are provided with the tools to enable self-help and self-regulation. All of this is achieved against an underlying theme that presumes the ultimate result will be a healthy lifestyle that is equated with an ethical lifestyle as decided by those in authority (government, science/medicine, education). The term "ethical" in this instance refers to the behavior of the individual adhering to guidelines offered by these institutions that enables their health to be maintained without treatment and cost to the health service and the government.

As mentioned earlier there is a recent move to identify obesity as a personal problem that requires a personal solution, which is part of a centuries-old and complex dialog between science, medicine, and government that uses the obese body as a model of ill health and unethical behavior to be compared to the ideal body as a paradigm of good health and ethical conduct. *Supersize vs. Superskinny* in particular uses this model in a televisual manner by employing a narrative arc that uses characters, aesthetics, and genre conventions to convince and persuade audiences. The observational and documentary-like form of the program also encourages a belief in the show as authentic and "true" that adds to its ability to alter perceptions. As part of this social commentary emerging from the program, in a comparative and critical display the underweight body is also regarded as unhealthy and unethical, thereby revealing a concern over the recent rise of anorexia.

Alongside the obesity epidemic there has also surfaced media representations of the equally extreme anorexia problem. Although the anorexic body is aesthetically opposed to the obese body, it still demonstrates a similar medicalization and association with social and cultural power relations. As Sharlene Hesse-Biber (1996) identifies, the cult of thinness is related to anorexia and even exhibits some of the same eating behaviors and disorders. She locates it as a primarily female practice/disease and traces it back as far as Aristotle and his contemplation of the female body as one rooted in the physical world whereas the male body was considered to be unimportant compared to his "Pure Mind" connected to his "divine Soul." This historical context led to women's bodies taking precedence over their minds and even led to the Victorian society actively discouraging women from being educated in case intellectual engagement adversely affected their reproductive system. Hesse-Biber also relates the female body directly to the rise of capitalism and consumer culture in the nineteenth century where women became the major consumer of goods, but at the same time their bodies became objectified as commodities. A woman's dependency on marriage for a financially stable and happy life meant having to conform to a feminine ideal dictated by male ideology, thereby placing her body and its appearance as her central focus requiring constant attendance. Even with the rise of independence for women in the twentieth century, the rigorous attention to appearance was demanded by a consumer culture obsessed with body image and being able to "purchase" the ideal physical transformation, be it through dieting, cosmetics, or surgery:

> These activities continue to divert economic and emotional capital away from other investments women might make, like political activism, education, and careers. These investments could empower women, and change their thinking about mind and body.
>
> Hesse-Biber 1996: 26–27

This is most apparent in makeover texts like *The Swan*, where the women are unable to function successfully because of their appearance. Their preoccupation with being unable to measure up to the ideal images permeating the media renders them inert and powerless to move outside their current role. In *The Swan*, once transformed into the ideal body, you would expect the women's situation to change but their preoccupation alters rather than disappears. Instead of a lack of self-esteem through anxiety over their appearance, this is replaced with a constant need to attend to and maintain the transformation, which once more "paralyses" them into a political inactivity. In her seminal text *The Beauty Myth*, Naomi Wolf explores the relationship between "female liberation and female beauty" and as she states,

> Reproductive rights gave Western women control over our own bodies; [however] the weight of fashion models plummeted to 23 percent below that of ordinary women, eating disorders rose exponentially, and a mass neurosis was promoted that used food and weight to strip women of that sense of control.
>
> Wolf 2002: 9

This notion of freedom then can be recognized as an artfully constructed illusion. Women are no longer prescribed a specific gender role and are not openly ostracized for penetrating its boundaries. However, the bombardment of ideal images from the media dictates what is desirable and desired.

Although the ideal body image shifted rapidly and fairly drastically throughout the twentieth century from the flat-chested and boyish figure of the 1920s "flapper," to the pneumatic and curvy form of the 1950s, back to the slender and diminished ideal of the 1960s, it can always be identified as responding to cultural and political shifts in women's social position. It appears that each time women began to gain some progress in the way of empowerment, consumer-led society would respond by supplying ever more stringent and demanding criteria for their body image to adhere to. The cult of thinness that exists today is one that emerges from a long-term and firmly established political need to maintain control over women by controlling the ideal image made available to them through the media. Yet whilst the obese body in contemporary culture can be recognized as either male or female in the context of globesity, the thin body seems to be predominantly female and is considered mainly in the context of feminism. As previously established, the meaning of the obese body also circulates within a political field and the fat female body is considered as an undisciplined body that resists the patriarchal control that typifies the thin body. As Kathleen Le Besco states,

> Viewed, then, as both unhealthy and unattractive, fat people are widely represented in popular culture and in interpersonal interactions as revolting— they are agents of abhorrence and disgust. But if we think about "revolting" in a different way, we can recognize fat as neither simply an aesthetic state nor

a medical condition, but a *political* situation. If we think of revolting in terms of overthrowing authority, rebelling, protesting, and rejecting, then corpulence carries a whole new weight as a subversive cultural practice that calls into question received notions about health, beauty, and nature.

Le Besco 2004: 2

This proposes the fat body as a resistant and political figure to be admired for its radical form that denies patriarchal control. As Orbach argues, an obese person challenges "the ability of culture to turn women into mere products" (Orbach 1998: 21). However, this is also a body that is attempting to defy the whole weight of modern scientific and medical "evidence" that names it as dangerous, unhealthy, and, both socially and personally, irresponsible. Aesthetically the thin body has become more acceptable and even desirable because it conforms more closely to the ideal body, and can be seen as disciplined because it demands constant attention to maintain its weight. As Rutledge Shields notes,

> these competing discourses surrounding body reduction help to position the discourse of thinness with that of health, thereby placing weightiness or fatness in binary opposition with health, as "disease."

Rutledge Shields 2002: 102

This typifies thinness as healthier than obesity, and critical studies of the thin body, such as Hesse-Biber's *Am I Thin Enough Yet?: The Cult of Thinness and the Commercialization of Identity* (1996) and Orbach's *Bodies*, also reveal the condition of anorexia as a form of resistance, that is capable of empowering women in particular, as they can feel they have taken back control of their life by controlling their body weight.

However, in *Supersize vs. Superskinny* the two extremes, excessive flesh and excessive thinness, are both regarded as unhealthy owing to their distance from the ideal image and its representation of ideal health rather than just ideal appearance. These aspects are signified by the body's enhanced physical function and appearance and evidenced by the participant's ultimate expression of happiness and well-being at the completion of the 3-month diet change. What both extreme bodies exemplify in the process of their transformation is the cultural and political forces at work upon their behavior and therefore also upon their flesh. Their diminishing or expanding physical presence on the television screen represents a move away from the gendered positioning of both obesity and thinness. Instead what we are witness to is Murray's "social ordering" at a distance or, in more traditional terms, Foucault's disciplining of the body by social institutions. These bodies, whether male or female, denote in their extreme form a resistance to the authority of the ideal body. These unregulated and disobedient bodies have to be corrected to return them to a normative state that expresses ethical behavior as stipulated by dominant ideology. Therefore, the transforming or transformed body becomes a site of contestation and struggle for political and cultural power relations.

These power relations are best observed at work in contemporary culture in television texts that provide an instructional model for healthy eating and living and thereby support this perspective of ethical behavior as an ideological ideal. Programs like *Supersize vs. Superskinny* clearly offer examples of ethical embodiment where the ethical (or unethical) behavior of the subjects offer models for audiences to adhere to or avoid.

Supersize vs. Superskinny and the ethical narrative of abjection

The typical narrative format of *Supersize vs. Superskinny* is integral to this process and demonstrates a storyline that inspires through its salvation of its subjects. After the initial introduction to the two subjects' extreme and unhealthy diets, they are brought under the instruction of Dr Christian Jessen into what is officially called a "feeding clinic." They live here for a week, without contact with their normal lives or families, each having to survive on the other's unhealthy and excessive regime. The expectation is that seeing someone else eating these meals will effect an epiphany, and each will see the error of their ways. As with *The Swan*, the structure of the program is based upon a biographical narrative of the participants' lives for purposes of close identification but also to demonstrate the "truth" or reality of the program. Kristeva's (1982) notion of the abject is also employed by this chapter to investigate how it operates to simultaneously repel audiences and also reinforce the concept of the ideal body, with visceral images of the interior and exterior of the extreme body.

The episode of *Supersize vs. Superskinny* that I have chosen for a case study is Tiffany and Keith (Series 2, Episode 7, first shown on Tuesday 24 February 2009). It is particularly relevant for inclusion of both male and female bodies and because of its inclusion of a gastric bypass operation. This allows an investigation of both the male and female bodies and how they are represented, thereby moving away from the concept of the gendered body and also exemplifies the notion of the abject at work in the programs. At the beginning of each program, we first meet the participants at home where we are treated to a visual feast of their respective extreme eating habits. In the case of the Supersize, a miniature camera is attached to whichever particular eating implement is being used, and the audience is carried, along with the food, directly into the mouth of the overweight contestant. Here aspects of the abject are being directly engaged with. We are given a privileged view of the internal cavities of a transgressive body. Kristeva identifies one aspect of abjection as "*exclusion* or taboo (dietary or other)" and another as "transgression" —both of which she closely relates to the Christian concept of sin. These bodies have pushed at the boundaries that remind us of death. The supersize body of Keith, consistently and excessively fed with "bad" or sinful foods—fats, sugars, processed foods,—literally becomes what it eats. The view inside the mouth reinforces that the food and the body consuming the food are abject, as Kristeva explains,

> "subject" [Keith] and "object" [food] ... confront each other, collapse, and start again—inseparable, contaminated, condemned, at the boundaries of what is assimilable, thinkable: abject.
>
> Kristeva 1982: 18

Here she is actually speaking of the abject in relation to Christianity and the sacred, and how it exists at the level of primal repression, always kept at bay by the rejection and denial of a "civilized" society. In association with the concept of the loss of meta-narratives, such as religion, these texts visually return us to the time of primal repression as they display abject bodies (reminding us of death— Dr Jessen introduces them as being "morbidly obese" and as "consuming their own bodies") who begin a purification process, which turns them from abject (or immoral) bodies into ethical bodies.

Against Keith is positioned the Superskinny (Tiffany) whose rejection of food sees her only eating a tiny amount of the full portion she serves herself. By denying herself what she sees as abject (in this case the food), her body begins to "eat" itself in order to survive, bringing her into close contact with the abject view of pollution by food. Kristeva identifies this as the boundary between "nature and culture, between the human and non-human" (Kristeva 1982: 75). Tiffany controls the pollution of her body by keeping the "non-human" consumption to a minimum, but ultimately by rejecting the abject she actually *becomes* the abject—a skeletal figure that firmly reminds us of the ultimate abject—the corpse.

At a weigh-in reminiscent of a prize fight, where both participants are exposed as transgressive by the extreme nature of their flesh, they are brought together in flesh-colored underwear to effect a visual comparison of the abject bodies. Keith is almost five times the size of Tiffany at 29 stone (about 340 pounds) and his leg is almost the same girth as her torso. With no normative figure to compare them to, the contrast between the two is rendered even more extreme. However, what is particularly significant is the method of comparison of their diets. The program makers set up two "food tubes," which they fill up with the appalling diets of the two contestants.

The voiceover that accompanies this process is explicit in its factual condemnation of their eating habits. Tiffany's meager daily diet is first to trickle into the tube as we are simultaneously informed that,

> An average calorie intake for a woman is 2000 calories per day. With her hectic lifestyle and an intake of just 1800 Tiff is under-eating by 1400 calories a week, making it impossible for her to gain weight.
>
> SS vs. SS, S2, E7, 2009

As we regard Keith's tube become rapidly engorged with processed, fatty foods we are told,

> The average calorie intake for a man is 2500 calories per day. On his worst days Keith is devouring a colossal 6000 calories. That's a whopping over-eat of 9 and half days' worth of food a week.
>
> SS vs. SS, S2, E7, 2009

The facts we are supplied with are scientifically calculated and therefore resonate with an authority and command that is designed to shock, with its emphasis on the extreme behavior practiced by the participants, and also to instruct on correct and regulated food intake for the nation. Aesthetically, the visual effect as the food spills into the tubes is designed to revolt and repel the audience as it becomes clear that the tubes are an externalization of their intestines. Their daily intake of food is poured into the tubes to form a visually abhorrent simulation of the gut. The intention is to present the contestants' diets as disgusting, as "non-human" as "other" and so as abject, to them and to the audience. As Kristeva states, even in normal circumstances

> Food in this instance designates the other (the natural) that is opposed to the social condition of man and penetrates the self's clean and proper body.
>
> Kristeva 1982: 75

Obviously the contestants' "clean and proper bodies" have already been contaminated as their physical appearance offers evidence of the fact that an unethical use of food will produce an unethical body. Having gone through a form of diagnosis, they are then prescribed a remedy: the diet swap as a cure for both the physical and moral ailments they suffer from. For both this is a punishment, a "rite of passage" ordeal that must be endured in order to begin the process of purification. Both are disgusted at their own diets but even more so at each other's and so the extreme nature of the food they eat renders it even more difficult for them to tolerate the swap. We follow them through this daily process, but other more psychological aspects are added to simultaneously test them and manipulate them toward an ethical regard of food and their own bodies.

We are informed by the voiceover that the facts about Tiffany's malnourishment are "startling and Dr Jessen is hoping that a few shock tactics will get her to change her ways." To encourage her to eat healthily Tiffany is taken to a sparse white room resembling a gallery where photos of parts of her body have been enlarged and displayed. Each photo represents a deterioration of her health and her body that Dr Jesson wants to emphasize in order to encourage her to change. The first photo is of Tiffany's "boobs," which barely fill her tiny bra. Dr Jessen states that,

> This is something you see a lot in underweight women. They start to look rather androgynous. They start to develop a boyish figure rather than a feminine figure and that is sort of a warning sign if you like that weight is becoming a problem and the body is changing and re-absorbing itself. Which sounds a bit alarming doesn't it?
>
> SS vs. SS, S2, E7, 2009

They then go on to look at the effect of her diet on her hair and nails, where she is told that the worst-case scenario is baldness due to a lack of enough vital vitamins and minerals in her diet, which shocks and dismays her. Dr Jessen moves on to a photo of her tiny hips and almost concave stomach and agrees with Tiffany that they are like a child's.

He goes on to relate her childlike body to her childlike portions and tells her that she needs to eat "adult, 'lady' portions rather than little girl portions." As they are in a clinic and the presenter is a doctor, overall the discourse and the language are couched in medical terms. However, this particular scene has an underlying theme that resonates around the "feminine" rather than female body, which is part of a cultural discourse rather than a medical one. Tiffany's fragmented body in photos is held up for contemplation as a spectacle in accordance with Laura Mulvey's "gaze," maybe not for sexual gratification but still as a form of control. Specific parts of the female body are identified as needing to conform to the prescribed ideal in order to be regarded as feminine (breasts, hair and nails, and hips) and Tiffany's body is then diagnosed as unable to conform to this ideal as a direct result of her unethical behavior. Her "punishment" for this "sinful" behavior is to look androgynous and boyish and be in danger of suffering the ultimate in the de-gendering of her body by going bald. Her lack of adult responsibility for her body is then emphasized, as the blame for her "condition" is placed firmly on her childish eating directly resulting in her childish body. The shock tactic employed by Dr Jessen concludes in Tiffany's identity as a woman being deconstructed. As diagnosed and confirmed by a doctor, she has lost contact with the "feminine" and has become de-gendered and de-sexed, returning to a childlike state that can only be remedied by adhering to a prescribed course of action.

The concept of the abject as theorized by Kristeva is used as a shock tactic throughout the program to reinforce the lesson to be learned regarding healthy and responsible eating by using the bodies of the participants as exemplars. The correlation of Tiffany's body with a corpse is visually supported by her photos: her bones are clearly visible through her skin and, according to Kristeva,

> It is as if the skin, a fragile container, no longer guaranteed the integrity of one's "own and clean self" but, scraped or transparent, invisible or taut, gave way before the dejection of its contents.
>
> Kristeva 1982: 53

Tiffany's internal/external boundaries have become so insubstantial that she has become an object of abjection. When this is made apparent to her, through Dr Jessen's shock tactics of forcing her to contemplate her own body, she moves up a level in the process of her purification as she begins to emotionally engage with her body once more. She begins to view food not as a pollutant or "other" or abject but as part of that process of purification enabling a move closer to the concept of the ethical body.

Keith's purification is necessarily different from Tiffany's and involves a visit to see an abject body that is an example of his possible future. Lisa is morbidly obese and is in hospital to have part of her stomach removed in a gastric sleeve operation; Keith is taken to meet her and learns the reasons for her plight and realizes he is headed in the same direction. Lisa is used as an object of educational spectacle (much like Foucault's poor bodies in the clinic) that is a warning to Keith and the nation alike. As they stand in the sterile white corridors of a hospital, Dr Jessen tells Keith,

> I have brought you here today because I want to make you realise that balanced and sensible diet and exercise is by far the best way to control your weight. I'm going to show you something that I think is probably going to shock you quite a lot but I hope will make you realise that it's not a situation you ever want to find yourself in.
>
> SS vs. SS, S2, E7, 2009

Against funereal background music, we then view Lisa's obese body in slow motion as she is undressed, laying bare her dimpled and distorted, transgressive flesh, in order to demonstrate the vast distance between her body and the ideal. The spectacle of her vast body, fragmented in much the same way as Tiffany's, is offered up for contemplation and simultaneously for condemnation and pity.

Her dependent state is illustrative of how disabling extreme obesity can be, and as the camera scans over her body like a mountain range the audience can only wonder at the extremes that the human body is capable of. The voiceover is also revealing of how we are expected to read and interpret this and other obese bodies, like Keith's.

> Over the last five weeks we have followed Lisa Wheeler's preparation for weight loss surgery. At 46 years old she weighs 26 stone making her morbidly obese. With a BMI of 66 she battles with her body every day. After a 10 year wait she's minutes away from major surgery to remove two thirds of her stomach and address her obesity nightmares for good.
>
> SS vs. SS, S2, E7, 2009

As Keith sits perched on a hospital chair with an expression of fear and trepidation on his face, Dr Jessen tells him that Lisa will never be able to eat a proper meal again, and as a consequence of her long-term obesity she has a list of ailments that require constant treatment. These conditions are firstly identified as those that are common to most obese people and are then recited by the voiceover as they are listed on the screen to reinforce the dangers of obesity. These include high blood pressure, DVT, constant back pain, a hernia, sciatica, and asthma. As Keith sits holding Lisa's hand he obviously struggles with anxiety and dread not only over the operation but for his own future. Dr Jessen steps in to reassure him by saying,

This is something you can do Keith. It's completely in your hands. It just requires self-discipline and I am hoping that now you've seen all this and once you've seen the operation that will give you the impetus to really go for it.

SS vs. SS, S2, E7, 2009

The screen then switches directly to the operating theater, and as we and Keith view Lisa's gastric sleeve operation, several aspects of the abject are brought into play. The voiceover explains that Keith is about to gain an internal view of the drastic effects of over-eating. Again we experience a breaking down of barriers, between the internal and the external, as large plugs are inserted on either side of Lisa's abdomen to facilitate insertion of the camera and the stapler into her internal cavity. We are then privileged to a scene inside Lisa's body via a large screen used during the operation, usually only experienced by surgeons and their staff. As the surgeon, Mr Ahmed, pokes and prods Lisa's internal viscera he points out the copious amounts of yellow fat evident around the stomach. Keith's reaction is one typically experienced when coming into contact with the abject as he states, "Looking at that fat is just making me feel … uhh … that is disgusting!" After locating the stomach, Mr Ahmed grasps it firmly with serrated tongs and applies the stapler. The visual juxtaposition of the hard, metal instruments against Lisa's soft and vulnerable internal organs follows horror film conventions by evoking a visceral reaction. The effect on the viewer is as Kristeva states: "These body fluids, this defilement, this shit are what life withstands, hardly and with difficulty, on the part of death. There I am at the border of my condition as a living being" (Kristeva 1982: 3).

Death is the literal breakdown between subject and object and as the majority of Lisa's stomach is wrenched out of a hole in her flesh we are forced to confront our own frailty and mortality. What was represented at the beginning of the program by a large plastic food tube has now become flesh; the internal has truly become external. The voiceover then emphasizes the seriousness of the procedure by quoting the statistic of one in a hundred operations ending in fatality and the complications that can ensue, such as leakage and infection from the stapled area. For Lisa this is a radical part of the purification process and is represented as an extreme aspect of the "rite of passage" technique that it is best to avoid. For Keith this close encounter with the abject is a lesson in morality; his ethical behavior (eating) has to improve in order to avoid the same fate. Kristeva states that when we speak of or confront the abject that there " … takes place a crossing over of the dichotomous categories of Pure and

Impure, Prohibition and Sin, Morality and Immorality" (1982: 16). For Keith, this crossing over leads to an epiphany that sees his purification process firmly established as he makes a connection between the food that he eats and the scene inside Lisa's body. Lisa's confrontation with the abject is a final attempt to transform her from abject to ethical and engages with Foucault's notion of "model-man" as its extreme opposite but capable in its impurity and immorality of advising how not to live.

Finally, having completed the diet-swap week and the activities designed to shock and motivate them, the two subjects are sent away to follow a strict and "healthy" diet regime compiled for them by Dr Jessen in the manner of a prescription on how to live. Our next encounter with them is when they return 3 months later for a final weigh-in and comparison with their pre-diet bodies and with each other. According to the conventions of makeover programs there is an understated final reveal, where the two are brought back together in order for them and the audience to see the results. Much like the reveal for makeover programs like *The Swan*, the unflattering white underwear is replaced with more becoming black underwear and their exposed bodies physically demonstrate signs of their ethical eating. They are not drastically transformed, as in the extreme makeover of *The Swan*; however, the signs of change can be traced on their faces and bodies. Dr Jessen deals with Tiffany first, giving her the good news that as a result of her ethical behavior she has gained five pounds. The voiceover also informs us that she has also gained "a healthy three and half inch gain overall." Healthier skin, hair, and teeth and no exposed bony joints also signal the transition from abject to ethical for superskinny Tiffany. Her body no longer resembles the corpselike reminder of death that it did. The layer of flesh and fat she has worked to gain is physical evidence of her healthy/ethical behavior. The program has used her transformation as a narrative myth of morality and change where the actual fabric of her body acts not only as evidence of moral rectitude but also as a register of difference. She is developing into Foucault's "model man" whose very being is instructional and motivational.

Keith has also altered, reducing in size and gaining in confidence. Dr Jessen informs him that he lost three stone and nine pounds and the voiceover tells the audience that he has a loss of "seventeen inches overall." His loss of flesh is also a monitor of his ethical behavior, charting his journey from undisciplined obesity to controlled weight loss. His body is used as an indicator and paradigm of model behavior that is also an exemplar of how a healthy and ethical conduct leads to happiness and success. The abject flesh that is symptomatic of iniquitous and unruly action begins to reduce, demonstrating an ethical commitment to self-improvement. Keith's physical transformation correlates with his narrative transformation, revealing a compelling story of ethical and corporeal struggle that serves as an allegorical lesson for society to follow.

Both Tiffany's and Keith's post-transformation interviews reveal a psychological change that has occurred along with the physical change. As the camera sweeps across her more substantial but still slim body, Tiffany reveals that,

> Since the swap, everything seems healthy about me now. My skin, my nails, there's a bounce in my step. People say I'm glowing!
>
> SS vs. SS, S2, E7, 2009

Keith's final words are accompanied by a full-length shot of his slimmer figure and his smiling face, demonstrating his newfound confidence and satisfaction at moving closer to the ideal image through the practicing of ethical behavior.

> Losing the weight has made me feel fantastic. I feel like a teenager again. I feel at ease around ladies. And they feel at ease around me and I'm having fun. I'm having fun again. And I'd forgotten what that was like.
>
> SS vs. SS, S2, E7, 2009

These final words and images are instrumental in constructing and maintaining the myth of healthy behavior as ethical behavior. Their ethical behavior is not recognizable in the conventional sense of the word as correct and ethical behavior, but as in the sense of practicing ethical conduct (healthy eating and exercise) to produce an ethical body (conforming to the ideal). Tiffany's speech demonstrates her belief that her skin and hair being "healthy" has reconstructed her as attractive (glowing) and confident (with a bounce in her step). Hence, her ethical behavior has resulted in happiness and satisfaction by becoming more feminine. Keith's words reveal his conviction that his weight loss has made him younger (like a teenager), more attractive (at ease around the ladies), and happy (having fun), so that his ethical conduct can be seen to have returned his self-esteem and his masculinity. The de-gendering they have both suffered due to their transgressive bodies is reversed and they are ready again to take up their assigned gender roles. Through the employment of ethical behavior both bodies have managed to move closer to the ideal image and via this achievement attained the happiness and satisfaction that result from social acceptance. The ideological resonance of their bodies for the audience is therefore instructional and hegemonic in the sense that they provide lifestyle models that are ideologically prescriptive and designed to maintain specific power-relations.

References

10 Years Younger. 2004–2009. Maverick Television. Channel 4. UK.

Biggest Loser USA, The. 2004–. NBC. 25/7 Productions.

Blythman, Joanna. 2006. *Bad Food Britain.* London: Fourth Estate.

Bordo, Susan. 2003. *Unbearable Weight: Feminism, Western Culture and the Body* (10th edition). LA, London: University of California Press.

Extreme Makeover. 2002–2010. Lighthearted entertainment, new screen entertainment, living TV.

Fat March USA. 2007. Ricochet television, ABC.

Foucault, Michel. 1991. *The Birth of the Clinic.* London: Routledge.

Gard, Michael, and Wright, Jan. 2005. *The Obesity Epidemic: Science, Morality and Ideology.* Abingdon: Routledge.

Gilman, Sander L. 2010. *Obesity: The Biography.* Oxford: Oxford University Press.

Hesse-Biber, Sharlene. 1996. *Am I Thin Enough Yet?: The Cult of Thinness and the Commercialization of Identity.* Oxford: Oxford University Press.

Jamie's Ministry of Food. 2008. Fresh One Productions, Channel 4.

Jamie's School Dinners. 2005. Fresh One Productions, Channel 4.

Kristeva, Julia. 1982. *Powers of Horror: An Essay on Abjection.* New York: Columbia University Press.

Le Besco, Kathleen. 2004. *Revolting Bodies? The Struggle to Redefine Fat Identity.* Amherst, MA: University of Massachusetts Press.

Murray, Samantha. 2008. *The 'Fat' Female Body.* Basingstoke: Palgrave Macmillan.

Orbach, Susie. 1998. *Fat is a Feminist Issue: The Anti-Diet Guide for Women.* London: Arrow.

Rutledge Shields, Vickie. 2002. *Measuring Up: How Advertising Affects Self-Image.* Philadelphia: University of Pennsylvania Press.

Supersize vs. Superskinny. 2009. Series 2, Episode 7. Remarkable Television, Channel 4, UK, 24th February, 2000 hrs.

Swan, The. 2006–2009. Galen Productions, Living TV.

You are What You Eat. 2004–2006. Celador Productions, Channel 4.

Wolf, Naomi. 2002. *The Beauty Myth: How Images of Beauty Are Used Against Women.* New York: First Perennial Edition.

4

Competence in Your Own Enactment: Subjectivity and the Theorization of Participatory Art

Simon Grennan
Independent Researcher

This chapter will attempt to utilize the work of Erving Goffman and some of the ideas associated with it in order to frame three works of art made by artists Rirkrit Tiravanija (in 1996), Santiago Sierra (in 2000), and Jeremy Deller (in 2001) and to consider existing theoretical approaches to them.

These artists methodologically include the real-time experiences of other people as content in their work. In each case this is a complex strategy that requires the creation of a matrix of firmly held dialectical and discursive positions that focus as much on a sociology of practice as on the theorization of art. As Claire Bishop comments of artists who practice in this way: "... these artists have internalised a huge amount of pressure to bear the burden of devising new models of social and political organisation ... " (Bishop 2012: 284). Their work belongs to theoretical and practical traditions of performance, conceptual, and installation art with roots that can be traced to the early twentieth century, which Bishop terms "participatory" (Bishop 2012: 12). Although their works do not necessarily share particular precedents with each other, as discourse they share a number of assumptions out of which their contemporary works arise.

The tradition of participatory arts practice has precedents in the process and protest art of the early 1970s, founded upon two motivating ideas: the indivisibility of art activities from social activities and the conviction that art practice is a defining practice of everyday life. In the last 25 years, this tradition has been theorized as political activism or "interventionism" (Foster 1998), as ecological path-finding or "New Genre" (Gablik 1994), and as a type of methodological wholism or "relational aesthetics" (Bourriaud 1998). In 2010,

Bucharest Biennial curator Felix Vogel used the word *handlung* ("acting" in English) to describe a revived theorization of social antagonism as a key dynamic of this type of practice (Vogel 2010). These existing theoretical approaches are characterized by the fundamental consideration of the social infrastructure for the production, presentation, and consumption of artworks, making discourse a core aspect of the work itself. This is often ideologically opposed to an approach to artworks that pretends to transcend the social circumstances of its own creation and consumption.

Generally, the theorizing of this tradition focuses heavily on ideas of social exchange, gift-giving, and generosity as paradigms for community cohesion and the subsuming of social hierarchy in social consensus. This approach was developed in the early 1990s by curators Mary Jane Jacob, Valerie Smith, and Yves Aupetitallot, in three exhibitions in France and the United States (Smith 1993, Decter 1994, Jacob 1995). The Land Foundation in Chaing Mai (1992–present) and Project Row Houses in Houston (1993–present) are two artists' initiatives that seek to practically manifest the theorization of exchange, supporting a position that makes a direct link between the representation of consensus and social benefit. Two subsequent events secured this broad approach to making and consuming artworks as a theoretical orthodoxy of contemporary participatory art: the exhibition "Traffic" at CAPC Musée d'art Contemporain, Bordeaux (Bourriaud 1996), and the publication "Relational Aesthetics" (Bourriaud 1998), both produced by curator Nicolas Bourriaud. Counter-arguments in this theorization have largely arisen from outside the tradition itself. Cultural philosopher Arthur Danto and art historian Mi Won Kwon both have argued that the theorization of social consensus in art is an end-game response to a broader culture spiritually debased by commodification (Danto 1996, Kwon 2004).

A third general position is emerging in the work of curator Felix Vogel, who is developing the theoretical base of the tradition rather than seeking to assault it. Vogel's *handlung* focuses on the antagonistic manipulation of social difference in participatory practice, as a proactive intervention in political and ethical life, rather than the presumption of beneficial social consensus often criticized for underpinning the idea of social exchange.

Rikrit Tiravanija's participatory artwork "Untitled (Tomorrow Is Another Day)" (1996) was a 100 percent scale replica of the inside of the artist's New York apartment constructed at the Kölnischer Kunstverein and open 24 hours a day for visitors to use in order to cook, sleep, meet each other, throw parties, study, and whatever else they might have wished to make use of a residential apartment in the center of Cologne for.

Santiago Sierra's "Workers Who Cannot Be Paid, Remunerated To Remain Inside Cardboard Boxes" (2000) constituted an exhibit at Kunst-Werke Berlin in which status-pending immigrants to Germany (who were not legally allowed to receive pay for work) were paid minimum wage to sit in individual, closed cardboard boxes during the opening hours of the exhibition.

Jeremy Deller's "The Battle of Orgreave" (2001) was the reenactment on 17 June 2011 at the same site, of a violent political skirmish between approximately 5,000 striking coal workers and 8,000 police at the village of Orgreave, United Kingdom, in 1984. The 1984 event was one of the most high profile in the most recent national struggle between organized labor and the British Government. The reenactment was achieved by members of 20 historic reenactment societies with the participation of people who had taken part in the 1984 clash and people local to Orgreave. The reenactment event was the subject of a documentary film broadcast the same year on national television, a publication, and an archive now housed at Tate Britain, one of the country's foremost contemporary art museums.

Figure 4.1 The Battle of Orgreave. Jeremy Deller 2001. An Artangel commission.

Production photograph by Martin Jenkinson.

Tiravanija's "Untitled (Tomorrow ...)" provided an " ... impressive experience of togetherness ... The art space lost its institutional function and finally turned into a free social space ... " according to critic Udo Kittleman, writing in the catalog that accompanied the exhibition (Kittleman 1996: np). If true, the work well represents the "criteria of co-existence" posited by curator Nicolas Bourriaud in his manifesto of art practices that methodologically include the experiences of other people as content (Bourriaud 1998). He proposes that the social situation manipulated by the artist (in this case signified by the Cologne museum) prompts a particular type of audience behavior, defined by self-questioning and a plurality of pragmatic or reflective responses, differing from habitual behaviors characterizing the activities of visitors to the museum.

The work's effect on the social situation in which it emerged constitutes the content of the work for Bourriaud (i.e. the change from one type of behavior undertaken by visitors to a museum, to other types). Although Bishop criticizes Bourriaud's theorization of this effect as the substitution of "ethicopolitical judgment" (*sic*) for aesthetic judgment (Bishop 2004: 65), she fails to grasp that these appellations only have meaning for Bourriaud as descriptions of types of social activity relative to the work, rather than as epistemological categories or criteria for adjudication independent of the social situation in which they are made.

Alternatively, according to theorist and critic Grant Kester, Sierra's "Workers ... " reproduced the economics of global capitalism as a spectacle for visitors to the Berlin museum and in doing so sought " ... to rob the bourgeois viewer of the solace of art as a space for spiritual recreation insulated from the contradictions of social life" (Kester 2011: 163). Kester argues that this effect is negated on the one hand by Sierra's theoretical reduction of museum-goers to a monolithic, complicit class of economic privilege/oppression, and on the other, by the undisturbed similarity of social hierarchy of the situations in which an unexpected encounter with a wage-slave, beggar, homeless person, or immigrant might occur, in or out of the museum.

It is the same, Kester concludes (and I paraphrase), for a class of museum visitor to walk past an immigrant in the street as to encounter that person on display in a museum as spectacle (Kester 2011: 165). In one sense, there is a rationale for Ketser's critique, based solely on an intuition (nothing more) of the experience of the people employed to sit in cardboard boxes themselves. They cannot be seen, they are silent, and they are earning very low wages illegally for demeaning and repetitive work. So much is, for them, life as usual as pending-status immigrants. It is only their place and type of work that have changed, for the duration of the exhibition. In Sierra's work, their performance, and that of the museum visitor, is utterly habitual.

Unlike both Tiravanija's "Tomorrow..." and Sierra's "Workers...," "The Battle of Orgreave" was described by Deller as a postmortem for an actual historic event that had been hastily passed over both in the public imagination and in the media in 1984 (Slyce 2003). In the sense of retrospective reenactment, reconsideration, and reevaluation, "The Battle of Orgreave" required a degree of prior knowledge of the event itself in order for it to become meaningful, but this prior knowledge was not considered a guarantee of any type of accurate recreation. Rather, despite the literal participation in the reenactment of a number of the 1984 event's original protagonists, the practical guarantee of versimilitude in "The Battle ... "'s presentation of a contemporary, 2001 view of an event in 1984 resided with the teams of historic reenactment experts employed to create it. The reenactment participants were required to conform to Deller's script and dress code in order to participate (Deller 2002: 154). The work's originality, in this way, resided in the application of a professionalized reenactment process, usually used to re-create key events of centuries past, to an event that took place in the very recent past.

In these three works, a shared discourse is produced in each case in widely different ways. This shared discourse has various causes and motivations, the scrutiny and discussion of which forms a major part of the art historical response to the works (see Bishop 2004 and 2012, Kester 2011, Beech 2002 et al.). The characteristics of the discourse itself, that is, the conditions that underlie the production of the works, might be summarized as follows. As discourse, the work of these artists appears to assume that behaviors that signify people as members of an audience are unspecified, incidental, or unimportant. It assumes that the physical location of the work is determined through an analysis of the social situation of the work in that location. It assumes that effecting instrumental changes in this social situation through the manipulation of the behaviors of everyone co-present produces the content of the work. That is also to say that effecting such instrumental changes becomes meaningful as historic commentary upon the social situation that has been changed or upon situations that it implies are similar to the one that has been changed.

This discourse constitutes a way of producing art that is singularly difficult to theorize utilizing art-historical methods, due in large part to the ways in which it problematizes rather than consolidates any role for a member of an audience or, more strictly, any participant whose activity is delimited primarily through reflective consideration of the work, including the art historian. This type of participant in the works I shall call participant-viewers.

Bishop describes succinctly a tenet of the discipline of art-history when she writes that "...art is given to be seen by others" (Bishop 2012: 241). This description neatly outlines the way in which the experience of a participant-viewer is placed theoretically beyond the discourse of the work in any way other than as a distinct situation in which, alone, a view can be taken. In effect, this theoretical delimitation of the experience of an audience is an art-historical definition of the work of art itself. For art-historians, it makes the task of responding critically to situations that contradict this discourse a very difficult one. Indeed, both Bishop and Kester describe participation-viewing in each work (which is the category to which their own participation belongs), as meta-participation, in which the entire situation of these works is available for an audience to view whilst being categorically separate from them.

On this basis, both Kester and Bishop are able to conclude that these works are more or less meaningful in as much as they provide a spectacle of ethically motivated art, intending to signal if not facilitate beneficial social engagement for someone or other, with the spectacle itself constituting an object of criticism. Kester writes that the motivation for art made this way is "...the transformation of human consciousness in a way that enhances our capacity for the compassionate recognition of difference, both within ourselves and in others" (Kester 2011: 185). Bishop writes that the goal of the work is "...to emancipate (an audience) from a state of alienation induced by dominant ideological order..." (Bishop 2012: 275). It is not surprising that both art-historians feel that the spectacle of ethical action in each work is underwhelming or that the ethics themselves are failed or misguided. They are considering the works from a largely unselfconscious position of meta-participation in which the whole work is considered available to view whilst the proscribed limits of participation as a viewer render it subjectively unaffecting (Bishop 2012: 284 and Kester 2011: 165).

The dissonance between the discursive methodologies of the artworks of Tiravanija, Sierra, and Deller and the subsequent theorization of the works by Bishop and Kester represent an antithetical difference in approaches to art practice as discourse. Furthermore, it could be argued that both artworks and theorizations themselves constitute a debate about the different types of discourse through which experiences of art are derived. Put this way, it is possible to outline in greater depth the ideological underpinnings of the type of discourse that constitutes the practices of Tiravanija, Deller, and Sierra other than those present in either Bishop's or Kester's critiques.

Bourriaud's conception of "relational aesthetics" provides a clue, in that he claims that the content of these artworks derives wholly from their capacity to affect the social situations in which they emerge. Thus, "relational aesthetics" conceives of a model of social relations in which each subject is both constrained and enabled in their actions by the context in which they act. Each subject experiences these opportunities and prohibitions as self-consciousness, meaning that the subject produces themselves through the reciprocal relationship between agency and social structure. This conception of discourse is a commonplace of contemporary sociology and can be traced through the work of Erving Goffman and G. H. Mead, ultimately to Georg Hegel (Goffman 1959, Mead 1967, Hegel 1979).

Goffman considers that any absolute ontology of the subject is ramified by social participation in the form of enactment, or the continual adaptation of individual behaviors according to desirable social typifications (Goffman 1959, 1967). In *The Presentation of Self in Everyday Life* (1959), he makes an analogy between the subject and the theatrical stage. He describes the subject as the product of the relationship between an unproduced or offstage self and enacted or onstage selves.

In this dramaturgic model of co-present, interpersonal interaction, the subject orients itself to each social situation in the form of an enactment of personal traits according to the requirements of the situation itself, relative to the existence of the unproduced or un-enacted self. Hence, Goffman's subject is bifurcated as a condition of subjectivity itself. Although he describes the offstage self as a private self, this privacy does not constitute the unmediated subject alone, for it only exists relative to the subject's enacted selves. Rather, the private self simply remains unproduced, un-enacted, and experienced by the subject alone. In one sense, the subject's un-enacted self is the enduring audience for the subject's enacted selves, taking a role relative to them that evidences a structural similarity with the social participants in every enactment, or the co-present other subjects.

It is important to avoid possible confusion between Goffman's theoretically bifurcated subject and the id–ego relationship theorized in psychoanalysis. In Goffman's terms, the id–ego is an attribute of the private self, remaining unproduced except through enactments. Sociologically, Goffman describes the subject as emerging in the relationship between produced and unproduced selves, that is, enacted and un-enacted selves. In taking this approach, his dramaturgic model is more akin to the relationship between consciousness and self-consciousness described by Hegel as a social foundation (Hegel 1979, Honneth 1995), which I shall return to later in this chapter. The appearance of a unified subject is a product of the relationship between the conscious subject and the self-conscious subject. This appearance is the basis both for the recognition of other subjects and for social normalcy, tying the emergence of the subject to the structure of social relationships and characterizing the limits of agency.

Self-enactment is then a constant negotiation between private and enacted selves as well as the continual attempt to orient the enacted self toward social normalcy, or rather the hard-won condition of intersubjective equilibrium, through the production of typified behaviors. Goffman writes that "…our intersubjective situations are governed by rules of interaction…a sustainable sense of self is intimately bound to these rules. We must abide by…such rules…if a (socially normative) sense of self is to be preserved" (Goffman 1968: 24).

Social normalcy results when private and enacted selves produce behaviors that conform to the constraints and opportunities indicated by social typification, or within what Bakhtin calls a "horizon of expectations" (Bakhtin 1985: 131). Because these horizons are habitually experienced, but not fixed, they only emerge moment by moment in each co-present situation. Enacting behaviors within them requires constant reorientation of the subject toward the situation on the part of every participant.

By definition, in any situation, social normalcy appears as an uninflected continuum of resolved contradictions, characterized by the absence of dissent and the absence of antagonism. In fact, the condition of normalcy is maintained only through the precarious equilibrium of contradictory subjective desires, enactment competencies, and the abilities and inabilities of all of the participants to influence or to be coerced by each other, or to collaborate or disagree. How extraordinary, then, is the quality of invisibility and lack of availability to critique, of any enacted behaviors that are produced within a specific horizon of expectation. The intersubjective relationships that sustain normal behaviors elude scrutiny in themselves, precisely because they operate through enacted conformity. Therefore, levels of competence in self-enactment produce meaningful social distinctions in themselves. Because competences in self-enactment are a condition of subjectivity, at a social level, each one of us exists in the continual demonstration of particular types of self-expertise.

If we consider the particular shared discourse of the three artworks from the point of view of Goffman's self-enactment, they can be described and adjudicated in quite a different way to that adopted by Bishop and Kester. Goffman's theory deftly provides a generalization of the process of subjective self-consciousness and accounts for the detail of the emergence of every social situation, institution, and interpersonal exchange, formally connecting the self and the society.

According to Goffman, we must consider enacted behaviors to be constrained by social habituation, including the delimitation of behaviors theorized as meta-participation. For example, it might be possible to argue that visitors to museums of contemporary art habitually behave as though they were art-historically idealized viewers, enacting meta-participation as self-production. Even so, it is not possible to extradite any behavior from the wider social situation in which it is produced. In the case of the museum visitor, this enactment always occurs relative to other visitors, to museum staff, to people hanging around the entrance to the building, to people on the street, and to the people responsible at points past for the facture of the artworks and the building and for the habits of their social use.

Hence, Goffman's theory extends an entire social ontology at the widest horizon of experience. As I have outlined, self-enactment is not a surface function of a private, individual self, but the arena in which both subject and world come into being. Of course, it could also be argued that this approach to theorizing the experience of the visitor to the museum can be applied with little distinction to a person's experience of an old master painting and the experience of Sierra's "Workers ... ". However, this is not the case. The differences in detail of the self-enactments constituting an experience of visiting a museum and looking at an old master painting and visiting a museum and experiencing Sierra's "Workers ... " cannot be elided, in Goffman's sense, although they might share significant similarities.

Crucially, the shared discourse of the artworks under discussion, by Tiravanija, Deller, and Sierra, is not the discourse of any artwork by an old master, although both can be found in the museum. The discourse conditioning the three artworks offers a specific affordance to each museum visitor in the social situation of the museum. According to this discourse, the visitor's response contributes to the content of each work only in so much as it constitutes a change in the habitual behavior of museum visitors, including reflection on past habitual behaviors. In the experience of these works, content is the relative enactments that constitute them. In "The Battle of Orgreave," it is even difficult to identify where an experience of the artwork takes place. Was the artwork constituted by an experience of the 2001 event, or is the artwork constituted by an experience of the documentary film or archive of the event? If it was the former, then any retrospective experience of the traces of the work belong to another register of experience in the museum and the work itself no longer exists.

We must keep in mind that, according to the discourse that these works embody, audience behavior relative to content is unspecified, incidental, or unimportant and the production of each work rests upon an adjudication of the whole social milieu in which it is experienced. Unlike the old master painting, these artworks beg a question as to the status and origins of people's social behavior relative to themselves, an occurrence for which a theoretical model of meta-participation, or viewing without affect, is unable to account. However, we might consider some of the deeper implications of this approach by utilizing Goffman's dramaturgic model to elucidate the co-presence of these works.

Key for an understanding of the discursive methodology emerging in the three artworks by Travanija, Deller, and Sierra is the notion that distinctions that we make about others and ourselves create both our subjectivity and society at once and that, on this basis, we live within a matrix of both social and self-constraints and opportunities. Modeling the relationship between individual agency and the influence of social structure, our self-enactments are not choices made from a possible range of behaviors, but the whole experience of being or the subject's constant struggle to achieve stability on the axis of social constraint and opportunity. This does not mean that we have no individual agency but, instead, that rather than modeling our behaviors according to some self-conscious schema, we are continually struggling to enact behaviors that increase our capacity to influence others on the basis of desire and self-observation.

When discussing the relative capacities of the participants in Sierra's "Workers..." Kester describes the no-status immigrants as having no agency. Although he criticizes Sierra for contributing to a state of affairs that negates each immigrants' agency, writing that "Only the viewer or public retains the power to act decisively..." (Kester 2011: 171), he fails to describe his own relationship with them, except as someone who is constrained to approach the work as a meta-participant. Rather, the people sitting in cardboard boxes have, exactly, the power of being themselves relative to Kester, to each other, and to Sierra.

At another level, the people sitting in cardboard boxes are coerced by the German state, chronically inhibited by poverty and lack of political capacity to influence and habitually typified as other in national media. This may, quite naturally, have rendered them desperate enough to take the "work" offered by Sierra in the face of greater poverty or more unpleasant and lowly paid work.

"Workers..." can indeed be described as a situation that putatively typifies particular people and offers them to other types of people as spectacle, but only if everyone, including the participant-viewer, remains unselfconsciously within constraint.

Kester writes that the participant-viewer will care no more about the people in Sierra's show than if they passed them in the street. He may be right, but the ethical imperative sidestepped in his description misrepresents the situation in Sierra's work. Unlike an old painting, of which the protagonists are long gone and other constraints on behavior are in place, the participant-viewer's response to the people involved in Sierra's work constitutes the content of the work. In the sense of an enacted self, that is, in Goffman's sense, the work is difficult because of the possibility that it holds for members of an audience to enact other selves relative to the social situation: simply, perhaps, to lift the lid of a box and see who is inside or speak to the other people involved.

The immigrants had also adopted a code for their behavior dictated by their relative capacity to bargain for their labor with Sierra. The participant-viewer enacts another role dictated by their agreement to behave in a particular way in a museum. Kester's criticism is telling because he bases it in his habitual response to art in a museum, but, in a very different way to a painting, the people in Sierra's "Workers..." are the participants in a social situation that requires both dis-habituation and a change in Kester's behavior.

Goffman proposes that the relationship between un-enacted selves and enacted selves underwrites not only our subjectivity but also our behavior relative to others. This proposal also underwrites the shared discourse in the three artworks that, in assuming that the content of the work emerges through instrumental changes in an existing social situation, propose that all of the participating subjects recognize that they are alike. Hence, the participant-viewer of "Workers..." might place themselves in the experience of an immigrant sitting in a box in a museum, or vice versa, something that is not formally possible with a painting or the content of a work of theatre. Tiravanija seems straightforwardly to give the imperative "you be me" to the people who hung out in the reproduction of his flat in "Untitled (Tomorrow...)." On the one hand, in "The Battle of Orgreave," Deller seems to prefigure Judith Butler's notion that self-enactment incorporates the present enactment of past selves (Butler 2005) and, on the other hand, provide an opportunity for self-enactment through consciously behaving as someone else, within the historicized constraints of another time.

Within the discourse of the artworks, these situational devices constitute formal actions designed by the artists to bring about either changes in subjectivity or opportunities to reflect upon the implications of the idea of a change in subjectivity, as content. In this, they find precedent in the work of sociologist George Mead as well as Hegel and Goffman.

Mead describes two aspects of consciousness that produce subjectivity in relation to each other: "I" and "Me." For Mead, "I" equates to consciousness alone, as Hegel defines, whereas "Me" describes consciousness's image of itself, as Hegel's self-consciousness. "I" and "Me" also neatly describe Goffman's private and enacted selves. Mead also follows Hegel and Goffman in rejecting an epistemological description of self-consciousness. Rather, he accords perception a mediating role in our consciousness of the world. "I" and "Me" are only perceptible in physical terms. They have no meaningful private aspect. Mead's "Me" results from a process of engagement with a differentiated other (initially the self-experiencing "I") based on an agreement of "intention to affect." In this way, Mead argues, the relationship between "I" and "Me" accounts for reflection and collaboration in every social situation, reproducing the structure of self-consciousness as society (Mead 1967, 1982).

It is instructive to note that, arising from the theories of Hegel, Goffman, and Mead, the adoption by one person of another's behaviors is a foundational method of sociological enquiry, conceived in order to provide both direct experience for the researcher and material for reflection. The fieldwork of sociologist Loic Wacquant comes to mind as an example. In the early 1990s, Wacquant joined a boxing gym in Chicago and trained and competed as a boxer, in order to underwrite a sociology of Chicago south-side boxing. His capacity to reflect upon the experience derived from his utter dis-habituation to the people and locale of semi-pro boxing as much as his training as a sociologist (Wacquant 2007).

In a sense, the three works in discussion, considered as contrived situations designed to articulate and reveal the functions of subjectivity themselves, are perhaps more easily comprehensible as sociological method than as artworks, hence their availability to the theoretical tools of Hegel, Goffman, and Mead.

However, this methodology chimes with art theorist Bourriaud's definition of artworks made in this way as "microtopian," or requiring commonality of experience in order to be understood (Bourriaud 1998). This term has been discussed as a fiction of social harmony (Bishop 2004:68), foregrounding the idea that there is no possibility of social inclusion without concomitant social exclusion. However, the idea that social relationships articulate binary opposites of inclusion and exclusion is essentially psychoanalytic in origin, deriving from a conception of the subject as failed, producing either a need for validation or social antagonism. As Ernest Laclau and Chantal Mouffe write: " ... the presence of the 'Other' prevents me from being totally myself" (Laclau and Mouffe 1985: 125). In fact, it is possible to argue that the commonality of experience that Bourriaud calls "microtopia" is not a function of inclusivity at all. Rather, it is the mutual process of self-enactment within the constraints of the artwork as a social situation, that is, the dealing of all the participants with each other. What the participants have in common in these works is, precisely, their experiences of each other.

Instead, the opportunities and constraints determining social self-enactment in any situation derive not from psychic failure or inhibition, but from habituation relative to the selves that we are capable of enacting at any moment. Habituation is constituted by participation in the specific intersubjective constraints and mandates that create every situation, producing social conventions at every level. Bakhtin writes that these must be considered " ... as a temporal process of the continual founding and altering of horizons (founded upon) ... the nonteleological concept of the playing out of a limited number of possibilities" (Bakhtin 1985: 132). Habituation provides a historic aspect to behavior in as much as it produced effects in the present that derive from a many-layered past of social behaviors. In a sense, the specifics of this capacity to adopt the behaviors of another are the focus of both sociological method, derived in part from the ideas of Hegel, Goffman, and Mead, and the content of artworks such as Tiravanija's, Deller's, and Sierra's.

The changes in subjectivity that the three artworks facilitate and open to self-scrutiny, as content, through the instrumental manipulation of social situations, do not constitute what Bishop terms a "double ontology," or the utilization by the artists of " ... people as a medium ... " (Bishop 2012: 284). As I have discussed, the artworks make little sense if their participating subjects are reified or a participant-viewer adopts the role of meta-participant. Theorizing exactly this, Janet Kraynak writes that Tiravanija's work relies upon the " ... covert equivalence between Tiravanija's work and self... The artist, repositioned as both the source and arbiter of meaning, is embraced as the pure embodiment of (his)...identity, guaranteeing both the authenticity and political efficacy of (his) work" (Kraynak 1998: 28). Despite Tiravanija's work having been discussed in terms of his reification as an artist, the social proposition that "Untitled (Tomorrow ...)"

makes still has its effect. In whatever way "Untitled (Tomorrow ...)" is inflected by relative celebrity, authority, or status of the artist, the work still makes the invitation to change and scrutinize self-enactment: you be me.

This chapter has discussed these artworks from the point of view of the relative competencies of participants in self-enactment, considering the functions of intersubjectivity according to a Hegelian model extrapolated in contemporary sociology. It outlines a theoretically formal approach that connects self and society, agency and social structure, discussing the roles of social habituation and normalcy. Discussing the three works by Tiravanija, Deller, and Sierra, it describes ways in which they constitute strategies for dis-habituation and subjective revision that are unavailable to critique from the position of a meta-participant. Self-expertise is produced by habitual enactors: ex-miners alone are competent in the enactment of the behaviors of ex-miners, for example. This approach shifts the status of Deller's, Tiravanija's, and Sierra's artworks from meta-narrative to social proposition, according to the habitual type of self-performances that appear relative to each other in the situations that they create, that is, according to the competence of all of the participants in becoming themselves.

References

Bakhtin, Mikhail. 1985. *Speech Genres and Other Late Essays.* Austin: University of Texas Press.

Beech, Dave. 2002. "'The reign of the workers and peasants will never end': Politics and politicisation, art and the politics of political art". *Third Text, 16*, no. 4, p. 387.

Bishop, Claire. 2004. "Antagonism and relational aesthetics". *October 110*, Fall, pp. 51-79.

Bishop, Claire. 2012. *Artificial Hells: Participatory Art and the Politics of Spectatorship.* London: Verso.

Bourriaud, Nicolas. 1996. *Traffic.* Bordeaux: CAPC Musée d'art contemporain.

Bourriaud, Nicolas. 1998. *Relational Aesthetics.* Dijon: Les Presse Du Reel.

Butler, Judith. 2005. *Giving an Account of Oneself.* New York: Fordham University Press.

Danto, Arthur C. 1996. *After the End of Art.* Princeton: Princeton University Press.

Deller, Jeremy. 2002. *The English Civil War Part II: Personal Accounts of the 1984–85 Miners' Strike.* London: Artangel.

Foster, Stephen C. 1998. *Hans Richter: Activism, Modernism and the Avant-Garde.* Cambridge MA: MIT Press.

Gablik, Suzi. 1994. *The Reenchantment of Art.* New York: Thames and Hudson.

Goffman, Erving. 1959. *The Presentation of Self in Everyday Life*. New York: Anchor Books.

Goffman, Erving. 1967. *Interaction Ritual: Essays on Face-to-face Behaviour*. New York: Anchor Books.

Goffman, Erving. 1968. *Stigma*. Harmondsworth: Penguin.

Hegel, Georg. 1979. *The Phenomenology of Spirit*. Oxford: Clarendon.

Honneth, Axel. 1995. *The Struggle for Recognition*. Cambridge: Polity.

Jacob, Mary Jane. 1995. *Culture in Action: A Public Art Programme of Sculpture Chicago*. Chicago: Bay Press.

Kester, Grant. 2011. *The One and the Many: Contemporary Collaborative Art in a Global Context*. Durham and London: Duke University Press.

Kittelman, Udo. 1996. *Rirkrit Tiravanija*. Cologne: Salon Verlag and Kölnischer Kunstverein.

Kraynak, Janet. 1998. Tiravanija's Liability. *Documents 13*, Fall, pp. 26-40.

Kwon, Mi Won. 2004. *One Place After Another: Site-Specific Art and Locational Identity*. Cambridge MA: MIT Press.

Laclau, Ernesto and Mouffe, Chantal. 1985. *Hegemony and Socialist Strategy*. London: Routledge

Mead, George H. 1967. *Mind, Self, Society*. Chicago: University of Chicago Press.

Mead, George H. 1982. *The Individual and the Social Self: Unpublished Essays by G. H. Mead*. Edited David L. Miller. Chicago: University of Chicago Press.

Slyce, John. 2003. Jeremy Deller: Fables of the reconstruction. *Flash Art International* January–February, p. 76.

Smith, Valerie. 1993. *Sonsbeek 93*. Sonsbeek: Snoek-Ducaju & Zoon.

Vogel, Felix. 2010. "Handlung. On Producing Possibilities." *Reader of the Bucharest Biennale 4*. Bucharest: Pavilion.

Wacquant, Loïc. 2007. *Body and Soul: Notebooks of an Apprentice Boxer*. New York: OUP USA.

5

The Transformations of Harvey Pekar's *American Splendor*: "Ordinary Life Is Pretty Complex Stuff"

Julia Round
Bournemouth University, UK

Harvey Pekar's comic book *American Splendor* tells the story of "our man" across four decades, giving us his observations on everyday American life—and, in the case of *Our Movie Year* (2004), the not-so-everyday. It is a brilliant combination of the universal experience and the individual human condition, as Harvey offers us his acerbic opinions on everything from shopping queues to politics. Throughout its run, it has been illustrated by a stellar range of underground comics artists, including R. Crumb, Kevin Brown, Greg Budgett, Sean Carroll, Sue Cavey, Gary Dumm, Val Mayerik, and Gerry Shamray. The flexibility of the visuals attached to Harvey's instantly identifiable voice makes it an excellent example of adaptation in action, as this chapter will discuss.

Much has been written on the power of autobiography and the benefits of understanding this type of writing as a transformative and adaptive process in itself: where selection, point of view, and multiple other narrative devices are used to fictionalize the real (see William Labov and Joshua Waletzky's (1967) oral storytelling categories and Allan Bell's (1991) application of these to news stories). This chapter discusses the specific challenges of narrating "real life" in comics and documentary film, focusing on Harvey Pekar's *American Splendor* (both the comic book series and the 2003 movie). It will explore the conventions used in both to argue that the themes of the *American Splendor* comic and the movie's exploration of these, together with the latter's use of a comics aesthetic, allow this "documentary" to coexist in an intertextual relationship with the entire body of work that makes up the *American Splendor* story, rather than being outside it and "about it."

The award-winning body of work that makes up *American Splendor* crosses media, exceeding expectations of what started out as a small, self-published underground comic. The series has run for nearly 40 years (Harvey Pekar/various), published between 1976–2011 (self-published; Dark Horse; DC Comics), and has won various awards including the 1987 American Book Award (for the first *American Splendor* anthology) and the 1995 Harvey Award for Best Graphic Album of Original Work (for *Our Cancer Year*). There are also two larger graphic novels: *Our Movie Year* (Ballantine Books: 2004) and *Ego and Hubris: The Michael Malice Story* (Ballantine: 2006). Two of Harvey's other graphic novels can also be considered spin-offs and part of the *American Splendor* universe: *The Quitter*, which details Harvey's early life (DC Vertigo: 2005), *Our Cancer Year* (written with his wife Joyce Brabner, Four Walls Eight Windows: 1994), as well as further posthumous works such as *Cleveland* (ZIP Comics & Top Shelf: 2012). There have also been three *American Splendor* theater productions (1985, 1987, 1990) and a movie (2003), directed by Shari Springer Berman and Robert Pulcini, which won first honors at the Sundance Film Festival and the Writers Guild of America Award for best adapted screenplay.

Harvey Pekar's entry into comics came about through his friendship with Robert Crumb, who was the first artist to illustrate *American Splendor*. The two met in Cleveland in 1962 when Harvey was working as a hospital clerk for Veteran's Administration and Crumb was working for the American Greeting Card Company. A shared love of jazz records and Crumb's encouragement led Harvey to start writing his own scripts, and their first collaboration, a one-page comic called "Crazy Ed" was published in 1972 in *The People's Comics*. Harvey would collaborate on various pieces with a range of artists over the next few years, and the first issue of *American Splendor* was finally published in 1976. The comic ran consistently after this, maintaining strong sales, and finding its own niche in terms of both being a steady independent title and being a known place for new artists to get their work seen. By selling back issues it could hit 10,000 (as much as *Classics Illustrated* in the mainstream trade) and Harvey seldom allowed a comic to go out of print (Buhle 2010).

As Paul Buhle points out, Justin Green had introduced the autobiographical comic with *Binky Brown* (1972), and the "artist-self" could be found in many underground comics of the time. But even within this genre, Pekar was unique— he worked a "boring" job and wrote about "ordinary folks." What made Harvey's work unique was not just that his characters were "psychologically credible," but that "they were and remained mostly people out of everyday life, destined to remain unknown to anyone but their friends" (Buhle 2010: 193).

Narrative: Construction and reflection

However, *American Splendor* is not lifted straight from everyday life, it is a carefully constructed comic, which adapts everyday experience into a familiar narrative shape. Labov and Waletzky's (1967) linguistic study of oral storytelling identifies six core categories that people use when "storifying" their own life/experience: abstract, orientation, complicating action, resolution, evaluation, and coda. What is interesting about *American Splendor* is the way it uses all these categories very self-consciously in both word and image: making its storytelling processes overt so that these processes in fact become the focus of the story, rather than the anecdote itself.

Take this example from *American Splendor: Another Day*, the verbal narration to which begins as follows:

> Setting the scene: Harvey's wife Joyce has gone to San Francisco to visit a medical specialist and stay a few days with her sister, leaving Harvey alone with his foster daughter, Danielle.
>
> Danielle and Harvey have never been alone together and Harvey does not relish his role as boss of the household. He has doubts about how much the sixteen year-old Danielle will respect him with Joyce, the leader of the family, away.
>
> Danielle has just come back from a weekend in Tennessee with a boyfriend which she feels pretty good about. She rode seventeen hours each way to get to Memphis, and is not likely to be easier to deal with when she's sleep deprived.
> "Yawn"
> Harvey is kind of a control freak, and his first day with Danielle has not gone all that well. They make an agreement which Danielle doesn't adhere to strictly.

Like all narratives, then, this story is selected (as is the point at which we join and leave it), reshaped, and book-ended. Not only does the opening sentence serve as the abstract (which Labov and Waletzky claim should signal that the story is about to begin by way of a short, summarizing statement), but also flags this up with its comment "setting the scene." The second half of the sentence proceeds directly to the orientation, answering questions of time, place, who is involved, and so forth, which the following sentences add to. The comic then proceeds to the complicating action(s): Danielle goes out later than promised and does not answer her phone; Harvey has not been paid by the *NY Times* for a story he wrote; Phoebe, the cat, goes missing; Harvey is concerned his book sales are falling; Danielle sneaks out of the house and then returns. The resolution (the final key event, often the last of the narrative clauses that make up the complicating action) takes place on the final page, as Harvey stands triumphantly with hands on hips, and a thought bubble reads: "Whew, well I got the problems with *The Times*, my book sales and Danielle straightened out. I sure feel a lot better than I did a couple hours ago." Evaluation has taken place at various stages throughout the narrative, as this linguistic model allows: for example, when Harvey explains to Danielle, "You can go anywhere you want [...] Just please tell me so I know what's going on. You know I'm a compulsive worrier, and I'll worry about you if I have no idea where you are." Harvey's explanation justifies the abstract by clarifying his personality and relationship with Danielle, and indicates the point of the narrative (that this has been a stressful day). A final evaluation and the coda conclude the story in the final three panels, as Phoebe the cat returns at 3 a.m. to wake Harvey, who asks: "Phoebe, where'd you come from? All these problems pop up and then get solved in about 24 hours. Wow!" This statement both clarifies the point of the story (evaluation: that problems appear and are resolved) and signals its end through a generality (coda).

Here, narrative distance is also used to extrapolate themes and meaning and to comment on the events themselves. However, the creation of an ideological subtext (e.g. of everyman Harvey struggling against social norms such as age, gender, large corporations, and so forth) is resisted by Harvey's simultaneous assertion of individuality (Witek: 149). Harvey's tales are *so* excessively inward-looking, for example, reflecting on his own personal reasoning, faults, differences, temper, and so forth, that we (the reader) resist the temptation to make him into *us*. Charles Hatfield echoes this point, arguing that: "Thus autobiography in comics, as in prose, often zeroes in on the contact surface between cultural environment and individual identity" (2005: 113). As such, autobiographical comics, unlike many of the genres more commonly published in the comics medium, can be read as "a literature that pushes people into their lives rather than helping people escape from them" (Hatfield 2005: 113).

However, and as Joseph Witek points out, *American Splendor*'s postscripted morals often feel tacked on with deliberate irony and stories frequently end on "an offhand moral" or a "reflective/ambiguous note" (Witek 1989: 123, 133). As Harvey says: "plot means nothing to me" (cited by Witek 1989: 135), an attitude that reinforces the personal and autobiographical nature of his tales. These are stories about conjuring atmosphere, about response and evaluation, and seldom really about the humdrum event itself. The scenario is realized through Harvey's musician's ear, which allows him to use the poetic rhythm of daily speech to reinforce the universalities of his experiences, rather than generalizing his values or events using historical or critical distance (Witek 1989).

Visualization: Objectifying the self

Harvey Pekar's overt reflection on his morals and the conspicuous narrativizing process he uses are a type of *ironic authentication*, where the appearance of honesty is given by denying the possibility of truth or emphasizing inauthentic elements about the text (such as the "tacked on" morals). This process is also apparent in the visual aspect of his works, where our protagonist is a shifting image, due to being drawn differently by various artists. Critic Charles Hatfield discusses a number of underground comics creators who use similar tactics to reinforce the truth claims of their work, including Daniel Clowes ("Just Another Day"), R. Crumb ("The Many Faces of R. Crumb"), and Jamie Hernandez ("Love Book"). Hatfield's discussion centers on the use of "successive selves" by these creators, who produce multiple, contradictory versions of themselves on the page (Hatfield 2005: 117–124).

Visual mobility is something that *American Splendor* makes great use of throughout. A standard approach would be for Harvey's cartoon persona/narrator to provide continuity while the stories offered variety; however, this is frequently subverted in *American Splendor*. Although the text is idiosyncratic and strongly narrated, our narrator remains multiple and variable. Witek (1989: 123) draws attention to the use of "multiple fictional autobiographical personae," including "Harvey Pekar," "Herschel," "Our Man," "Our Hero," and "Jack the Bellboy." However, even when our protagonist is most clearly identified with/named directly as "Harvey Pekar," the visual collaboration of *American Splendor* undercuts this. As Paul Buhle argues: "Harvey was forced (but also allowed) to work with all kinds of artists, across every possible generational and other barrier, thus creating in his own way a comic art with extraordinary breadth and complexity" (2010: 191).

Both the writing and art of *American Splendor* lift it above the everyday, breaking with many assumptions made about comics' fantastic and sensational content. As Witek (1989: 128) says: "Pekar's aesthetic of aggressively humdrum realism struggles against the tide of decades of comic-book fantasy and escapism." Just as the mundane content of *American Splendor* goes against traditional comics genres like the superhero, so too does its use of visual style.

The basis of cartooning lies in stereotyping (the use of physical features to represent personality), and so such images have frequently been used in comics to engage viewers, sustain interest, and create familiarity and immediacy, as "it is inherent to narrative art that the *requirement* on the viewer is not so much analysis as *recognition*" (Eisner 1990: 38). Critic Scott McCloud puts forward a similar argument, claiming that the level of detail and artistic style directly affects universality and narrative identity: "The more cartoony a face is, for instance, the more people it could be said to *describe*" (McCloud 1993: 31).

Both Eisner and McCloud are two of the first wave of comics creators-turned-critics, and their ideas and theories tend toward privileging the visual in this way. Other creators such as Art Spiegelman have argued that comics in fact have the power to *individualize* and *dismantle* stereotypes, by using sustained narrative to undercut expectations (cited in Hatfield 2005: 115).

The depiction of Harvey by completely different artists, often appearing in the same collected volume, both refutes and sustains these ideas about the use of comics art. In a sense, it is similar to long-running superhero series, where different writers and artists will have a well-publicized "run" on the title, with obvious stylistic variations. *American Splendor*, however, takes this one step further by making the variation overt and commenting upon it in its own text. For example, in "A Marriage Album" (*American Splendor* #10 (1985)) Joyce Brabner (Harvey's wife) visualizes a range of "Harveys" before meeting Harvey for the first time, as her only knowledge of him is taken from the comics themselves. She reflects on her anxiety, while the text reincorporates some of the different artistic ways he has been represented into a single panel containing a montage of "Harveys."

Charles Hatfield (2005: 115) comments that "Objectification of the self, through visual representation, may actually enable the autobiographer to articulate and uphold his or her own sense of identity" and the cartoon image therefore offers a unique way for the comics creator to externalize his/her subjectivity. It is the seeing of the protagonist by the reader that objectifies him/her enough for his/her story to go beyond subjectivity. Hatfield (117) claims that Harvey Pekar's creative process in particular "precisely mirrors this transition," as Harvey draws stick figures and then passes these to the artist to realize, as noted. This process allows Harvey to use his writerly skills "to abstract his own character, in the form of simplified diagrams and nuanced dialogue" (117). Hatfield ultimately uses this observation to support his own theory: that it is comics' tensions (here between visual and verbal; although Hatfield's theory defines this tension as just one of four) that allow this self-referential type of representation and encourage intertextual or meta-textual commentary.

American Splendor certainly does not simplify the concept of narrative identity. As Harvey asks himself at one point: "Am I some guy who writes about himself in a comic book called *American Splendor*? … Or am I just a character in that book?" (Pekar, Brabner and Stack, *Our Cancer Year*) McCloud's treatment of narrative identity offers the fairly simplistic argument that the abstraction of cartooning allows greater engagement with characters seen on the comics page: "When you look at a photo or realistic drawing of a face—you see it as the face of *another*. But when you enter the world of the *cartoon*—you see *yourself*" (1993: 36). In contrast, the Harvey Pekars of *American Splendor* reinforce the tension between the individual and his environment by being both aggressively individual yet also multiple and adaptive. These multiple realizations of Harvey (and other characters) as drawn by so many different artists also allow a myriad of different responses to the character, as is commented upon by the *American Splendor* movie, which uses storytelling conventions of the documentary genre alongside a distinctly comics narratology, as will now be discussed.

Comics conventions on screen? Documentary and adaptation

It is surely not an accident that the *American Splendor* movie opens with an assertion of identity, as we are introduced to "our man" as a pre-teen boy out trick-or-treating with his friends (all dressed as comic book superheroes while Harvey has no costume). In response to the confused homeowner's questions: "And what about you, young man?" "Who are you supposed to be?" Harvey replies "What about what?" "I'm Harvey Pekar. […] I ain't no superhero, lady. I'm just a kid from the neighborhood, all right?"

Written and directed by documentarians Shari Springer Berman and Robert Pulcini, this ambitious movie mixes media and techniques from an array of different genres. Interviews with the "real" Harvey Pekar (in a white studio with no furnishings), footage from previous television appearances, dramatization with Hollywood actors, cameo appearances from other "real" characters playing themselves (such as Harvey's co-worker Toby Radloff), and re-enactments of other versions such as the *American Splendor* stage play are all woven together to make a documentary whose claims to realism rest entirely on the use of ironic authentication. *American Splendor* is a "drama documentary" (Hight: 180) that uses a collage of techniques to "make[s] stylistic forays into comic-book aesthetics, including animated sequences and illustrated frames" (West et al.: 40), although it also revolves around a central emotional storyline: that of a love affair between a man and his comics and what that brought him. However, here too it ironically follows the tone of the overall corpus, as some critics found the ending "trite and incongruously upbeat" (West et al.: 40)—recalling the "offhand" and "ambiguous" endings Witek identifies in Harvey Pekar's comics.

This is a documentary that interrogates and problematizes notions of reality and the representation of experience; as Pulcini comments: "we're also playing with the idea of reality versus nonreality, what's real and what's not, and all of that that interests us as documentary filmmakers" (West et al.: 42). The movie offers us multiple "Harveys" (Daniel Tay, Paul Giametti, Harvey Pekar himself, Donal Logue (in the *American Splendor* stage play clip shown) and animated version(s)). Even the "real" Harvey is complicated by inclusion of clips from his appearances on *Late Night with David Letterman* in the 1980s and the 1990s—is this the "same" person as our self-conscious narrator? The animated, acted, and actual versions of Harvey are used "in a way not unlike how a documentary would use all available footage and materials" (Sperb: 124). However, a consequence of this is that it simultaneously makes *American Splendor* "an antithetical act of documentation, because it is an autobiography which resists a central, implied assumption of autobiographies—there is no single, definitive Harvey to reclaim narratively" (Sperb: 124).

Alongside multiple Harveys, key scenes are also duplicated and revisited multiple times in the film. After seeing Harvey and Joyce's (played by Giametti and Davis) disastrous first date, we later see the couple in the theater watching this scene being re-enacted (by Logue and Shannon). There are also translations of key scenes from the comic that *already* contain their own reflexivity and multiplicity, such as a mixed-media scene in the movie that merges animation and acted footage as Harvey and Joyce first meet at an airport (see Figure 5.1 below). This revisits the montage panel from "A Marriage Album," which displays Joyce's multiple imaginations of Harvey, as mentioned above. These tensions interrogate notions of experience and narrative identity, which Charles Hatfield argues are the broader issues at work in *American Splendor*: "how we fashion our very selves through the stories we tell. Who is Harvey—creator, creation, both?" (109) However, these questions are also addressed within the story proper, as in the scene near the end where Harvey, midway through cancer treatment, asks himself: "Who am I? [...] Am I some guy who writes about himself in a comic book called

American Splendor? … Or am I just a character in that book?" This is taken from *Our Cancer Year*, allowing the real-life comic to exist "paradoxically and literally—both inside and outside the film" (Sperb: 127).

Figure 5.1 *American Splendor* (2003). Directed by Shari Springer Berman and Robert Pulcini.

Other more light-hearted scenes serve a similar purpose: for example, a scene between Paul Giametti and Judah Friedlander (playing Toby Radloff) where Radloff wants to go and see *Revenge of the Nerds* play at a cinema. Radloff (who has appeared in Harvey's comics for decades) in fact starred in the low-budget, cult horror films *Killer Nerd* and *Bride of Killer Nerd* during the 1980s and so their argument (Harvey claims these films are about middle-class characters, not actual nerds, and Toby should not bother going) has meta-significance, as Harvey self-reflexively states: "Those people on the screen ain't even supposed to be you ... [T]his *Revenge of the Nerds* ain't reality."

Sperb therefore argues that the *American Splendor* movie "foregrounds Harvey as always in a state of simulation" and that in so doing it celebrates the "unrepresentability of Pekar's life" (Sperb: 124). He also notes "multiple deconstructive asides" (124), for example, scenes of Harvey reading his voice-over direct from the script in an all-white room, and his comments, which frequently expose the technical processes behind constructing the film (such as "you should be able to cut something together from that"). Director Pulcini comments:

> We wanted a very different style for the documentary parts of the film. We decided that would be the place where we'd have a very artificial look, where we'd create a comic book panel look, with very vibrant colors and just a few well-placed items in the frame amidst a lot of empty, white space.
>
> West et al.: 42

Showing Harvey reading the script (and admitting he has not read or rehearsed it!) is a "*staging* of his real presence" (Sperb: 137).

Just like Harvey's comics, which always introduce his character with subjective referents such as "our man," "*American Splendor* never offers a fixed point for the act of documentation" (136). Listening to the real Harvey Pekar describe his character in third person situates him "both inside and outside the character" (Sperb 2006: 131). Director Pulcini comments that: "We also thought it [using Harvey as narrator] would give Harvey the opportunity to debunk the whole idea of making a movie about him as we made it, which is very true to *American Splendor*" (West et al.: 41). Craig Hight (2007: 193) also notes that Joyce Brabner's voice in the interview sections of the film provides another critique of Harvey's work as "selective" and "negative."

In this sense *American Splendor* can be read as a postmodern "attempt to obliterate some supposed central truth and replace it instead with the surface of images" (Sperb 2006: 125). However, it is also an interrogation of the nature of identity: a "*socially antithetical autobiography*, which documents Harvey's experience by resisting overt claims to definitively representing his experiences" (Sperb: 128–129, my emphasis). It asserts a divide between Harvey's aesthetic life and his biographical life, while simultaneously asserting that neither can be mastered by an *outside* observer (Sperb: 125). As such, it seems appropriate that the film ends with a reassertion of the "real" characters of Harvey, Joyce, Danielle, Toby, and other friends, as the movie's wrap party is staged for the camera. Hight (2007: 197) notes that at this point the boundaries between the different formats collapse, as the camera tracks from Paul Giametti in his final take over to the real Harvey Pekar conversing with Toby Radloff off-camera at the catering table. The following sequence shows Toby being photographed while talking in (scripted) voice-over about his friendship with Harvey. These cuts and combinations, Hight argues, explicitly rupture the fourth wall of both the narrative sequences and documentary sequences. The film then closes in a typically reflexive manner, with a shot of the cover of the comic *American Splendor: Our Movie Year*, which, of course, Harvey has written about his experiences around making the movie.

Movie conventions on the page? *American Splendor: Our Movie Year*

So it may seem that life becomes comic, becomes film, and becomes comic once again. However, I would like to instead suggest that neither the comic nor the film has final authority within the *American Splendor* oeuvre. The collected *American Splendor: Our Movie Year* reprints a number of Harvey's freelance pieces reflecting on various aspects of the movie experience. The theme that runs through the whole collection is a dichotomy between Harvey's amazement that people like the movie and his ongoing fears that even cinematic critical acclaim will not translate into the extra work or money he claims he so desperately needs.

The stories in the collection all connect with the film, albeit sometimes in tenuous ways. There is the retelling of the *American Splendor* history at its widest level (Harvey works as a filing clerk, he meets Robert Crumb, they become friends, and Crumb offers to illustrate some of Harvey's scripts, critical acclaim follows); stories that focus on Harvey's post-movie experiences (promotion, celebrity); unrelated stories (Harvey's car breakdown, his cat's visit to the vet); a series of one-off strips called "Lost and Found" that focus on various writers, movies, musicians; and "Liner Notes," which discusses the movie's soundtrack and is followed by a series of individual pieces focusing on the musicians featured. Just as comics are used to shape the aesthetic of the movie (e.g., in the clean set used for the "real" Harvey and his voice-over, which conforms to Michael Cohen's (2007) ideas regarding a comics aesthetic in *Dick Tracy*, where bright colors and empty surfaces are used to refer to the appearance of comics art), so in this collection we can see the use of televisual styles, such as MTV in the story "Hollywood Reporter," which tells of Toby Radcliff's rise to fame. After mentioning his work with "Big Harv" and conducting a short interview about his "socko" new film *Townies*, the story concludes with Radcliff directly facing and addressing the reader, gripping the edge of the panel with his fingers, and breaking the fourth wall to announce: "Yeah, my next movie will be called *Fanboy*. It'll be about a crazed comic book fan who follows this comic writer around" (22).

Within this collection the *American Splendor* movie story is also retold multiple times and with multiple collaborators. There is a ten-part strip ("The American Splendor Movie" by Harvey Pekar with Mark Zingarelli), a six-page story for a national magazine ("My Movie Year" by Harvey Pekar with Gary and Laura Dumm), and multiple stories about the post-movie experience, such as Harvey's trips to Cannes and Sundance film festivals, Great Britain, and so forth. These are written for different publications, including *American Splendor* the comic, *Empire* film magazine, and so forth, and so each retelling has a different focus. Between them events are revisited and revalued: for example, Harvey sees Al Gore on his flight and in one story is impressed (13), whereas in another tale this proves completely irrelevant (86).

Similarly, images from the movie are drawn back into the comic of *Our Movie Year*, again emphasizing processes of simulation and simulacra. These options "to assess the characters from more than one standpoint" (Pekar 2004: 15) are exactly what the collection as a whole offers—a series of stories told and retold, each capturing a slightly different element of the movie experience, even when they deal with the same exact events. In this way both the movie and its comic become incorporated *into* the *American Splendor* story rather than being "about it" or "outside it."

American Splendor and adaptation

Walter Metz writes that "If one stops to think about it, documentaries should have always been the stuff of adaptation of non-fiction writing" (2007: 311).

However, as an adaptation of *fictional* writing (as demonstrated above by analyzing the way Harvey shapes his tales), *American Splendor* the film displays the inadequacy of early adaptation theory. Geoffrey Wagner (1975) divides adaptation into the three categories of translation, commentary, or analogy, but *American Splendor* is not an easy fit for any of these. What is being adapted here? Is it the events of Harvey Pekar's life, or (more accurately) his interpretation of his own experiences, with all the complications of subjective perspective that this awareness brings?

The *American Splendor* movie crosses categories and comments upon Harvey Pekar's comics techniques by analogously translating them into film. Its use of ironic authentication to create a type of interrogated realism illustrates the interesting postmodern condition of fictional truth, linked by Mark Currie to narrative identity and defined as follows: "When I tell my own story, I must deny that I am inventing myself in the process in order to believe that I am discovering myself" (1998: 131). *American Splendor* shows the process of invention in this way, as a process of discovery. Witek claims that Harvey's stories become "increasingly self-reflexive" as the series continues: and that the body of work goes far beyond the comics themselves. All of its narratives (videos of the *Letterman* show, the comic itself, news, or magazine articles about the comic or film release) bring different nuances, and Harvey's life is perhaps best defined as a "nexus" they revolve around, rather than being the stable referent of the tales (Witek 1989: 143).

As such, *American Splendor* requires us to apply a richer notion of intertextuality as argued for by many theorists of adaptation studies (Sanders 2006, Albrecht-Crane and Cutchins 2010). Texts like the Letterman television show, its reappearance within the movie, the framing scenes with Giametti, and its reinterpretation into the drawn comic book are cross-fertilized by their interactions and recontextualizations. They both produce art and affirm difference. Albrecht-Crane and Cutchins (2010: 20) argue that creation and reaction cannot be grounded in reality and notions of fidelity are insufficient to understand texts such as these. Instead, they suggest, we must examine the complex relations between texts-as-satellites. This seems epitomized by the *American Splendor* body of work.

In this way, *American Splendor* represents the Derridean *aporia* of texts (1993) as containing a promise that is impossible yet inevitable. As Sperb (2006: 139) claims about the movie: "*American Splendor* is an autobiography which wishes deeply to document an experience it senses is always—in some way—removed."

The processes of comics creation allow, of course, for removal from the writer's experience: as event becomes script, which in turn is reinterpreted by a variable artist for the page, and this is echoed in the movie whose use of direct address and multiple actors problematizes Harvey's position still further—is he writer, subject, narrator, or commentator? *American Splendor* thereby becomes a self-conscious interrogation of what constitutes "real" life as its texts explore multiple possibilities of representation. Perhaps then they are best understood as a multidirectional interaction between Harvey and his audience, as we are all encouraged to reflect with, and about, "our man."

References

Albrecht-Crane, Christa, and Dennis Cutchins, eds. 2010. *Adaptation Studies: New Approaches*. Cranbury, NJ: Associated University Presses.

Bell, Allan. 1991. *The Language of News Media*. Oxford: Wiley Blackwell.

Berman, Shari Springer, and Robert Pulcini, dirs. 2003. *American Splendor*. Fine Line Productions.

Buhle, Paul. 2010. "Harvey Pekar, in memory." *Studies in Comics 1*, no. *2*, 191–195.

Cohen, Michael. 2007. "Dick Tracy: In pursuit of a comics aesthetic." In *Film and Comic Books*, edited by Gordon, Ian, Mark Jancovich, and Matthew P. McAllister, 13–36. Jackson, MS: University Press of Mississippi.

Currie, Mark. 1998. *Postmodern Narrative Theory*. Basingstoke, Hampshire: Macmillan.

Derrida, Jacques. 1993. *Aporias*. Stanford, CA: Stanford University Press.

Eisner, Will. 1990 [1985]. *Comics and Sequential Art*, expanded edn. Tamarac, FL: Poorhouse Press.

Green, Justin. 1972. *Binky Brown Meets the Holy Virgin Mary*. San Francisco, CA: Last Gasp Eco Funnies.

Hatfield, Charles. 2005. *Alternative Comics*. Jackson, MS: University Press of Mississippi.

Hight, Craig. 2007. "*American Splendor*: Translating comic autobiography into drama-documentary." In *Film and Comic Books*, edited by Gordon, Ian, Mark Jancovich, and Matthew P. McAllister, 180–198. Jackson, MS: University Press of Mississippi.

Labov, William, and Joshua Waletzky. 1967. "Narrative analysis: Oral versions of personal experience." In *Essays on the Verbal and Visual Arts*, edited by J. Helm, 12–44. Seattle: University of Washington Press.

McCloud, Scott. 1993. *Understanding Comics*. New York: Paradox Press.

Metz, Walter. 2007. "Documentary as adaptation." *Literature/Film Quarterly 35*, no. *4*, 307–312.

Pekar, Harvey et al. 1985. *American Splendor* #10. Cleveland: Harvey Pekar.

Pekar, Harvey et al. 2004. *American Splendor: Our Movie Year*. New York: Ballantine Books.

Pekar, Harvey et al. 2007. *American Splendor: Another Day*. London: Titan Books.

Pekar, Harvey, Joyce Brabner and Frank Stack 1994. *Our Cancer Year*. Cambridge, Massachusetts: Da Capo Press.

Sanders, Julie. 2006. *Adaptation and Appropriation*. London: Routledge.

Sperb, Jason. 2006. "Removing the experience: Simulacrum as an autobiographical act in *American Splendor*." *Biography 29*, no. *1* (Winter 2006), 123–139.

Wagner, Geoffrey. 1975. *The Novel and the Cinema*. Cranbury, NJ: Fairleigh Dickinson University Press.

West, Dennis, and Joan M. West, with Anne Gilbert. 2003. "Splendid misery: An interview with Robert Pulcini, and Shari Springer Berman." *Cineaste 28*, no. *4* (Fall 2003), 40–43.

Witek, Joseph. 1989. *Comic Books as History*. Jackson, MS: University Press of Mississippi.

Part 3

The Politics of Representing Real People

6

Narratives of Trauma Re-lived: The Ethnographer's Paradox and Other Tales

Marina Lambrou,
Kingston University, UK

And I never know, I never know how I'm going to be when I tell the story but it doesn't matter I have to tell the story…

Herb Ouida, April 2010

Introduction

This chapter sets out to discuss some of the key issues that arose during an ethnographic study involving participants who were interviewed for their personal experiences. I initially set out to interview individuals who had experienced the terrible events of the London 7/7 terrorist bombings in 2005 but went on to investigate personal narratives of those affected by New York's 9/11 terrorist attacks in 2001. The aim was to gather a corpus of personal narratives to understand the discourse of trauma and to identify the linguistic markers and story macro-structure for their telling (see Lambrou forthcoming 2014). Although the spoken data—or narratives—were the central object of study using ethnographic methodological approaches, it became apparent during the process just how complex researching personal narratives about real experiences can be when faced with the prospect of interviewing real people for their traumatic experiences. For example, there were a number of issues I was unable to anticipate prior to the study, such as the matter of what I call the "Ethnographer's Paradox" and its effects in a constrained dialogic speech event. I was also unprepared for the sensitive and upsetting content of people's experiences and had not anticipated the level of difficulty—at both a personal and practical level—that I would encounter during the study. Other important issues were ethical considerations to ensure confidentiality, which is fundamental to a study of this kind. This level of intersubjectivity, nevertheless, produced a context for the sharing of some extraordinary stories. This chapter will discuss my experience as an ethnographer by focusing on the process of researching sensitive data rather than on the data itself. The case study that will be central to this discussion is the personal experience of a father who lost his son in New York's terrorist bombings in 2001.

Background: Narrating our experiences

Sharing personal experiences through narrating stories is generally accepted as a universal activity, and one that aids socialization. Bruner (1990) refers to our readiness to learn and produce narratives as a "push" to construct narratives and claims that this innateness explains children's ability to adopt the grammatical forms to create them. These cognitive story structures enable readers and listeners to comprehend and make sense of stories and to produce and perform them. Narratologists, sociolinguists, and psychologists have proposed various models for the analysis of narratives that focus on the macro- and microstructures of the narrative form and function.[1] The model of narrative that I work with for the analysis of personal experiences is one developed by Labov and Waletzky (1967), who proposed that a prototypical structure of a narrative comprises six stages or schemas formed of an Abstract, an Orientation, a Complicating Action, an Evaluation, a Resolution, and a Coda.

A further, nonlinguistic factor—the "reportability" value of a story—was also considered essential by Labov (1997) in his later work on personal narratives, and can be likened to the categories for newsworthiness in news reporting where newsworthiness describes those stories that are worthy of broad coverage because they fulfill a number of key criteria (see Bell 1991; Galtung and Ruge 1973). In narratives detailing traumatic loss as experienced by those involved in 9/11 and 7/7, there is no doubt that the notion of reportability is very much foregrounded as personal experiences as a consequence of world events are shared through the telling of oral narratives. It is the emotional content of these types of experiences that Wilce (2009: 13) in his work on "Language and Emotion" describes as a form of action that does things to the world, including the subjective and intersubjective worlds of experience ... Among the acts performed by talk are identificatory acts, the proper focus of an adequate theorization of language as emotional object. Such linguistic-identificatory acts exemplify the profoundly interactive nature of emotion-in-talk.

The personal narrative that will be discussed in this chapter is in response to an interview question, in a semi-formal interview setting. Because of the nature of the emotion talk, the dialogic features of storytelling soon come into play, despite my aim to remain neutral and uninvolved. This interaction is one of the issues explored.

Motivation for this study: The London 7/7 bombings and a survivor's story

It is worth saying a few words about the motivation for this study. My interest in narratives of trauma began as a result of a friend who experienced the London 7/7 terrorist attack in July 2005: he was commuting to work on the Piccadilly line tube when it exploded. He was physically uninjured and was able to make his way out of the tunnel. He was interviewed within moments of exiting the train station by a television reporter and his story was broadcasted globally. I heard his account and many retellings after this terrible experience and was intrigued by the linguistic strategies including lexical choices he used in his narrative account of what happened that day. I then interviewed him two and a half years after the first interview for an account of what happened on the morning of 7/7/05 as I was also interested in the idea of "telling the same story twice" (Polanyi 1981), to understand which of the prototypical features of a personal narrative—at the level of both the macrostructure and microstructure—remain constant over time. Analysis of those narratives revealed a number of lexico-grammatical features that were unexpected and required further examination (see Lambrou forthcoming 2014). Unable to confirm whether these findings were idiosyncratic and specific to the narrator or linguistic features commonly found in the personal narratives about trauma, I set about widening my research to collect personal narratives from other individuals involved in 7/7 and then extending it further to 9/11 as a comparative source of data.

Ethnography as methodology

My role as researcher involved collecting personal narratives from individuals using ethnographic research methods to interview participants in the study. Ethnographic research is usually associated with studies undertaken by anthropologists who conduct fieldwork by immersing themselves in cultures as participant observers, primarily to understand behavioral practices. It is fundamentally about collecting data in a natural setting. Malinowski (1922: 25), one of the earliest ethnographers, states the main goal of ethnography is to "grasp the native's point of view, his relation to life, to realise his vision of the world." For those interested in linguistic behaviors, ethnographic methods provide a way of investigating "patterns of speaking in relation to ethnic and social groups and cultural differences" (Wales 2001: 136). Moreover, ethnography can offer linguistics a non-deterministic perspective on data, whereas linguistics can offer ethnography a range of established procedures for identifying discursive structures (see Rampton 2007 in Litosseliti 2010). In these studies, the interview is used as an empirical method to collect qualitative data usually with the aim of identifying linguistic patterns, whether at the phoneme, lexical, syntactical, or functional levels of speech, for example, and correlating them to an individual's social factors such as class, gender, ethnicity, age, and so forth. Many groundbreaking sociolinguistic studies focusing on variation in language adopted ethnographic methods to collect linguistic data from informants from various speech communities (Labov and Waletzky 1967, Trudgill 1974, Milroy 1980, Cheshire 1978).

Ethics

Before undertaking any research, a number of considerations have to be made by a researcher regarding professional behavior. One of these is ensuring that ethical codes are adhered to, especially where informants are involved. According to Murphy and Dingwall (2001: 339), "ethnographers have a responsibility not only to protect research participants from harm, but also to have regard to their rights." When using informants, for example in interviews, it is important to establish trust between the researcher and the informant. Cameron, in her paper "'Respect please!' Subjects and objects in sociolinguistics" (unpublished paper in Stockwell 2003), describes the ethical responsibilities in a study she conducted in Southwark where it was important to be sensitive to the community being researched. In addition to ensuring the welfare of those involved, the researcher should also clarify the purpose of the study in a format that they can understand.

One way of establishing trust from the outset and ensuring that an ethical code is in place is to provide a letter for informants to sign outlining the aims of the study. The letter should be written in a style that is clear and free from jargon and acts as written consent, giving permission for the informant's involvement in the study and the option of anonymity. If the data from the research is likely to be published at a later date, used in a classroom setting for teaching purposes, or presented in a conference paper, for example, it is also important to include that information so informants are aware that anything they say might become publicly available. It is therefore important to give those involved in the study the option of whether they want their identity to remain confidential and undisclosed or known. The letter should be signed and dated and a copy given to informants to keep. A copy of the letter I developed for this research is provided below as an example. The letter explains the aims of the research and gives informants the choice of anonymity (the letter is presented here as a model for other researchers as there are very few examples available).[2]

Letter of permission and confidentiality

Dear []

Thank you for agreeing to take part in my research.

I am an academic based at a London university researching personal narratives (or stories about real experiences). I am looking at personal stories that describe traumatic experiences, such as those experienced by people who survived the 9/11 terrorist attacks. I am interested in how stories are told, especially the language that is used to evaluate and describe these experiences. (I turned to analysing these types of narratives after a close friend survived the London 7/7 tube and bus bombings. Thankfully, he was unhurt.) I am currently working with people who were involved in London's 7/7 bombings and would like to extend my research by looking at the narratives of survivors of 9/11.

For this research, I would like to interview you to ask you to recall your experience of that day. (If at anytime you would like to stop the interview, please indicate this.) I will record the interview, which I will then go on to transcribe. Your story may be reproduced for discussion and publication. You have a choice as to whether you would prefer to remain anonymous in any subsequent discussion involving your experience or, whether you would be happy for your name to be cited. Please tick your preference, below:

_____ I prefer that my identity remains anonymous and my name is not given out (e.g. informant A)

_____ I am happy for my name to be given in discussions that refer to my story (e.g. John C)

Please sign below to confirm that you agree to the above and give permission for your story to be reproduced for this study.

Name of informant (signature) ....

Name of informant (in capitals) ....

Occupation: (if retired, at the time of 9/11) ....

....

Age .... Male/Female

Thank you. I appreciate your willingness to take part in what is a sensitive subject.

Dr. Marina Lambrou

Principal Lecturer in English Language and Communication

Method

The first challenge in any ethnographic study is finding informants who are willing to take part. Living in London, finding informants for their 7/7 experiences would be more straightforward. I used social media, such as Facebook, asked friends if they knew of anyone, and even contacted individuals directly who had published accounts of their experiences (identified via newspaper reports, autobiographical accounts in books, and the internet). In one case, I gave a seminar at a local university and was approached after my talk by a student who informed me her neighbor had survived the attacks and would be willing to be interviewed.

Finding informants who had experienced the terrorist attacks on 9/11, however, was much more difficult. My university had given me a sabbatical and I decided to use my time to go to New York for a short period of time to interview individuals such as firefighters, first responders, and those who were involved in, witnessed, or survived the attacks. It was important to try to set up some meetings while I was still in London and so I emailed various organizations—including the Uniformed Firefighters Association, the FDNY Union—hoping they would be able to help. Unfortunately, none of the replies were positive and I flew to New York with no interviews arranged. I did, however, manage to secure a space to work from at New York University, thanks to the help of a very generous Professor, who not only gave me an office to work from but also gave my research some authority by association.

In New York, I spent a number of days knocking on the doors of FDNY stations, which was not easy. The response was negative. (It was only later that I discovered that many of the firefighters in 2001 had since retired and that many of those currently employed joined the FDNY Department after the attacks.) My breakthrough in finding informants came after visiting the 9/11 Memorial Preview Site, a museum for the events and items of 9/11, near Ground Zero, the location of the attacks. After speaking to one of the administrators, I was put in touch with the 9/11 listserv webmaster and was able to write and ask if there was anybody willing to take part in my study. See email below (again, this is presented to show the transparency of my research aims to potential informants).

Dear Members

I am an academic based at a London university researching personal narratives (or stories about real experiences). I am looking at personal stories that describe traumatic experiences, such as those experienced by people who survived the 9/11 terrorist attacks. I am interested in how stories are told, especially the language that is used to evaluate and describe these experiences. I am currently working with people who were involved in London's 7/7 bombings and have extended my research by looking at the narratives of survivors of 9/11. (I turned to analysing these types of narratives after a close friend survived the London 7/7 tube and bus bombings. Thankfully, he was unhurt.)

I would very much like to interview people who were directly involved in the events of 9/11 to record their recollection of their experience of that day, whether New York Firefighters, Rescue Unit members, office workers, or people on the ground who escaped the terrible dust and debris. I am based at New York University until 21st April and would be happy to come out to wherever it is convenient to conduct my research. I can be contacted on m.lambrou@kingston.ac.uk.

Thank you.

Dr M Lambrou

(University website link)

In my email, I not only shared information about myself with regard to my reasons for conducting this study but also provided a link to my university website. It was important to establish trust at the outset by providing some information about myself. Moreover, I wanted to show that despite the purpose of the study—to collect spoken data from informants—I was getting involved with real people and emotions and it was necessary to show a sensitivity toward the subject I was dealing with. By revealing some personal information about myself and my friend's involvement with London's terrorist bombings, I hoped that this self-disclosure would help reduce the level of asymmetry in the power relationship between the researcher and the informant and make the interview less formal.

The replies that followed were overwhelming. To give an example, I list some of these below—cut and pasted from email—but have removed names of senders, shown only as [XX] apart from the final email, which is the case study in this chapter:

Are you looking for family members … or only people that were there that day? [XX] sister of FF [XX], Ladder 7, FDNY

Dr. Lambrou, I was involved in the rescue effort on September 11th. I was working with my unit, Ladder 113, trying to rescue trapped firefighters from the lobby after the south tower fell. I was injured and hospitalized after the north tower fell. Feel free to contact me. [XX] (Retired Lieutenant Ladder 113)

Just a brief note of introduction, my name is [XX] my wife, [XX] and I lost our daughter, [XX] aged 26, on September 11,2001 at the WTC. [XX] was an employee of Cantor-Fitzgerald, a newly wed married less than a year. I understand your focus is on those who survived, but wanted to share [XX's] story with you as well.

i am a surviving fdny firefighter i have sent you copy of story i had written just days after the attack thanks [XX] you may contact me by email if you would like to discuss these events with me

I was a First Responder chaplain at the WTC 19 DAYS gave last rights to the victims and did search for bodies will be happy to talk to you by phone i live in Ohio I also now very ill from the toxic air at ground o dying nothing more can be done for me hospice cares for me at home, if interested my number is [xxx], Thank you, [XX]

Please visit http://www.mybuddytodd.org Herb Ouida

I responded to each email by compiling a carefully worded email of condolence—a type of response I had not anticipated writing—tailored to each respondent. I was surprised and moved by the number of people who responded and were willing to share their stories. I had imagined the opposite as this was a subject that was personal and upsetting and the events were relatively recent. It was later when I interviewed Herb Ouida, father of Todd, that I understood why so many were willing to be involved and for their story to be told.

Todd's story by his father Herb

One of the 9/11 list members who replied to my email was Herb Ouida, who wrote to me about his son Todd, with a weblink attached. We arranged that I would interview Herb at his house in New Jersey.

Todd was just 25 and worked for Cantor Fitzgerald on the 105th floor of the North Tower. Cantor Fitzgerald occupied the 101st to the 105th floors of One World Trade Center—the North Tower. Approximately 2,000 people died in the North Tower that day, with Cantor Fitzgerald suffering the greatest loss of life when 658 of its 960 employees, nearly two-thirds of its workforce, perished in the attacks. American Airlines Flight 11 crashed into floors 94–98 and Todd's office was above the impact zone. His father Herb worked on the 77th floor and managed to escape. Todd did not survive.

Trauma re-lived

I began the interview with one question: "Can you tell me what happened on September 11th 2001?" My approach was to ask one question and allow the speaker to narrate his story with as little interference from me as possible—I did not want to "influence" the direction of the telling in any way. More importantly, I wanted to remain neutral so asking one question rather than a series of structured interview questions would not only elicit an account of the events of that day but would also elicit the experience in the form of an uninterrupted personal narrative.

Herb was a very eloquent narrator who spoke with great emotion and warmth about his son and of the Foundation that had since been set up in Todd's name to help children with mental health issues (see weblink at the end of this chapter). Until the interview, I was unaware that Herb had also been working in the North Tower on the 77th floor and survived the terrorist attack. Below is an excerpt from Herb's story describing the events following the collapse of the South Tower (Two World Trade Center):

> Then they told me as I walked there was no more World Trade Centre. How could that be? 8.46 the- [] 9.02 the other building was hit and then at 9.58 the other building collapsed first! The building that was hit second collapsed first because it was hit at a much more ferocious speed and at a lower point, it was about the 60th floor. All that I found out later but I thought about 8.46 I am out of the building and Todd still has 28 minutes, I calculated. From 9.58 when I got out to 10.26 when my building collapsed the other building collapsed at 10.02. Now in that time I said 'He's younger than me, he is stronger than me. He only has 28 flights to go down. I am on the 77th he is on 105th. He'd certainly make it.' But I did not know there was no way out. The building was on fire, the staircases were destroyed. The entire building above where the plane hit was a prison. There was no staircase. They tried to go up some of them they wanted to get the helicopter. The doors were locked. The helicopter couldn't land anyway. I walked to my daughter's house and then I saw on tv what had happened but like everyone, all of us, I knew Todd had gotten out, I was sure he had gotten out and he was going to call me. And we spent the time going to the hospitals, we spent the time looking. Everybody put up the pictures. My wife said to me before I could admit it that Todd was lost. I did not believe that. It was Tuesday morning September 11th. It was a beautiful morning. It reminds me from this song from Les Miserables. Can such evil happen on such a beautiful day? Can young men die on such a beautiful day? Yes. We waited and prayed, we prepared and then on September 30th, it was a Sunday, we had a memorial service for Todd. Nobody was allowed to speak except someone who knew him. We did not want anybody to come in just with phrases, meaningless phrases, it had a comfort knowing him.

Herb's moving experience was filled with many factual details about specific events within his personal story as well as what Labov and Waletzky (1967) describe as "evaluation," which reveals what the narrator felt at the time through their assessment of the events. It was during Herb's narration that I came to understand the reason for the overwhelming number of responses to my email on the 9/11 listserv asking for members to contact me to take part in my research. As Herb explained:

> I want to tell the story and I want to tell I think it primarily, honestly for my own healing but I also think it is important to tell the story because Todd's story in his life touches people that are alive, touches their lives, so in a way Todd lives because his life touches other lives and changes those lives hopefully, because our work is very much dedicated to helping children who suffer.

Herb also explained that

> "Telling the story is therapeutic … it's important …" "There was a Todd Ouida … he walked this earth … "

Members of the 9/11 listserv and other informants who took part in this study responded wanting to tell their story because "the story" celebrates the life rather than the death of individuals who died in the attacks. Tuval-Mashiach et al. (2004: 281) explain that

> People infuse meaning into their lives, into the events they have experienced, and into the choices they have made, through the stories they tell about themselves. As such, the life-story is not only a format for telling oneself (and others) about one's life but is also the means by which one's identity takes shape (Bruner 1990; Giddens 1991; MacAdams 1988; Polkinghorne 1988; Rosenwald and Ochberg 1992). On the one hand, the story expresses the identity of the narrator, on the other it shapes and influences the transformations of that identity. This is because it is through their stories that individuals come to know themselves or to reveal themselves to others.

Narrative storytelling, therefore, is one way of coping with traumatic events as it allows the narrator to understand the events through the construction of a story. The story itself allows the narrator "to charge the event with personal meaning and to place it as part of the rest of his life, as opposed to being its focus" (Tuval-Mashiach et al. 2004: 291). It would be an understatement to say I was very moved—I sobbed throughout the interview as I heard Herb narrate his own personal experiences of that day and also details of Todd's loss. The intersubjective nature and situated activity of storytelling provides a context for the display of emotion where it is acceptable and allowed, despite my attempts to remain neutral. In a generous act of sensitivity, Herb apologized to me for my visible distress even though these painful experiences were his:

> I am sorry to put so much pain out for you but you asked me to tell you the story.

And,

> That's my story. [7 second pause.] I feel as if I have almost imposed on you this story but um you have been very kind. When I saw your message that you were looking, I knew I would be interested so even when you said there was some difficulty in the travel I offered to do it on the phone. And I never know, I never know how I'm going to be when I tell the story but it doesn't matter I have to tell the story. It's a good story in many parts too you know if you think about it. There's all that part of the story where he overcomes these problems and like so many of the September the 11th families so many of them—we went to a support group for many years my wife and I.

My emotional response to Herb's story made me reflect on my own behavior as an ethnographer and raised the question of what I call The Ethnographer's Paradox and, particularly, how should the ethnographer respond in an interview setting: is there a right or a wrong way?

The Ethnographer's Paradox

Prior to the interview I had decided that I would remain silent after the initial question, where I asked Herb to tell me what happened on the morning of September 11, 2001. I was aware that I did not want to affect the storytelling process with any additional verbal or nonlinguistic cues. However, this is problematic on two levels. First, a position of impartiality, as Gobo (2008: 141) states, is "impossible to apply in practice." He argues that

> Our emotions and inclinations make us prefer some relationships to others: we find some participants morelikeable than others; we feel affinities with some of them but may be entirely indifferent to the rest.

Second, storytelling is a social activity, a naturally dynamic speech event that requires an audience (real or idealized) to collaborate and co-construct its formation. It is usually natural for the narrator to receive signs of engagement through a number of linguistic and nonlinguistic cues, such as the use of minimal responses and back-channeling, as well as through paralinguistic signals such as laughing and nodding. The dilemma or the "paradox" for the ethnographer is whether it is in fact natural to remain silent to avoid the story becoming tailored to the ethnographer as listener and audience. The paradox is that while trying to remain neutral, other nonverbal signals, such as crying and silence, communicate a response and engagement with the narration nevertheless, and the ethnographer is positioned as an empathetic listener. The interview as methodology for collecting data therefore has to be reevaluated, as "the interview can no longer be viewed as a unilaterally guided means of excavating information. It is being reevaluated in terms of its structure, interactional dynamics, situational responsiveness, and discursive dimensions" (Gubrium and Holstein 2012: 27). There is, therefore, a need to reconceptualize the role of the interviewer as an active and involved participant in the interview event that becomes transformative for both the informant and the researcher.

And what of the lasting effects … ?

Apart from the obvious outcomes of the study, that is, a corpus of spoken narratives of traumatic experiences, both the ethnographer and the informants gain in different ways from the experience. As an ethnographer, the opportunity to undertake a study of this kind and to meet such generous people willing to share their stories is an incredible and humbling experience. I was able to collect authentic, natural, personal narratives to begin my analysis to understand the language of trauma and the structure of this sub-genre of narratives. On the way, I also came to understand the complexities involved in researching real people and real lives for their stories. (On the downside, it was suggested to me by a therapist speaking on behalf of one of the 9/11 informants that I should seek counseling to deal with the traumatic content of the stories I had encountered. This was another methodological issue I had not anticipated.) A "relationship" with the informants, to keep in touch by email, can also be established, if both sides are willing. For the informants in the study, there is a context for telling their story and giving meaning to these life-changing events through narrating their experiences. Poignantly, to reiterate Herb Ouida, "Telling the story is therapeutic … it's important … " "There was a Todd Ouida … he walked this earth … "

Informants also receive a copy of the transcribed interview to thank them for their involvement in my research.

Coda

Researching narratives of trauma raises a number of issues on the practicalities of undertaking ethnographic research, highlighting questions such as *What does it mean to interview someone?* and *What are the real issues for the ethnographer?* Despite the conventional role of ethnographers as passive participants in an interactive interview event, there are situations, as illustrated in this chapter, where the Ethnographer's Paradox comes into play and engagement is shown to be a natural consequence of storytelling. To reiterate Gubrium and Holstein (2012: 27), "the interview can no longer be viewed as a unilaterally guided means of excavating information. It is being re-evaluated in terms of its structure, interactional dynamics, situational responsiveness, and discursive dimensions." For those participants who experienced the traumas of the London 7/7 and New York 9/11 terrorist attacks, narrating personal stories provides a chance to make sense of the events through their articulation and construction as a story. Finally, for Strejilevich, personal narratives are testimony and she argues that they are "a means for working through traumatic memories and for social and cultural resistance—a must for the ethical recovery of a community after the experience of utmost exclusion" (2006: 701).

Notes

1   See Prince 1973, Todorov 1969 and Chatman 1978 for literary models of narrative; Labov and Waletzky 1967; and Labov 1972 for sociolinguistic models of narrative; Bartlett 1932; and van Dijk and Kintsch 1983 for psychological models or narrative, for example.

2   The British Association of Applied Linguists (BAAL) provides extensive information and advice on ethical priorities in their paper "Recommendations on Good Practice in Applied Linguistics." Available at http://www.baal.org.uk/dox/goodpractice_full.pdf

Acknowledgments

To find out more about the "Todd Ouida Children's Foundation" please visit: http://www.mybuddytodd.org

I would like to say a huge thank you to Professor David Hoover of New York University (NYU) for his generosity in letting me have the use of his office and for his great sense of humor.

References

Bartlett, Frederic C. 1932. *Remembering*. Cambridge: Cambridge University Press.

Bell, Allan. 1991. *The Language of News Media*. Oxford: Blackwell.

Bruner, Jerome. 1990. *Acts of Meaning*. Cambridge MA and London: Harvard University Press.

Chatman, Seymour. 1978. *Story and Discourse: Narrative Structure in Fiction and Film*. New York: Cornell University Press.

Cheshire, Jenny. 1978. *Variation in an English Dialect*. Cambridge: Cambridge University Press.

Galtung, Johan and Marie Ruge. 1973. "Structuring and selecting news." In *The Manufacture of News: Social Problems, Deviance, and the Class Media*, edited by Stanley Cohen and Jock Young, 62–67. London: Constable.

Gobo, Giampetro. 2008. *Doing Ethnography*. London: SAGE.

Gubrium, Jaber, F. and James A. Holstein 2012. "Narrative practice and the transformation of interview subjectivity." In *The SAGE Handbook of Interview Research*, edited by Jaber F. Gubrium, James A. Holstein, Amir Marvasti, and Karyn D. McKinney, 27–43. London: SAGE. 2nd edition.

Labov, William. 1972. *Language in the Inner City*. Philadelphia: University of Pennsylvania Press.

Labov, William. 1997. "Further steps in narrative analysis."*Journal of Narrative and Life History 7*, no. *1–4*: 395–415.

Labov, William and Joshua Waletzky. 1967. "Narrative Analysis: Oral Versions of Personal Experience." In *Essays on the Verbal and Visual Arts: Proceedings of the 1966 Annual Spring Meeting of the American Ethnologic Society*, edited by June Helm, 12–45. Seattle, WA: University of Washington Press.

Lambrou, Marina. Forthcoming 2014. "Narrative, text and time: Telling the same story twice in the oral narrative reporting of 7/7." *Language and Literature 23(1)*.

Litosseliti, Lia. 2010. *Research Methods in Linguistics*. London: Continuum.

Malinowski, Bronislaw. 1922. *Argonauts of the Western Pacific*. London: Routledge and Kegan.

Milroy, Lesley. 1980. *Language and Social Networks*. Oxford: Blackwell.

Murphy, Elizabeth, and Robert Dingwall 2001. "The ethics of ethnography." In *Handbook of Ethnography*, edited by Paul. Atkinson, Amanda Coffey, Sara Delamont, John Lofland, and Lyn Lofland. 339–351. London: SAGE.

Polanyi, Livia. 1981. "Telling the same story twice." *Text 1*, no. 4: 315–336.

Prince, Gerald. 1973. *A Grammar of Stories*. The Hague: Mouton.

Rampton, Ben. 2007. "Neo-Hymesian linguistic ethnography in the United Kingdom." *Journal of Sociolinguistics 11*, no. 5: 584–607.

Stockwell, Peter. 2003. *Sociolinguistics*. London: Routledge.

Strejilevich, Nora. 2006. "Testimony: Beyond the language of truth." *Human Rights Quarterly 28*, no 3: 701–713.

Todorov, Tzvetan. 1969. "Structural analysis of narrative." *Novel 3*: 70–76.

Trudgill, Peter. 1974. *The Social Differentiation of English in Norwich*. Cambridge: Cambridge University Press.

Tuval-Mashiach, Rivka, Sara Freedman, Neta Bargai, Rut Boker, Hilit Hadar, and Arieh Y. Shalev. 2004. "Coping with trauma: Narrative and cognitive perspectives." *Psychiatry 67*, no. 3: 280–293.

Wales, Katie. 2001. *A Dictionary of Stylistics*. Longman: Harlow.

Wilce, James, M. 2009. *Language and Emotion*. Cambridge: Cambridge University Press.

van Dijk, T. and Walter Kintsch 1983. *Strategies of Discourse Comprehension*. New York: Academic Press.

7

Autobiography and Political Marketing: Narrative and the Obama Brand

Darren G. Lilleker
Bournemouth University, UK

Introduction

When storytelling and politics are mentioned in the same sentence, it may conjure images of spin or lying. However, political communication has a strong oral tradition. The power of rhetorical speech was discussed by Aristotle, recognizing it can manipulate man for good or ill. Before Aristotle, Plato was intensely critical of the use of sophistry. He argued that this form of combining manipulation with moralization was the endeavor of those with little knowledge of the "truth." Although in the modern age we would recognize there is no single fundamental truth, one can only wonder how Plato would view our political communication. Would the stories embedded in political campaigns, press calls, policy launches, or consultation processes be viewed as rhetorical manipulation for the benefit of society or just sophistry? The answer is perhaps a matter of perspectives, on what is said and on the person speaking. The twenty-first-century citizen is deemed to possess the tools to avoid being beguiled by colorful imagery, carefully crafted words, and verbal hyperbole; political communicators on the other hand attempt all the more sophisticated means to manipulate the emotions of the citizenry: to win their support, votes, and donations. It is with this critical eye that we approach the study of narratives in political communication. We recognize politics is built around stories. National histories and revolutionary events create stories that shape understanding; equally, our understanding of events is shaped by the narratives that are woven by those involved. Journalistic and analytical reflections add layers to these narratives, giving depth and embedding them in popular culture. Increasingly, narratives are also used as integral parts of marketing campaigns designed to sell candidates and parties bidding for votes to the highest offices.

One of the most successful and innovative marketing campaigns of recent years was built by and around Barack Obama during his bid for the US Presidency in 2007–2008. His victory in 2008 was testament to innovations in campaigning certainly, but behind the campaign was the creation of the Obama brand. Central to the Obama brand was a set of core values, values that epitomized the American dream, winning government back for the people and fundamentally changing the relations between the citizens and the state. The campaign positioned Obama as the perfect candidate to lead America and heal the gulf between citizen and government post George W. Bush. The Obama brand was built through a range of media appearances, his advertising campaign, and innovative use of social networking. In themselves, these developed a compelling narrative around the Obama brand. However, his brand narrative is best viewed within two books that were authored prior to him deciding to run for the US presidency but were clearly expressions about the man, his politics, and his vision for the nation. Obama's autobiography *Dreams from my Father: a story of race and inheritance* (Obama 1996/2004) and statement of political values *The Audacity of Hope* (Obama 2006) offer a carefully constructed brand narrative that would underpin his communication and shape the perceptions of an Obama presidency. Through a process of discourse analysis producing a thick descriptive narrative this chapter explores what Obama said and did not say, how he positioned himself vis-à-vis American society and the political system, and built a platform from which to engage with new segments of the American electorate. The core argument is that by producing a narrative that identified with both the actual and aspirational personae of young Americans, he made an in-depth connection with an untapped source of electoral support. Our analysis allows us to then offer some thoughts on the role of narratives in political communication.

Psychology, narratives, and branding

Narratives play a fundamental role in much persuasive communication in the postmodern age. They offer symbolic structures through which complex and intangible ideas can be understood and contextualized within the daily lives of audience members (Mumby 1987: 118). Folk stories, personal, tribal, and national histories, passed down through generations, revised, repackaged, and given a modern spin by Hollywood or Bollywood—all tell stories about who and what "we" are, why we are not "them," and why the differences are important. In these ways it is argued that narratives are central features to "the structuration of cultural life" (White 1987: 34) and our understanding of histories (Thomson 1984). Narratives are simply stories, sometimes a blending of fact and fiction, sometimes simply fictional, yet they are frequently used to present compelling images of a future. History is not simply telling us about "our" past, but also gives shape to a collective future (White 1987, Wertsch 2008). Narratives play a role of sense making for audiences; however, for the creators of narratives they give sense to ideas. Narratives are also interpreted by audience members, and this interpretive cognitive effort, which positions the story's narrative juxtaposed to personal lived experiences, allows for sense to be made (Clegg 1975). This is argued to be particularly the case with autobiographies, which connect the author to the life of the reader and vice versa (Linde, 1987a, Linde, 1987b, and Peacock and Holland 1993). However, power over the interpreting and decoding of narratives can lie as much with the narrator as with their audience. The encoding of narratives to elicit specific emotional responses can cloud judgment, lead to a suspension of disbelief (Escobar 2011), and lead to a single collective interpretation to emerge from exposure to the narrative (Giddens 1981). The well-constructed narrative will thus have one single intended interpretation and this should be shared by the narrator and his or her intended receiver, if not by every possible member of the audience.

One can thus talk of the teleological nature of narratives. Stories that instill and/or reinforce religious beliefs, social attitudes and behaviors, moral values and codes, and the role of citizens share a strategic purpose. The power of the narrative is not in its use of persuasion, it is the power to take an audience on a journey that will often describe a reality, a process of transformation, and an alternative future, be that future personal or collective. Allegories underpinning Greek and Roman myths, Aesop's fables, much of the old testament of the Bible—each transmits moral values to a wider society. The normative instruction is embedded in the story, played out in metaphor. White (1987) describes such narratives as providing meta-code, a shared reality that we cognitively inhabit and that shapes our behavior toward one another and toward the society. Although many moral narratives are timeless in terms of reflecting and further embedding deeply held social mores, other narratives can be limited spatially and temporally (Linde 2010). Portelli (1981) talks of the role of life histories in building class identity. In discussing the linkages between the personal, collective, and institutional narratives that shape identity, Portelli argues that these "are never entirely separate and discrete since they all run simultaneously and mix together in the way people think and tell their lives" (171). Thus, what is suggested here is that narratives are most effective when they meet points of shared consciousness, when the narratives reflect key elements that are central to personal and collective identities, and are also embedded within the narrative of institutions that represent, or claim to be supportive of the goals of, a social group. One can perhaps suggest that there have been key points in history when individual workers, their Trade Unions, and the UK Labour party have been seen to share a common narrative that has led to collective action, although these may be argued to be few and far between (Calhoun 1976). The danger with this is that the rhetoric employed to encode organizational narratives can create false consciousnesses. Belief in the meta-code and identification with a collective that adheres to rules portrayed within narratives can leave one susceptible to believing that those who reflect the meta-code values should be within our cognition of who we are, the "us" as opposed to "them." Thus, narratives can play a profoundly obscurant role.

Persuasive communication, to be successful, must find points of agreement between the persuader and his or her audience. It is argued that every individual has a latitude of acceptance on a range of argument positions (Sherif and Hovland 1961); these can be trivial likes and dislikes or be linked directly to a meta-code of a collective. Positions linked to a meta-code will be the most powerful as these directly link to perceptions of personal and collective identity. Because individuals seek heuristic cues to aid their decisions on who is right or wrong, closest or furthest from their position, relating to simple meta-code positions can be used to sway significant numbers within any audience (Simon 2002). The meta-code contained within political meta-narratives relating to "the American Dream," socialism, fascism, or more radical theories around anarcho-syndicalism, environmentalism, or feminism are often related directly to deeply held social values of a type not unfamiliar to devotees of religious sects and movements. It is the link to the meta-code that makes them persuasive and so attractive to those susceptible to elements within the core ideas of any argument (Westen 2007). It does not mean that those seeking agreement versus disagreement are "pensée sauvage" individuals who are politically unconscious, blinded by imaginary solutions linked to repressed historical contradictions (Jameson, 2006 and Greimas 1987), though one can see evidence for this in the myth of the Aryan race as propounded by the distinctly non-Aryan leaders of the German National Socialist Party in the 1930s. What it does suggest though is that if agreement is recognized and the institutional narrative conflates with personal and collective narratives, it has clear potential for gaining support within a population with latent dissatisfaction with the reality they face and a desire for something different.

Linde (1986) distinguishes between three types of narrative. The event structure provides the building blocks for society by informing us about choices, the selection process, and their outcomes. Evaluative narratives inform about importance and priority and ask audiences to consider carefully choices they are being requested to make; the information is encoded to shape perceptions of "the way things are, the way things ought to be, and the kind of person the speaker [or source] is" (Linde 1986: 187). This neatly links to two elements of persuasion—the logos (messages) and the ethos (nature of the speaker and their goodwill)—but also heavily relies on the shaping of the pathos (the nature of the audience). Linking to meta-codes within the collective to which the audience belongs increases the likelihood of a receptive pathos. Explanatory narratives are the most direct and inform how things are, with a clear link to cause and effect. These may often link with evaluations of what is right and wrong, depending on context, and carry an exceptionalist discourse regarding "others"; those who are wrong and disagree and maybe are causes of events that have negative, "wrong," consequences, which defy meta-codes. Plausibility of the description of events, evaluations, and related explanations are key to entering the audience members' latitudes of acceptance and agreement; the tighter the overlap of a narrative with widely accepted other narratives, and the synergy with meta-codes, theoretically the more likely they are to be accepted. Being aware of what Miller et al. (2009) call referential restraints is important in gaining high levels of acceptance and avoiding obscuring the narrative through the use of hyperbole and empty rhetoric.

In the field of political communication, narratives are omnipresent but seldom a focus of research. Yet the histories of parties, their leaders, and events in politics are often presented as narratives. The parties or individuals themselves, opposition forces, journalists, even citizens may well have their own stories (Burgess 2006). The greatest strategic focus is on the creation of the narrative around the party or candidate, and here it is useful to perceive them as a brand. Branding is the process of "assembling and maintaining in a brand a mix of values, both tangible and intangible, which are relevant to consumers and which meaningfully and appropriately distinguish one supplier's brand from that of another" (Murphy 1988: 4). As relevant in politics as in any other field of strategic communication is the argument that "what is underneath the label should be in line with the personal values of today's consumer" (Rooney 1995: 49). Transplanting the language of values with meta-code and consumer as audience, one can instantly link the process of branding to that of the construction of persuasive political narratives. Connections made through narratives involve the invocation of schema items that lead to automatic inferences being made and arguments being accepted (Gerrig and Egidi 2003). Bruner (1990) suggests the primary way people make sense of others, real or fictional, is through stories. Building on the perspective, Shank (1990) argues that all human knowledge is stored in the form of narratives. The power of the metaphorical narrative is also noted, because metaphors that are embedded within cultures facilitate the acceptance of abstract notions (Lakoff and Johnson, 1980). Thus, narratives play an important role in constructing a political brand personality. Whereas in corporate branding the challenge is to construct a story that facilitates the portrayal of the brand (Deighton, Romer, and McQueen 1989), politics presents its own story. The centrality of individuals to stories is facilitated even better within candidate-centered systems (Johansen 2012), where the candidate becomes the embodiment of a party or movement, the heart of the political and ideological values (Lilleker 2005). The US system is perfect to understand how the individual candidate narrative, in the context of a presidential election contest, is constructed and what this indicates about branding narratives within a political communication context.

Analyzing narrative: A brief methodological note

It could be argued that the successful campaigns for the Democratic nomination and subsequently the US presidency of Barack Obama in 2007–2008 were exceptional. The level of innovation in connecting to and with the voter, the projection of Obama as a brand symbolizing change, and the interest in him as the first colored man to have a realistic chance of becoming president all mark out the contest as unique (Sevin et al. 2011). Yet, despite the unique qualities of the contest, Obama was simply engaging in an activity that has preoccupied probably all candidates for the US presidency: winning voters. Furthermore, the use of autobiographical material is not unique to Obama; advertisements have long been used to present images of the candidates to the electorate (Jamieson 1996). Although unique to an extent, Obama's autobiography had been released some years prior to him standing for the Democratic Party nomination. His first book *Dreams from my Father* was first published in 1995, prior to his first attempt at getting elected to the House of Representatives but after his election as the first black president of the Harvard Law Review, which gained him media attention and a book contract. The second book *The Audacity of Hope* can be viewed more as a manifesto being published in 2006. However, the fact that both became bestsellers during his campaigns indicate their importance as campaign artifacts, ones that informed numerous television interviews, articles in the media, including five cover stories on *Time* magazine, as well as shaping perceptions of him as a man and potential president. It is therefore these books that this chapter focuses on as representations of the Obama brand narrative. The argument is not that these were strategic productions, aimed at winning support, but that they are representations of Obama by Obama and thus indicate how he wanted people to view him as a man (Linde 1993).

The analysis seeks to identify the appeals made within the texts. First, the appeals to collective meta-codes, the values held by those who might support his presidency and if we can identify particular references that point to a shared consciousness, shared values, and normative realities. Second, we focus on issues of identity and how Obama positions himself throughout the texts, both in the way he constructs the narratives about himself, the others in his life, and whether there is a discernible us and them narrative. Third, we identify how the texts use event, evaluative, and explanatory narratives to build arguments. The method develops a microanalysis of political communication, focusing on both meta-level and micro-level elements (Bull 2002). Meta-level analysis focuses on the key features and functions of the overall narrative, its structure and its encoding; these include meta-coding information, delivering the narrative in an event structure or as evaluative or explanatory stories. These meta-level features are then operationalized into specific devices within the text. The micro-level analysis explores these rhetorical devices that link to features identified within the meta-level of the narrative. Meta-coding will build identities, an us and them perhaps, and define the beliefs, values, and ideology (ethos) of the collective "us," which is intended to be internalized by the speaker; the ethos will be directly linked to an alternative, better, future to the present. One would expect meta-coded narratives to be constructed using an emotive tone and rhetorical devices.

It is expected that the rhetorical devices will be delivered in various ways. Event-based narratives will use case studies and factual evidence to highlight positive and negative outcomes of specific behaviors. The language will be de-personalized and will focus on a collective that is not necessarily internalized by the speaker but perhaps empowered or constructed by the narrative. This will focus on normative statements about what "ought" to be, and be instructive. A similar structure, but focusing on more emotive reasoning, would identify narratives designed to be evaluative. There will be a clearly identifiable tone with direct statements of right and wrong with details of rewards and punishments and the nature of choices that are required of the audience. Factual evidence may be employed to reinforce the arguments for one course of action but the argument will also be personalized and delivered as informed opinion. Explanatory narratives will combine the factual and the emotive, in particular drawing in general beliefs as evidence. These will be used to link actions to outcomes with a clear sense of which course of action is correct and how that is shared with a broader collective. Explanatory narratives are likely to have a historical dimension from which predictions are drawn that have a strong emotive component and link the personal ethos of the speaker to that of the broader collective. While each feature could exclusively dominate any single piece of communication, given the complexity of autobiographical works it is expected that features and devices will complement one another to construct a brand image. The identification of these rhetorical vehicles aids the identification of what is referred to as the "story logic" (Herman 2003: 13), that which the author is trying to impart to the reader, and how the author combines the narrator's roles of viewing, telling, acting, experiencing, and reflecting (Fludernik 1996). Combining these perspectives thus allows for an understanding to be gained of the way the narratives position Obama vis-à-vis the US society, its values, and how the narratives attempt to build a shared consciousness around his presidency. The chapter will now offer an overview of each text prior to drawing overall conclusions about the role these narratives played in building the Obama brand.

Dreams from my Father: Shaping the Obama brand

Dreams from my Father can be read as both a discussion of general American values and politics and a deeply personal narrative: the three parts, in turn, reflect on growing up as a mixed-race boy in 1960s' and 1970s' America, working in grassroots politics as a community organizer, and visiting his family in Kenya; each section connects to particular component parts of the job of the US President. Through the narratives, Obama demonstrates sharing the angst of many teenagers but particularly those of color, his caring for the ordinary American, particularly those living in poverty, and his unique perspective on global politics and America's role in the Third World. Alternatively, it is a deeply personal narrative on issues of race and racism, one that shaped the young Obama, and the narrative describes his search for his identity and a sense of belonging. Darsey (2009) argues Obama's personal journey is used as a metaphor, establishing a synergy between a personal journey, the journey of African Americans from slavery to the legislature, and the broader American rags-to-riches journey that incorporates the meta-code of the American Dream (Howell 2008). Alternatively, the text is viewed as an expression of cosmopolitan post-racial American character (Hammack 2010). Arguably, therefore, the book talks to a number of audiences, exploring themes that will connect with the lives of many of those his campaign was to mobilize so successfully.

The personal nature of the narrative is stressed from the very start. Whether there was a strategy behind producing the text or not, the book is cast as an autobiography: "my past in a book, a past that left me feeling exposed, even slightly ashamed" (xiv). The preface also pitches the book as a personal journey, perhaps a metaphor as Darsey (2009) argues, a search for identity and direction in life, qualities that Howell argues make the author "genuinely likable and knowable" (2009: 188) because the narrative "smacks of authenticity" (2009: 189). The metaphor for the journey is in "a boy's search for his father, and through that search a workable meaning for his life as a black American" (Obama 2004: xvi). It is also the story of a search for community, one of color, a family, and one that is America as a society—themes that are made practical in *The Audacity of Hope*. While personal and most likely authentic, one can also see how the feelings of disconnection may resonate with broader currents of feelings within American society, and in particular the American youth mobilized during his campaign (Barr 2009).

The first section, "Origins," deals directly with his discovery of his place in society, one that was no longer segregated, was tolerant, but not necessarily accepting. The question "would you let your daughter marry one," asked of white parents; the puzzle for Obama was why his white grandparents had agreed to their daughter marrying his father (Obama 2004: 12). Obama shows he was protected from the racism prevalent in US society, but using a series of event narratives talks of exposure to issues such as black men undergoing chemical treatments to bleach their skin. He records being profoundly shocked (30), even when he is reading about the practice from faraway Indonesia. The young Obama became aware of what now would be called institutional racism: "I began to notice that Cosby never got the girl on *I Spy*, that the black man on *Mission Impossible* spent all his time underground. I noticed there was nobody like me in the Sears, Roebuck Christmas catalog ... and that Santa was a white man" (52). He records this as evidence of being protected from exposure to issues of race, not whether this depressed his expectations. He does record an increasing feeling of not belonging, particular during his schooling (60) but, perhaps with hindsight, argues against arbitrary "rage at the white world" (81). The event narratives used as vehicles to explore issues such as black militancy, told through his memories of militant college friend Ray, lead into evaluative narratives that reflect on broader issues prevalent in modern-day US society. The record of his years in school and college expose him to a tapestry of all American society, his experiences those of every man (or perhaps woman) but tinged with a pain of lacking an identity, being neither black nor white, one that drove him away from the cocoon of Hawaii, his mother, and grandparents.

> What I needed was a community, I realized, a community that cut deeper than the common despair that black friends and I shared when reading the latest crime statistics, or the high fives I might exchange on a basketball court. A place where I could put down stakes and test my commitments. (115)

Such explanatory narratives are frequently deployed to show America as it is and how it ought to be with Obama emerging as a character with the higher understanding that is perhaps needed to complete America's journey.

The record of this period of Obama's life sees him politicized, pointing to issues that need change and proposing himself, perhaps, as the vehicle for that change. Hinting at the tactic he would exploit throughout his fight for the Democratic Party nomination and then the Presidency, Obama states, through an explanatory narrative that as a community organizer his mission was to bring about change. "Change will come from a mobilized grass roots ... I'll organize black folks. At the grass roots. For change" (133). However, introducing another theme of his election campaign, that of changing the interface between citizens and the state, his induction into community organizing in Chicago taught him that change frequently ran into the buffers of realpolitik. Interweaving event, evaluative, and explanatory narratives, Obama portrays how expediency defeated idealism, negotiation watered down not just radicalism but making any difference at all to the lives of the poorest black communities. The difference Obama would strive for, following the advice of mentor Marty, was to empower people and "move toward the center of people's lives" (188). Obama's idealism began to be tempered, he listened to the people he strove to help and learned their stories. Using accounts of his personal connections with the narratives of those he was helping, he builds a shared identity with "his" people, disadvantaged black America, but also links their plight to that of all Americans living on the breadline: the problem is politics not race. Successes were limited, he does not paint himself as the white knight who rode in and took residents of the poor neighborhood of Altgelt out of poverty, he even failed to get their toilets fixed (234), rather he touched a few lives without having any tangible impact. The impact was on Obama rather than those he helped. Event narratives portray how he learned of the hostility and mistrust within the black communities toward whites, he learned of the merits and flaws of black nationalism, and recognized the prejudices and bitterness in his own character. One of the few girlfriends who feature failed to understand his search for identity and apparently ended the relationship because "She couldn't be black" (211) and so was unable to grasp the emotional impact of prejudice on the young Obama. He also learned about community, though. He records the importance of "a sense ... that one has a stake in this order, a wish that, no matter how fluid this order sometimes appears, it will not drain out of the universe" (270). The order of which he speaks is both a temporal connection to your forebears as well as a horizontal connection to those around you. The connections are picked up as Pastor Jeremiah Wright's words are recounted. His rejection of class in black communities—as it encourages "them to think of 'we' and 'they' instead of US" (284)—indicates a disavowal of social distinctions to connect to the postmodern and post-racial America Hammack (2010) describes. Obama's embrace of religion, the cultural community of the church, and Wright's influence in giving him the title for his manifesto *The Audacity of Hope* provided him with a large piece of his jigsaw, he suggests. The final piece of his puzzle takes him to Kenya, the land of his father.

Despite this being an alien place, Obama records feeling at home: "My name belonged and so I belonged, drawn into a web of relationships, alliances, and grudges that I did not yet understand" (305). The purpose, however, is not to distance himself from America but to build an evaluative narrative that reflects on American society and asks whether it is really the land of the free. The majority of his recollections on the visit are personal, relating to him discovering his family for the first time. However, it is also recorded as a time of learning. In particular, he absorbs some of the thinking of his father, his family, and the African and so, perhaps, learns more about what it means to be an African American. Quoting his grandfather, he is happy to put into print an indictment of both the white and black races: "like an ant the white man works together ... he will follow his leaders and not question orders. Black men are not like this. Even the most foolish black man thinks he knows better than the wise man. That is why the black man will always lose" (417). But he finishes positively, connecting the threads of his journey. The concluding highly evaluative narrative positions Obama as connecting to the meta-code that all Americans are dissatisfied with the inequalities in society and dysfunction of its politics. Obama tries to connect to both the black and white communities, despite the book taking the perspective of a boy who discovers he is black: "Black and white, they make their claim on this community we call America. They choose our better history" (439). In statements such as this Obama makes an explicit link to the American Dream meta-code. Should this be seen as a call to overcome the prejudices that have separated Americans along racial lines, should it be a sign to strive for a better future, is it a statement of values designed to position Obama as the bridge between black and white, past and future.

The Audacity of Hope: **The personal made political**

Dreams from my Father sets up *The Audacity of Hope* perfectly, it is the personal made practical; as Howell describes it "one part policy, one party historical synthesis, and one part personal narrative" (2009: 188). Obama describes the book as "personal reflections on those values and ideals that have led me into public life ... based on my experience as a senator and lawyer, husband and father, Christian and skeptic" (9). As such therefore it is not a Democratic manifesto but a personal one with Obama as both the character and the narrator; it is a personal journey through life and politics and how life shaped his personal vision for a political future.

A key theme of the book is to identify himself with the masses. Many a personal reflection is positioned as a representation of every man. For example, "one of those flaws had proven to be a chronic restlessness; an inability to appreciate, no matter how well things were going, those blessings that were right there in front of me. It's a flaw that is endemic to modern life, I think—endemic, too, in the American culture" (2). The representation of himself as everyone, perhaps capturing the idea of being both the ordinary man but also the persona of superman with higher values and understanding (Nietzsche 2005 [1885]), is extended to him embodying mass opinion: "the standards and principles that the majority of Americans deem important in their lives, and in the life of the country—should be the heart of our politics, the cornerstone of any meaningful debate about budgets and projects, regulations and policies" (52). Obama also presents himself as having a connection with a global political desire for "four essential freedoms": of speech and worship; from want and from fear (317). Alongside these broad rhetorical devices are specific event and evaluative narratives that appear designed to reach the latitudes of acceptance of mass American society.

Politics and politicians are often seen as out of touch, a perception often countered with photo opportunities with ordinary people. Obama presented him being in touch more directly.

> I listened to people talk... what struck me was just how modest people's hopes were ... I told them they were right: government couldn't solve all their problems. But with a slight change in priorities we could make sure every child had a decent shot at life... More often than not, folks would nod in agreement and ask how they could get involved ... I knew once again why I'd gone into politics.(6–7)

The combination of the event and explanatory narratives that employ both case studies and personal judgments makes the persuasive element of the overall narrative more powerful. For example, Obama argues listening is not sufficient, he describes his connection to the people at the more fundamental level of empathy: "a sense of empathy is one I find myself appreciating more and more ... It is at the heart of my moral code ... a call to stand in somebody else's shoes and see through their eyes" (66). Here Obama invokes the essence of a line delivered by Atticus Finch to his daughter in Lee Harper's 1960 tale of heroism in the face of racism *To Kill a Mockingbird* and a quotation attributed to the Muslim faith "To understand a man, you've got to walk a mile in his shoes, whether they fit or not." Obama attributes the ideal to his "mother's simple principle—'How would that make you feel?'" (67). Obama extends this explanatory evaluative into a political doctrine that argues if empathy was at the heart of politics the balance would be redressed in favor of those struggling in the US society. Obama's empathy is not contained within the borders of the United States. As he explores his time in both Indonesia and Kenya in *Dreams from my Father*, he uses these also when discussing the American world role. Indonesia, in particular, he uses as a metaphor for understanding the world "beyond our borders" where the US "record is mixed…farsighted, simultaneously serving our national interests, our ideas, and the interests of other nations. At other times…misguided, based on false assumptions…" (279). Such evaluative narratives juxtapose Obama with his predecessor explicitly, he stands as "the antithesis of, but the antidote to, the Bush era" (Escobar 2011: 114). But largely criticism is leveled at a more amorphous and exclusive political system, one that is out of touch with the ordinary people, which shaped Obama's narrative. The theme of Obama as outsider, a change agent, versus a system of pork barrels and filibuster, corporate funding and lobbying, would run through his campaign advertisements (Lilleker and Scullion 2009), positioning him as a Weberian ideal-type president.

Through his narrative Obama presents a gulf between himself and US politics as he found it, observing "In the world's greatest deliberative body, no-one is listening" (15). In such phrases Obama juxtaposes his belief in the American polity and the ideals on which the branches of government were formed and the way that governance is practiced. Obama argues for a rebalancing of power as "in a democracy, the most important office is the office of citizen" (135). Socialism seems at times recommended as he juxtaposes the traditions of the New Deal "We're all in it together" philosophy with the conservative and republic view of society based on ownership where "You're on your own" (178). Obama also offers a personal and moral case for redistribution, arguing "those of us who benefited most from this new economy can best afford to shoulder the obligation of ensuring every American child has a chance for that same success" (193). Yet there is also an element of defeatism. He accepts the reality of politics and the chase for money that "eliminated any shame I once had in asking strangers for money" (113). Equally, he shows in event narratives—about meetings with President George W. Bush and Republicans—a sense that politics is out of touch and in ways that are not easily fixable.

The gulf between the ideals of the US political system and how politics is practiced is just one of the many paradoxes and contradictions in the Obama narrative. The internal contradictions within his own thinking, stemming from his experiences as both a man and a politician, are often faced, recognized as a product of having empathy with citizens and elites, principles and realities. This leads to pragmatism in his argument that may be a reflection of growing up American or positioning himself as both the outsider and the insider: one that is socialized and strategic. For example, on state intervention, Obama argues "we will do collectively, through our government, only those things that we cannot do well or at all individually and privately. In other words, we should be guided by what works" (159). The contradictions are also discussed in terms of his views on religion. From his mother Obama learned religion to be "an expression of human culture ... not its wellspring" (204). In Chicago, however, Obama found the community within which his ideals and beliefs were shared, something his mother lacked. Within this, Obama perhaps makes a metaphorical link with the broader American society and the sense of shared culture, identity, and values that he argues is central to the national character elsewhere in the book. The national character is one that is fair and equal, one accepting of difference, one that is explicitly visualized through the eyes of a "child of a black man and a white woman, someone who was born in the racial melting pot of Hawaii" (231). He does not, however, suggest that racial inequalities are of historical significance only. In discussing the contradictions in his own views of prejudice, he explores tensions between different racial groups, his own dissonance at seeing the Mexican flag adorning the US streets, but in the end builds a shared entity that is America. The evaluative narrative exploring issues of race and color that emerges is one of structural inequality: "more minorities may be living the American Dream, but their hold on that dream remains tenuous" (243). Obama's vision, both personal and political, is that "America is big enough to accommodate all their dreams" (269). The contradictions return in his discussion of foreign policy that raises questions regarding the world role the United States has adopted but concludes with "Like it or not, if we want to make America more secure, we are going to have to help make the world more secure" (304). His proposal is to be the sheriff but with a more multinational accompanying posse, one that bridges many traditions of thinking within the United States. The same can be said of neoliberalism and national development, where he proposes that the flexibility of markets means "market-based liberal democracies offer people around the world their best chance at a better life" (316). Obama thus explains and evaluates all aspects of American politics and society, highlighting inconsistencies and offering solutions.

The final chapter is the most personal as it deals with family and offers insights into him meeting his wife Michelle, the birth of their daughters, and the challenges of being a long-distance parent, and how the years between the end of the first book and the start of his presidential race shaped his politics. Obama offers a perfect picture of family life in that of Michelle's, one that "stirred a longing for stability and a sense of place that I had not realized was there" (334); this is used as a metaphor for how family life should be and underpins his argument that "policies should strengthen marriage for those who choose it and that discourage unintended births outside of marriage are sensible goals to pursue" (334). Here again we see the contradiction; Obama's evaluative narrative shows a belief in conservative values but with individual choice allowed where the right choice is made. He uses his family as a metaphor for the busy working family, the juggler family (336), as well as broader failings in American and African American families, which mirror those he experienced: "my father's irresponsibility towards his children, my stepfather's remoteness, and my grandfather's failures" (346). He suggests that the American Dream is built upon high expectations for oneself, arguing that "if we want to pass on high expectations to our children, we have to have higher expectations for ourselves" (347). Such value-laden passages connect explicitly to the meta-codes of the American Dream that are so embedded in the American psychology.

The book's epilogue returns to the theme of the ordinary people and his empathy, those who he remembered in his 2004 speech to the Democratic convention. The people he introduces throughout the book are brought back as those he represents—ordinary Americans who struggle but who moved Obama through "their determination, their self-reliance, a relentless optimism in the face of hardship." He links these qualities together as the audacity he speaks about in the title and throughout, the "pervasive spirit of hope." The final metaphor, him walking onto the stage at the 2004 convention saying "let me tell their stories right," is one that reaches beyond any single event. It perhaps suggests not only Obama telling their stories, but retelling them in order to get policies enacted that will alleviate their struggles and help them realize their dreams. It is perhaps a metaphor for his vision of the presidency, and perhaps a hint of the philosophy of an Obama presidency, one that offers a perception of how he approaches walking on to a stage that acts as a metaphor for a national or world stage as leader, a platform where he can represent some or all of America better than his rivals, as much as it being the stage at the Democratic Party convention.

The Obama narrative: A meta-coded brand

The identity Obama offers is highly complex, embodying the history of racial segregation and the journey of the African American (Darsey 2009) as well as a post-racial America (Hammack 2010). The stronger meta-code invoked is that of the American Dream, the faith that an individual can attain success and virtue through strenuous effort, which Hochschild (1996: 36) argues to be the very soul of the American nation. His journey, how he advanced himself economically and intellectually, is how he positions himself as embodying the American Dream; it is a theme that runs through his narrative and, as Escobar (2011: 114) argues, was "a structuring theme for his best campaign performances." However, the American Dream needs to be facilitated. The values Obama expresses link him to any American who feels that the American Dream is not offered equally, to the African Americans in ghettoes like Altgelt but also a range of people who strive to keep themselves and their families out of poverty. The narratives thus try to connect with the stories of many ordinary Americans who feel disenchanted and disenfranchised and see the political system as exclusive and not inclusive. Obama thus held up a mirror to American society, reflecting public opinion to deliver a highly personal critique that many would have agreed with and, given the authenticity of his critique, accepted him as the best chance for change. Reflecting on the election campaign, one commentator argued that the lesson from Obama is that "Political success depends on becoming a collective representation" (Alexander 2011:53); it would seem a simple truism reflecting on the narrative that was developed through the 1995 autobiography, his philosophical political manifesto launched in 2006, and then the advertisements, performances, statements, and speeches that characterized his campaign.

The implied authenticity of the Obama narrative is driven by the structuring of his arguments around events, which are then explained and evaluated to reach a teleological conclusion; his personal narrative could be about any black man and to a point any man, thus connecting broad swathes of American society to his vision of a new politics. The case study approach Obama takes allows him to explore a range of issues through the eyes of others, with him as the commentator. These event narratives all explore periods of his life; the people he met are vehicles to explore specific viewpoints and roles, but each are geared toward shedding light on issues within the American society. Yet, Obama's event narratives are highly personalized accounts, no events are presented without evaluation, and his writing drifts easily between accounts of episodes in his life and offering a broader judgment based around his experiences. Obama's evaluations are highly judgmental, and clearly will connect to any reader who shares his values. Given the connections between his evaluations, basic human values, and the meta-code of the American Dream it is likely his evaluations would be shared by many readers of his works. Perhaps the most persuasive sections are the explanatory narratives that link the circumstances of an episode in his life, his judgments on those episodes, and a broader normative judgment on what needs to change. Selecting both positive and negative experiences, Obama skillfully links these both to his own values and to broader values of American society, accentuating how the positives mirror all that is good in America and how the negatives demonstrate the shortcomings. The solution is never to say that he should have political power; rather, that a change is required within the social and political arrangements. The readers, reading the reprints, which sold over 4 million copies in the United States alone, can make their own decision. Forming perceptions of Obama, connecting to his values, engaging with his arguments are all cognitive processes that are argued to lead to attitude formation and so drive behavior.

The Obama brand was, therefore, a synthesis of currents of thinking in American society, of "pluralism, multi-culturalism, and cosmopolitanism" (Hammack 2010: 183). However, at the mass opinion level, Obama also presented his thinking as a synthesis of currents of dissatisfaction, exclusion, disenfranchisement, and disadvantage. He may never have imagined going beyond pursuing a career in law when he wrote *Dreams from my Father*, and *The Audacity of Hope* may have been designed to start a debate rather than position him as advocate and solution, but the theme running through the books fed directly into his campaign. That theme is change, changes that have occurred within the American journey, changes for good and bad, and so changes that are still required. Obama presents a vision of change that encompasses all aspects of American society and politics, from cultural and inter-race relations to the US global role; it is positioned as a reflection of the true Obama, and the theme as an artifact of who he is and his personal and political philosophy. Thus, his campaign is positioned as authentic as his writings prior to entering the world of electoral politics. Many readers may well have felt the same feelings as reviewer Angela Howell, who states, "anyone who can read between the widest lines will get it: why he actually cares about working people, why he has this seemingly too-good-to-be-true empathy, and why he seems wise beyond his mere 47 years" (2009: 189). Perhaps these feelings were shared by many and the books were the start of a love affair with a character. From the perspective of branding that is a powerful persuasive tool, one that sold an idea of an Obama presidency, an idea that could perhaps only be fully constructed through complex narratives—narratives that were summarized, synthesized, and disseminated through offline and online media. It is impossible to measure systematically the impact of the Obama brand narrative, but it is possible to gain insights. Oliver Escobar summarizes research among viewers of the Obama campaign, thus: "for those of us who engaged emotionally with the Obama phenomenon, it became a medium of self-expression. We felt compelled by the possibility of projecting into politics not only frustration but also hope, a longing for humanistic leadership in an inhuman system" (Escobar 2011: 124). In invoking the American Dream, redesigning its central tenets for a post-racial America, and using it to critique the polity, Obama represented the epitome of change to all who sought something fresh, new, inclusive, and accessible. His narrative tells us the roots of his philosophy, the strength of attachment to his values and how that feeds a political philosophy; how could anyone who shared his aspirations for America not be persuaded.

Acknowledgments

The author would like to note a debt of gratitude to Britt Marie Zeidler for insightful conversations around this topic; it was a shame that ill health prevented her from co-authoring the chapter as her theoretical perspective on political autobiographies would have added a further dimension to this essay.

References

Alexander, Jeffrey C. 2011. *The Performance of Politics: Obama's Victory and the Democratic Struggle for Power*. Oxford: Oxford University Press.

Barr, Kathleen. 2009. "A perfect storm: The 2008 youth vote." In *Campaigning for President 2008: Strategy and Tactics, New Voices and New Techniques*, edited by D. Johnson, 105–125. London: Routledge.

Bruner, Jerome Seymour. 1990. *Acts of Meaning*. Cambridge, MA: Harvard University Press.

Bull, Peter. 2002. *Communication Under the Microscope: The Theory and Practice of Microanalysis*. London: Routledge.

Burgess, Jean. 2006. "Hearing ordinary voices: Cultural studies, vernacular creativity and digital storytelling." *Continuum: Journal of Media & Cultural Studies* 20, no. 2, 201–214.

Calhoun, Craig Jackson. 1976. "Continuity and change: The significance of time in the organization of experience." *International Review of Psycho-Analysis* 3, 291–304.

Clegg, Stewart. 1975. *The Theory of Power and Organisation*. London: Kogan Page.

Darsey, James. 2009. "Barack Obama and America's journey." *Southern Communication Journal* 74, no. 1, 88–103.

Deighton, John, Romer, Daniel, and McQueen, Josh. 1989. "Using drama to persuade." *Journal of Consumer Research* 16 December, 335–343.

Escobar, Oliver. 2011. "Suspending disbelief: Obama and the role of emotions in political communication." In *Politics and Emotions: The Obama Phenomenon*, edited by M. Engelken-Jorge, P. Ibarra Güell and C. Moreno del Rio, 109–128. Wiesbaden: VS Verla.

Fludernik, Monika. 1996. *Towards a 'Natural' Narratology*. London: Routledge.

Gerrig, Richard J and Egidi, Giovanna. 2003. "Cognitive physiological foundations of narrative experiences." In *Narrative Theory and the Cognitive Sciences*, edited by D. Herman, 33–55. Stanford: CSLI.

Giddens, Antony. 1981. *Modernity and Self-Identity: Self and Society in the Late Modern Age*. Stanford: Stanford University Press.

Greimas, Algirdas J. 1987. *De l'imperfection*. Périgueux: Pierre Fanlac.

Hammack, Phillip L. 2010. "The political psychology of personal narrative: The case of Barack Obama." *Analyses of Social Issues and Public Policy* 10, no. 1, 182–206.

Herman, David. 2003. "Introduction." In *Narrative Theory and the Cognitive Sciences*, edited by D. Herman, 1–30. Stanford: CSLI.

Hochschild, Jennifer,L. 1996. *Facing Up to the American Dream: Race, Class, and the Soul of the Nation*. Princeton: Princeton University Press.

Howell, Angela McMillan. 2009. "President-elect Obama: His symbolic importance in his own words." *Journal of African American Studies* 13, no. 2, 187–189.

Jameson, Fredric. 2006. *The Political Unconscious: Narrative as a Socially Symbolic Act*. London: Routledge.

Jamieson, Kathleen Hall. 1996. *Packaging the Presidency: A History and Criticism of Presidential Campaign Advertising*. New York, USA: Oxford University Press.

Johansen, Helena P M. 2012. *Relational Political Marketing in Party-Centred Democracies*. Farnham: Ashgate.

Lakoff, G. and Johnson, M. 1980. *Metaphors We Live By*. Chicago, IL: University of Chicago Press.

Lilleker, Darren, G.. 2005. "Political marketing: The cause of an emerging democratic deficit in Britain? " In *Current Issues in Political Marketing*, edited by W. Wymer and J. Lees-Marshment, 5–26. New York: Haworth.

Lilleker, D. G., and Scullion, R. 2009. "Political advertising." In *The Advertising Handbook (Vol. 4)*, edited by H. Powell, J. Hardy, S. Hawkin, and I. MacRury, 187–198. London: Routledge.

Linde, Charlotte. 1986. *Creation of Coherence in Life Stories*. London: Greenwood.

Linde, Charlotte. 1987a. "The life history: A temporally discontinuous discourse type." In *Psycholinguistic Models of Production*, edited by H W. Dechert and M. Raupach, 189–206. Norwood, NJ: Ablex.

Linde, Charlotte. 1987b. "Explanatory systems in oral life stories." In *Cultural Models in Language and Thought*, edited by D. Holland and N. Quinn, 343–366. NewYork: Cambridge University Press.

Linde, Charlotte. 1993. *Life Stories: The Creation of Coherence*. Oxford: Oxford University Press.

Linde, Charlotte. 2010. *Working the Past: Narrative and Institutional Memory*. Oxford: Oxford University Press.

Miller, Peggy J, Potts, Randolph, Fung, Heidi, Hoogstra, Lisa, and Mintz, Judy. 2009. "Narrative practices and the social construction of self in childhood." *American Ethnologist* 17, no. 2, 292–311.

Mumby, Dennis K. 1987. "The political function of narrative in organizations." *Communications Monographs* 54, no. 2, 113–127.

Murphy, John. 1988. "Branding." *Marketing Intelligence & Planning* 6, no. 4, 4–8.

Nietzsche, Freidrich. 2005[1885]. *Thus Spoke Zarathustra*. translated by Clancy Martin. London: Barnes and Noble.

Obama, Barack. 2004[1996]. *Dreams from my Father*. New York: Three Rivers Press.

Obama, Barack. 2006. *The Audacity of Hope*. New York: Crown.

Peacock, James L and Holland, Dorothy C. 1993. "The narrated self: Life stories in process." *Ethos* 21, no. 4, 367–383.

Portelli, Alessandro. 1981. "The time of my life: Functions of time in oral history." *International Journal of Oral History* 2, no. 3, 162–180.

Rooney, Joseph Arthur. 1995. "Branding: A trend for today and tomorrow." *Journal of Product & Brand Management* 4, no. 4, 48–55.

Sevin, Efe, Kimball, Spencer, and Khalil, Mohammed. 2011. "Listening to president Obama: A short examination of Obama's communication practices." *American Behavioral Scientist* 55, no. 6, 803–812.

Shank, Roger, C. 1990. *Tell Me a Story*. New York, NY: Macmillan Press.

Sherif, Muzafer and Hovland, CarlI. 1961. *Social Judgment*. New Haven: Yale University Press.

Simon, Adam, F. 2002. *The Winning Message*. Cambridge: Cambridge University Press.

Thomson, Paul. 1984. "History and community." In *Oral History: An Interdisciplinary Anthology*, edited by D. Dunaway and W. Baum, 37–50. Nashville, TN: American Association for State and Local History.

Wertsch, James V. 2008. "The narrative organization of collective memory." *Ethos* 36, no. 1, 120–135.

Westen, Drew. 2007. *The Political Brain: The Role of Emotion in Deciding the Fate of the Nation*. New York: Public Affairs.

White, Hayden. 1987. *The Content of the Form: Narrative Discourse and Historical Representation*. Baltimore, MD: Johns Hopkins University Press.

8

Merging Fact and Fiction: Cult Celebrity, Film Narrative, and the Henry Lee Lucas Story

Shaun Kimber

Bournemouth University, UK

Henry Lee Lucas has a central place within American serial killer history. Often referred to as the most atrocious serial killer of all time, he claimed to have murdered hundreds of people. Lucas's death sentence was commuted to a life sentence due to concerns over the veracity of his confessions. Although not as infamous as Jeffery Dahmer, Ted Bundy, Charles Manson, or Eddie Gein, Henry Lee Lucas holds a cult position within American and transnational popular cultures. Although difficult to define, cult is taken to refer to a designation conferred on a cultural artifact as a result of a recognition, by audiences, and the culture industries, of particular networks of relationships between texts, contexts, circulation, and reception (Mendick and Harper 2000 and Jancovich et al. 2003). These networks of relationships are often recognized as challenging widely held social, cultural, and moral norms and conventions circulating within societies.

Henry Lee Lucas's cult persona reflects in significant ways what Schmid (2006) has characterized as the status of the celebrity serial killer:

> The famous serial killer combines the roles of monster and celebrity in a particularly economic and charged way, and this is why famous serial killers are such a visible part of the contemporary American cultural landscape.
>
> 2006: 8

For Schmid celebrity serial killers, and the serial killer industry that has been established around them, are a consequence and manifestation of the rise of consumer and celebrity cultures during the twentieth century. He argues that a cultural transformation has taken place, which has witnessed a decline in fame linked to merit and a rise in celebrity based upon visibility and attention. What is pertinent to this analysis is the way this makeover has generated a morally neutral space within which serial killers were able to acquire the role and status of cult celebrities within popular cultures.

This chapter considers the combining of evidence and falsehood in the story of Henry Lee Lucas and the subsequent amalgamation of fact and fiction within the narratives of four films that have drawn inspiration from his story: *Henry: Portrait of a Serial Killer* (McNaughton 1986), *Confessions of a Serial Killer* (Blair 1987), *Henry: Portrait of a Serial Killer, Part 2* (Parrello 1996), and *Drifter: Henry Lee Lucas* (Feifer 2009a). The chapter evaluates the cultural work of these films' narratives in contributing to discourses circulating around Henry Lee Lucas that have helped mythologize his story and contribute to his cult celebrity status within intersecting fictional popular and factual true-crime cultures. As Schmid suggests, "… recent serial killers have a far more specific, individuated form of celebrity that enhances the figure's ability to do the cultural work that is required of it" (2006: 5).

The four case-study films contribute to Henry Lee Lucas's folklore and status through the foregrounding of three interrelated themes: the propensity and possibility of undetected random stranger violence in both real and fictional worlds; the ambiguous relationship among truth, memory, and lies within the Lucas story; and the complicity between Lucas, law enforcement agencies, and journalists during his confessions. These themes are linked to a number of wider contexts, for example, undetected and random stranger violence, with anxieties and attractions linked to the serial killer (Seltzer 1998, Simpson 2000, Schmid 2006, Kimber 2011); ambiguity between fact and fiction, with the problematizing of meta-narratives linked to objectivity and truth operating between fact and fiction, and history and film (Landy 2001, Rosenstone 2006); and complicity between Lucas and detectives, with the synergistic interrelationships between the law and law enforcement agencies, the culture industries and audiences in the hegemonic construction and propagation of celebrity serial killers (Schmid 2006). Lucas's mythology and celebrity are therefore informed by, and at the same time informs, a number of social, cultural, and economic contexts operating in relation to the role and function of serial killers nationally and transnationally. Outside the focus of this chapter the legend and infamy surrounding Lucas have also been underwritten by nonfiction TV documentaries, news reports, and paratexts, including *Acts of Violence* (Horvath 1985), *American Justice: Myth of a Serial Killer* (Kurtis 1992), *The Serial Killers: Henry Lee Lucas: The Confession Killer* (Ashford 1985), and *Murder by Numbers* (Hodges and Carlin 2004).

A defining feature of the Henry Lee Lucas story is its blending of proof and falsehood, making it an intriguing case study for filmmakers and fans of true-crimes. According to investigative criminologist Christopher Berry-Dee (2003), the precise details of Henry Lee Lucas's life are difficult to ascertain, owing to a lack of corroborative evidence and uncertainty surrounding his confessions. Despite this, the generally accepted facts of his life are that Henry Lee Lucas was born 23 August 1938 in Virginia, United States, and lived in deprived and abusive conditions. On 12 January 1960, aged 21, he murdered his mother, Viola. He was eventually charged with second-degree murder and sentenced to between 20 and 40 years in prison, although in June 1970, because of overcrowding, he was released. In 1977, living in Florida, Henry met Ottis Elwood Toole, who had also had a childhood of poverty and abuse. From 1978 Henry and Ottis were involved in a range of robberies, arson attacks, rapes, and murders, the most infamous of these incidents being the murder of an unidentified woman known as "Orange Socks." Henry (when 40 years old) fell for Ottis' niece Becky Powell (who was 13), which caused a rift between Ottis and Henry, as Ottis was in love with Henry. Henry and Ottis parted company in January 1982, and toward the end of August that year, Henry killed Becky after she tried to leave him. He also raped and killed Kate Rich, an 80-year-old widow with whom he and Becky had boarded, in exchange for Henry's labor as a handyman. Henry was eventually arrested for possession of a firearm, and on 1 October 1983 he pleaded guilty to the murder of Kate Rich, receiving a 75-year sentence. On 10 October he was sentenced to life imprisonment for the murder of Becky, and then claimed responsibility for the rape and murder of "Orange Socks." Henry was sentenced to death because the murder of "Orange Socks" was accompanied by another serious offence. Encouraged by law enforcement agencies who were keen to clear up as many unsolved murders as possible, Henry proceeded to confess to numerous crimes, but later retracted these confessions. In June 1998 Henry's death sentence was commuted to life imprisonment by the then Governor of Texas, George W. Bush, because of doubts over his guilt in the "Orange Socks" case. Henry died from a heart attack in prison on 12 March 2001. He was 64. Whilst Henry Lee Lucas may only have murdered a fraction of the people he confessed to killing, ethically it is acknowledged that at the heart of this chapter's analysis of the fictional handling of real stories are actual victims and their bereaved friends and families.

Henry Lee Lucas's story is so full of uncertainty, ambiguity, and contradiction that any focus on the fidelity of the adaptations within the case-study films would be misdirected. As Rosenstone (2006) suggests, films dealing with history inevitably go beyond simply constituting facts to inventing facts. For Rosenstone, this involves not only selecting moments from the past as important to the narrative but also extends to making up dialog, characters, and incidents. Landy (2001) supports this position advocating the conditional, partial, and re-negotiated nature of history and film's relationship to, and representation of, that history. He also flags up how films' engagement with the past tends to reflect in significant ways the anxieties and concerns of the contexts within which they are produced, circulated, and consumed (Landy 2001). This point can be extended to take into account what Schmid (2006) sees as the dialectical relationship society has with the celebrity of the serial killer:

> Our complicated relationship with celebrities, affective as well as intellectual, composed of admiration and resentment, envy and contempt, provides us with a lexicon through which we can manage our appalled and appalling fascination with the serial killer, contemporary American culture's ultimate deviant.
>
> 2006: 25

Schmid identifies a range of ambiguous and complex responses evoked by the celebrity serial killer. Within the context of true-crime narratives, serial killers can be seen to promote uncomfortable feelings by evoking a range of binary distinctions, including good/evil, normal/monster, known/unknown, insider/outsider, destructive/creative, and same/different. Serial killers can also simultaneously foster a range of overlapping and potentially unresolvable anxieties and pleasures incorporating revulsion, admiration, desire, hatred, and exhilaration.

Rosenstone (2006) recommends two useful ways of looking at the medium-specific characteristics of film and its relationship with history. First, how films help audiences think historically about the overall sense of the past the films are trying to convey, rather than just about the facts. Second, viewing films as offering a challenge to, or commentary upon, traditional historical discourses that seek to provide literal truths about the past. This view is reinforced by McCrisken and Pepper (2005), who advocate that films' engagement with history has the potential to both open up discussion, through the creation of revisionist accounts, and close down dialog, as a result of supporting dominant historical ideologies through their style, form, and content. It is interesting to note how the inventing of facts, through the reimagining of the Henry Lee Lucas story within each case-study film, invites viewers to think about not only his life, actions, and crimes but also the latent and manifest roles, functions, and status of serial killers within society. As such, this analysis is less interested in the factual accuracy of the films and more about how the fictional narrative constructions contribute to the public memory and personage of Henry Lee Lucas within national and transnational popular cultures.

The four case-study films occupy spaces within American cinema outside of Hollywood but linked to it, working as they do within and against Hollywood's generic, narrative, and formal codes, conventions, and thematic preoccupations. As commercial and relatively mainstream films, they are part of a medium within which storytelling is a key guiding principle. Within American cinema classical Hollywood narrative, recognized here as a range of tendencies rather than a set of absolutes, is the dominant storytelling paradigm (King 2005). All of the independently produced case-study films offer narratives in a form that is recognizable to audiences and critics versed in classical Hollywood narrative. For example, they all have conventional screen durations of around 85 minutes; the narratives are organized around a central character and his relationship with other characters, which move the narrative forward; each film narrative is progressed through a broad logic of cause and effect; and all of the films contain scenes of stylized Hollywood violence.

The case-study films are all realist horrors. For Freeland (1995) realist horror films reflect a postmodern blending of fact and fiction within contemporary culture that sees, for example, news stories used as the basis for film plots. All of the films are serial killer films, a subgenre of horror cinema that has expanded since the late 1960s as a result of increased sociocultural attention being paid to random stranger violence in both real and fictional contexts (Simpson 2000, Cettl 2003, Schmid 2006). These films also belong to a sub-subgenre of low-budget American exploitation and independent serial killer films that base their narratives on true-life crimes and which are often distributed straight to DVD. Examples include *Bundy* (Bright 2002), *Raising Jeffrey Dahmer* (Ambler 2006), *Chicago Massacre: Richard Speck* (Feifer 2007b), and *B.T.K* (Feifer 2008b). As such, the case-study films can be contrasted with more mainstream and big-budget true-crime serial killer films, for example, *Summer of Sam* (Lee 1999), *Monster* (Jenkins 2003), and *Zodiac* (Fincher 2007). Working within the predispositions of classical Hollywood narrative, the codes of the realist horror paradigm and the generic conventions of the true-crime serial killer film, each case-study film offers its own contribution to the mythologizing of the Henry Lee Lucas story and the cultural commodification of his cult celebrity status.

This is not to imply that genre and narrative are determining, but to recognize that they are two key constitutive frameworks, which help shape film industry, film audience, and film critical discourses. It is also recognized that audiences' extratextual knowledge of the Henry Lee Lucas story, allied with a range of pre-viewing contextual and individual factors, such as viewers' feelings on film violence and the relationship between real and reel violence, will all impact upon their engagement with these films (Hill 1997).

Henry: Portrait of a Serial Killer (1986) is an oblique fictional character study loosely based on the real-life crimes of Henry Lee Lucas. *Henry: Portrait of a Serial Killer* was the first independent feature film to be cowritten and directed by John McNaughton and was produced in Chicago, Illinois, in 1985 by Maljack Productions Incorporated (MPI). Michael Rooker plays Henry and the narrative documents a few weeks in his life living with Otis (*sic*) (Tom Towles) and Otis's sister Becky (Tracy Arnold). During the film Henry initiates Otis into the craft of undetected serial killing, until tensions get so great that Henry murders Otis and Becky before moving on. The concept came from the American news show *20:20*, which featured a segment on Henry Lee Lucas and Ottis Elwood Toole. The concept was then developed based on research material about Henry Lee Lucas in particular and serial killers in general, and creating a fictional dramatization of events taken from the mediated retelling of stories that Henry Lee Lucas had retracted in prison. For example, several of the film's tableaux scenes were based on crime scene photos taken from news footage, including the re-staging of the "Orange Socks" murder that opens the film. As Fuchs suggests, "John McNaughton has distilled some archetypal episodes from the case of Henry Lee Lucas ... for his low budget opus" (2003: 123).

The filmmakers also wanted to redefine and push the boundaries of horror films by presenting a human monster who exists next to us in the real world, taking spectators into the everyday life of a serial killer and encouraging them to sympathize with him, and refusing to offer a moral compass with which to judge Henry or the film. As such, McNaughton and co-writer Richard Fire were keen to remove the buffer of fantasy that allows audiences to view the spectacle of violence as entertainment whilst also implicating the filmmakers and audiences within this process. As the film's promotional tag line suggests, "He's not Freddy, he's not Jason ... He's Real." This blending of fact and fiction, with an emphasis placed on invented facts, within a self-reflexive narrative provoked controversy and debate by tapping into, and by deliberately not offering reassuring answers to, a range of anxieties and fascinations linked to serial killers circulating at the time. For example, fears of and an interest in random stranger violence; apprehensions and attractions linked to a heightened awareness of mediated real violence in the news and increasingly spectacular representations of fictional violence in films; and investment in and concerns about the dependability of FBI criminological profiling, behavioral psychological explanations and law-enforcement paradigms for dealing with serial killers (Kimber 2011). Although *Henry: Portrait of a Serial Killer* was produced during the boom in independent film production of the mid-1980s, it did not achieve mainstream circulation until the early 1990s because of challenges with its rating and distribution in the United States and the United Kingdom.

In 1987, the American company Cedarwood Productions produced a second film based on the Henry Lee Lucas story. *Confessions of a Serial Killer*, written and directed by Mark Blair, attempted to get closer to the nonfictional details of the Lucas story than *Henry: Portrait of a Serial Killer*. As Fuchs outlines, "Despite changing names and settings the film is closer to the biography of the travelling murder-machine Henry Lee Lucas than John McNaughton's rather free adaptation HENRY" (2002: 122). *Confessions of a Serial Killer* starred Robert A. Burns as Daniel Ray Hawkins, who is captured by the Texan police and invited by Sheriff Will Gaines (Berkley Garrett) to recount his motivations and version of events whilst confessing to a range of multijurisdictional murders. Daniel only starts to open up and recount his stories once the Sherriff offers him food, cigarettes, and eventually trips to visit crime scenes. The story also weaves into its narrative Daniel's relationships with Moon Lewton (Dennis Hill) and Molly Lewton (Sidney Brammer). During the early part of the narrative, questions are raised in relation to both the impetuses behind Daniel's crimes and also the trustworthiness of his admissions, but these themes are somewhat lost in the last half an hour when the film shifts into a more generically determined horror trajectory. That said, the final scene returns to Daniel in custody eating and expressing guilt over the murder of Molly and the impact it would have had upon Moon, before casually requesting another chocolate milkshake.

According to the cover of the United Kingdom 4 Digital Media DVD release: "CONFESSIONS OF A SERIAL KILLER, based on the true story of Henry Lee Lucas one of the most feared serial killers in American History is told through this grisly, gore-filled picture." *Confessions of a Serial Killer* adds to the developing myths and cult celebrity status of Henry Lee Lucas in two connected ways. First, by placing more of an emphasis upon constituent facts, the film is more consistent with what Schmid (2006) sees as an important aspect of the celebrity serial killer.

He suggests that a serial killer's identity and actions become fused and details from their life are seen as potentially contributing to an understanding of his/ her behavior and crimes. Second, by drawing attention to Daniel's growing awareness of his role as a knowing agent in the construction of his story, and the allied complicity between Daniel and the police, he is represented as becoming increasingly aware of his own status as a public figure with an audience within his unfolding story. This affords Daniel opportunities to capitalize on this status, such as bargaining for privileges in exchange for information and confessions. This creates a further link to the performative aspects of the celebrity serial killer theorized by Schmid (2006). Like *Henry: Portrait of a Serial Killer, Confessions of a Serial Killer* was shelved for several years, eventually being released direct-to-video in 1992. It has been largely overshadowed in the history of true-crime serial killer films by the controversies surrounding *Henry: Portrait of a Serial Killer*.

Henry: Portrait of a Serial Killer, Part 2 (1996) (also known as *Henry 2: Portrait of a Serial Killer* and *Henry: Portrait of a Serial Killer 2—Mask of Sanity*) is a fictional sequel to *Henry: Portrait of a Serial Killer* and was released in the United States in 1998. The film was written and directed by Chuck Parello, who worked for MPI. Parello has since directed the true-crime serial killer movies *Ed Gein* (Parello 2000) and *The Hillside Strangler* (Parello 2004). *Henry: Portrait of a Serial Killer, Part 2* was produced by MPI with several of the crew of the original film returning to work on the project. Neil Giuntoli plays the homeless drifter Henry and the film picks up where the original left off. Kai (Rich Komenich) and his wife Cricket (Kate Walsh) take in co-worker Henry. Henry earns extra money helping out Kai in his arson business and in exchange Henry introduces him to the random murder of strangers. Luisa (Carri Levinson), a troubled niece who lives with Kai and Cricket, falls for Henry. Tensions build between Kai, Luisa, and Cricket until Luisa commits suicide in front of Henry. Henry then shoots Kai and Cricket, puts his newly learnt skills into practice by burning down their house, before moving on once more. The packaging of the MPI (Dark Sky Films) DVD release of *Henry: Portrait of a Serial Killer, Part 2* makes no reference to Henry Lee Lucas, in its place it promotes itself as a follow-up to *Henry: Portrait of a Serial Killer*. As Cettl suggests, "This equally low budget and grim follow-up is more of a recapitulation, although there is some attempt to make Henry a more conflicted character…" (2003: 206). As such the film mainly underwrites wider historical discussions linked to Henry Lee Lucas through its inter- and extratextual fictional associations with *Henry: Portrait of a Serial Killer. Henry: Portrait of a Serial Killer, Part 2* is understood to be an attempt to further commodify the celebrity serial killer status of Henry Lee Lucas through franchising. Moreover, Parello (2002) stated that he could not rule out the possibility of *Henry 3* because of the track record and financial success of the *Henry* brand. This demonstrates the productive potential of the serial killer within consumer and celebrity cultures.

Directed and cowritten by Michael Feifer, *Drifter: Henry Lee Lucas* (2009a) (also known as *Henry Lee Lucas: Serial Killer*) was produced by Feifer Worldwide and Renegade Pictures. It is interesting to note that the film's title is presented as *Henry Lee Lucas: Serial Liar* in the title sequence of the United Kingdom Lionsgate DVD release. Feifer, like Parello before him, has made several true-crime serial killer films, including *Ed Gein: The Butcher of Plainfield* (Feifer 2007a) *Bundy: An American Icon* (Feifer 2008a), and *The Boston Strangler: The Untold Story* (Feifer 2008c). The narrative of *Drifter: Henry Lee Lucas* focuses upon the confessions of a captured Henry (Antonio Sabato Jr.) as he recounts his narcissistic motivations to police, a district attorney, and journalists. The story foregrounds selected constituent events in the Henry Lee Lucas story, from his childhood and his familial relationships through to his associations with Ottis (Kastas Sommer) and Becky (Kelly Curran). The director's commentary, which accompanies the DVD, suggests that lines of transcribed archive interviews with Henry Lee Lucas were integrated into key scenes within the film (2009b), indicating the literal commodification of aspects of his testimony within this fictional reimagining of his life story. *Drifter: Henry Lee Lucas* also questions the veracity of Henry's admissions and the complicity among him, law enforcement agencies, and the media in those confessions. The cover of the UK DVD release of *Drifter: Henry Lee Lucas* states, "Inspired by true events surrounding one of America's most prolific and controversial serial killers, this finely detailed film aims to set the historical record straight." *Drifter: Henry Lee Lucas* contributes to the developing myths and cult celebrity status of Henry Lee Lucas in two connected ways, which intensify the processes initiated with *Confessions of a Serial Killer*. First, by placing even more of an emphasis upon constituent facts, *Drifter: Henry Lee Lucas* further fuses identity and actions in an attempt to offer an explanatory framework for the actions and crimes of the celebrity serial killer (Schmid 2006). Second, by explicitly foregrounding Henry's narcissistic awareness of his role in the construction of his story, and also escalating the levels of mutual complicity and manipulation among himself, law enforcement agencies, journalists, and an implied public beyond, he is represented as being acutely aware of his performance in the manufacturing of his serial killer celebrity (Schmid 2006).

Contemporary critical reception of the case-study films often views them relationally and intertextually due to their connection to, and adaptation of, the Henry Lee Lucas story. *Henry: Portrait of a Serial Killer* tends to be recognized as the most interesting and challenging of the true-crime adaptations (Cettl 2003), *Confessions of a Serial Killer* is seen as a gritty and generally overlooked cult movie (Fuchs 2002) and *Drifter: Henry Lee Lucas* as competent but lacking the impact of previous films (Amanda by Night 2009). Owing to its status as a sequel, *Henry: Portrait of a Serial Killer, Part 2* is often marginalized and overlooked within reviews and commentary. When considering the production, circulation, and marketing of these films, with the exception of *Henry: Portrait of a Serial Killer, Part 2,* they all make claims to the "real" in relation to the Henry Lee Lucas story. This manifests in the realist and sub-subgeneric distinction made between fantasy monsters and real monsters; claims to actuality invoked by aligning their titles and narratives to a notorious real-life serial killer; and associated claims to authenticity by getting closer to the facts of the case and therefore the life of Henry Lee Lucas. This reinforces the role of the culture industries in the construction and perpetuation of the celebrity serial killer.

In terms of main characters, all four films focus directly on the story of Henry, or in the case of *Confessions of a Serial Killer*, Daniel, as the main driver of the narrative. This fits into what Simpson (2000) characterizes as psycho profile and masculine hero serial killer films. Although all of the films present their fictional versions of Henry as unredeemable, they all smooth out the rough edges of their monsters by offering varying degrees of motivations and justifications for his tendencies, thus allowing some narrative space for sympathy. Even in *Henry: Portrait of a Serial Killer*, the most ambiguous and oblique of the films, Henry is represented as an attractive man affected by childhood abuse and who attempts to protect Becky from Otis's incestuous advances and eventual rape. As character studies, the four case-study films all foreground restricted narration. This implies the framing of the narrative through the subjective point of view of the leading character (Bordwell and Thompson 2008). Each of the films presents its narrative through the direct experiences of their serial killer and his interactions with other characters. There are very few scenes in which the lead character is not present. This runs counter to the tendency in classical Hollywood narrative for unrestricted narration (Bordwell and Thompson 2008). All four of the case-study films promote cultural interest in Henry Lee Lucas by narrating their films from the subjective position of the serial killer, and thus offering potential insights into his life and criminal motivations. A critical reading derived from

Schmid (2006) is that by focusing on the subjectivity of the serial killer, and his interactions with police and victims, it enables audiences to disavow their complicity in the co-creation and co-maintenance of his celebrity.

With respect to key character relationships, the narrative of *Henry: Portrait of a Serial Killer* focuses on the Oedipal relations between Henry, Otis (*sic*), and Becky, and *Henry: Portrait of a Serial Killer, Part 2* the patriarchal interactions between Henry, Kai, Cricket, and Luisa. The narratives of *Confessions of a Serial Killer* and *Drifter: Henry Lee Lucas* are based around two character groupings—the complicit and manipulative relationships between Daniel and Henry and law enforcement agencies and, in the case of *Drifter*, journalists; and the pseudo-familial relationships between Daniel, Moon, and Molly or Henry, Ottis, and Becky. Therefore, *Henry: Portrait of a Serial Killer* and *Henry: Portrait of a Serial Killer, Part 2* can be seen to augment the mythology and cult celebrity of Henry Lee Lucas through the foregrounding of a range of fascinations and fears linked to not only Henry's crimes but also random stranger violence within wider society. In contrast, *Confessions of a Serial Killer* and *Drifter: Henry Lee Lucas* add to the folklore and public persona of Lucas by problematizing the collaborative, performative, and narcissistic processes linked to Henry Lee Lucas's confessions. These two films can be seen to foreground the synergistic relationships among serial killer, police, and the media in the manufacture of celebrity serial killers. All four films offer audiences opportunities to imaginatively participate with the cult celebrity serial killer in a safe environment that offers important ways of engaging with their anxieties and attractions whilst potentially enabling them to disavow culpability in their perpetuation.

When considering narrative structure and temporal patterning, *Henry: Portrait of a Serial Killer* and *Henry: Portrait of a Serial Killer, Part 2* both present conventional linear narratives whose plots unfold over weeks, with only occasional references to historical story events. *Henry: Portrait of a Serial Killer* offers a nightmarish vision of a serial killer who drifts unencumbered from one place to another, who can get close to people by establishing relationships with them, and when things get tricky, kills them, evades capture, and moves on undetected and unrepentant. Likewise, *Henry: Portrait of a Serial Killer, Part 2* adopts a similar narrative structure, progressing from Henry being free but destitute, to him finding work and moving in with Kai, Cricket, and Luisa, through to him killing them and then moving on again unnoticed with money and a car.

Spatially, *Henry: Portrait of a Serial Killer* and *Henry: Portrait of a Serial Killer, Part 2* focus their narratives on a limited number of geographically linked locales and spaces. These spaces are often associated with the private, such as domestic homes that the characters both live in and invade, and public, such as urban spaces associated with commerce and transit. The spatial patterns of the narrative design of these two case-study films are used to reflect the free and undetected movements of their serial killers through civic spaces. Thematically, both films present the mundane and everyday lives of the serial killer who is an adaptive and calculated craftsman, who avoids detection by keeping moving, varying their modus operandi, and murdering random strangers who cannot be traced back to them. Although both films work within the tendencies of classical Hollywood narratives, they do elide conventional storytelling practices by not offering any comforting resolution or restorative retribution against Henry as a result of their open-endings. Moreover, they are also characterized by the absence of law enforcement agencies and behavioral frameworks offering insights into their behaviors and motives. *Henry: Portrait of a Serial Killer*, directly, and *Henry: Portrait of a Serial Killer, Part 2,* indirectly, further contribute to the lore and cult celebrity of Henry Lee Lucas through the sustained promotion of worries and desires linked to random stranger violence, whilst also creating opportunities for audiences to disown their role in their prolongation.

Confessions of a Serial Killer and *Drifter: Henry Lee Lucas* both investigate the social and psychological motivations for the actions of their serial killers more directly than *Henry: Portrait of a Serial Killer* and *Henry: Portrait of a Serial Killer, Part 2*. This is achieved through directly intermingling biographical details from the Henry Lee Lucas story within their invented fictional narratives. *In Confessions of a Serial Killer,* the second flashback presents evidence of psychological abuse as a result of his mother bringing home clients to have sex with in front of him, his sister, and father. Later in the film Daniel explains some of the inconsistencies in his stories and recollections as being a consequence of alcohol and drug abuse. Moreover, the doctor who has been assessing Daniel's mental capacity in his feedback to the Sheriff discloses that Daniel had no clear father figure, an abusive mother who worked as a prostitute, 3rd grade education, and violent hostilities toward women. *Drifter: Henry Lee Lucas* devotes much more attention and screen time to the interrogation of Henry Lee Lucas's biography within its fictional narrative. The film presents a wide range of social, psychological, and economic explanations for Henry's actions taken directly from the Henry Lee Lucas story, for example, his impoverished upbringing, his physical, sexual, and emotional abuse at the hands of his prostitute mother— including sending him to school in a dress. Reference is made in the film to his accidents as a child resulting in him losing an eye, and his arrest and incarceration for stealing. The film also recreates Henry's murder of his mother, his attempted suicides as a result of his subsequent arrest and guilt over his mother's murder, his psychiatric treatment, his interstate roaming with Ottis and Becky, and his eventual murder of Becky. *Confessions of a Serial Killer* and in particular *Drifter: Henry Lee Lucas* actively contribute to the ongoing cult celebrity serial killer status and mythologizing of the Henry Lee Lucas story through their concerted blending of the constituent facts of his case within their invented narratives. This further shows the fusion of action and identity linked to the modern celebrity of the serial killer identified by Schmid (2006).

Confessions of a Serial Killer and *Drifter: Henry Lee Lucas* both employ structures that rely upon subjective flashbacks. As such, temporally both films weave together the past and present in their fictional explorations of the Henry Lee Lucas story. In *Confessions of a Serial Killer* Daniel is revealed to be within police custody, after a pre-credit sequence of him murdering a woman he had picked up after her car had broken down. It is from within this detention that Daniel recounts his story and confesses to several multijurisdictional crimes, whilst doctors and law enforcement agents try to ascertain the validity of his claims. *Drifter: Henry Lee Lucas* opens and closes with Henry in captivity having the veracity of his confessions questioned by a District Attorney. Insights into his childhood, his roaming crime spree with Becky and Ottis, and his life with the Texas rangers are all represented through flashbacks initiated by the interrogations. As such, in contradistinction to *Henry Portrait of a Serial Killer* and *Henry Portrait of a Serial Killer, Part 2,* both *Confessions of a Serial Killer* and *Drifter: Henry Lee Lucas* offer narratives of containment. Moreover, both films employ voice-overs during their flashback sequences as narrative devices. This use of first person voice-over formally bridges the gap between the past and the present. In the case of *Confessions of a Serial Killer*, of the eight flashback sequences, six are accompanied by Daniel's voice-over. The use of the voice-over also thematically foregrounds the subjective desire of the characters to nostalgically control the past from their present restricted situation (Hayward 2000), thus illustrating the trend identified above of serial killers' awareness of their function and performance in the assemblage of their story, mythology, and celebrity status.

These narratives of containment are structured around the conventional cause and effect logic of classical Hollywood narrative, where situations in the present initiate subjective flashbacks showing events from the past that seek to clarify or explain those enigmas (Hayward 2000). This foregrounding of memories through subjective flashback, and their suggested manipulation, can also be read as a gendered performance through which the serial killers seek to present themselves as self-reliant and in control within a context of physical confinement. As noted, the narrative of *Confessions of a Serial Killer* is structured around eight flashback sequences. Each flashback sequence is motivated by the line of questioning taking place during the interrogation of Daniel. The first hour is tightly structured around seven short flashback sequences; the final half hour is more loosely organized around the final extended flashback that culminates in Molly's murder and Daniel's arrest. A key theme emerging from these flashback sequences is the extent to which the police can trust Daniel's confessions. After several of his recollections, officers go off to check if Daniel's stories hold up against their records and the intelligence of other law enforcement agencies. In one scene, the Sheriff and the doctor who is assessing Daniel discuss his propensity for mixing lies with the truth.

Drifter: Henry Lee Lucas is particularly interesting in this respect due to its narrative being organized into a horseshoe structure. The film opens and closes with the murder of Becky told through flashbacks and overlaid with dialog between Henry and the District Attorney. The repetition of this event draws our attention to its narrative frequency and invites viewers to reflect upon its significance (Bordwell and Thompson 2008), in this case the questioning of the validity of his confession to multiple murders as a result of a mutually beneficial complicity with Texas rangers. Moreover, the second recounting of the event introduced at the end of the film includes Henry's admission that his confessions had been exaggerated to gain attention and to secure a better standard of living within his incarceration.

Therefore, in terms of narration, a key theme explored in *Confessions of a Serial Killer* and *Drifter: Henry Lee Lucas* is unreliable narration. This emphasis upon the untrustworthiness of the narration has increased through successive films. As we have seen in *Confessions of a Serial Killer* and especially in *Drifter: Henry Lee Lucas*, attention is explicitly focused upon the false testimony of their respective serial killers in an attempt to stay in the spotlight and maintain their privileges. This theme of unreliable narration can also be found in a key scene in *Henry: Portrait of a Serial Killer* where Henry and Becky are playing cards. After being prompted by Becky, Henry describes how he killed his mother, in three different ways, only correcting his story when Becky picks up on the inconsistencies in his recollection of events.

Spatially the two films also emphasize containment. This is reflected in the restricted physical mobility of Henry and Daniel within cells and interrogation rooms where they are only free to roam imaginatively, through their recollections and confessions, and physically through accompanied visits to potential crime scenes. *Confessions of a Serial Killer* and *Drifter: Henry Lee Lucas* both reinforce conventional storytelling structures by offering spatial narrative assurances of containment of the human monster, and advancing their narratives from a relative position of temporal safety, looking back at their violent transgressions. Both films' narratives also offer a strong degree of closure through the promise of future restorative legal justice and having tied up a range of narrative enigmas linked to how Henry and Daniel came to be incarcerated. As such both *Confessions of a Serial Killer* and *Drifter: Henry Lee Lucas* leave fewer narrative gaps and are characterized less by ambiguity and mystery than either *Henry: Portrait of a Serial Killer* or *Henry: Portrait of a Serial Killer, Part 2*. *Confessions of a Serial Killer* and *Drifter: Henry Lee Lucas* further contribute to the mythologizing of the Lucas story and his celebrity serial killer status by highlighting the performative and subjective nature of identity and truth; the unreliability of recollection and testimony; and the mutual manipulation among the serial killer, law enforcement agencies, and journalists in his confessions.

This chapter has investigated the blending of fact and fiction within the narratives of four independent American true-crime serial killer films, which have drawn inspiration from the Henry Lee Lucas story. It has been put forward that, owing to the intermingling of proof and conjecture within the story of Henry Lee Lucas, a focus on the fidelity of these film adaptations would have been unsuitable. It was then argued, that the four case-study films all contribute to the cult celebrity serial killer status of Henry Lee Lucas, and the continuing mythologizing of his life story and actions through the process of blending constituent facts with invented facts within their narratives. This has been achieved through the foregrounding of three interrelated themes within their narrative constructions. First, the propensity and possibility of undetected random stranger violence in both real and fictional worlds, which align with broader anxieties and attractions linked to serial killers. Second, the ambiguous relationship among truth, memory, and lies within the Henry Lee Lucas story, which can be viewed as symptomatic of the problematizing of meta-narratives linked to truth and objectivity within society and culture. Third, the complicity among Henry Lee Lucas, law enforcement agencies, and journalists during his confessions, which highlight not only the synergistic interrelationships between legal institutions and culture industries in the hegemonic construction and propagation of celebrity serial killers but also the way in which films can facilitate audience's disavowal of their complicity within these processes. The cultural work of these films can be seen not only in their contribution to ongoing debates linked to the public memory and cultural significance of the life and crimes of Henry Lee Lucas but also the perpetuation of the serial killer industry and more particularly the iconic status of serial killers within contemporary consumer and celebrity cultures.

References

Amanda by Night. 2009. *Drifter: Henry Lee Lucas*, http://www.planetfury.com/content/drifter-henry-lee-lucas-2009 [Accessed 26th March 2013].

Ambler, Rich. 2006. *Raising Jeffrey Dahmer*. USA: Renegade Pictures.

Ashford, Neal. 1985. *The Serial Killers: Henry Lee Lucas: The Confession Killer*. Season 1. Episode 3. USA: Mainline Television Productions.

Berry-Dee, Christopher. 2003. *Talking with Serial Killers: The Most Evil People in the World Tell Their Own Stories*. London: John Blake Publishing Ltd. 311–349.

Blair, Mark. 1987. *Confessions of a Serial Killer*. USA: Cedarwood Productions.

Bordwell, David, Thompson, Kristin. 2008. *Film Art: An Introduction*. 8th Edition. London: McGraw-Hill. 74–109.

Bright, Matthew. 2002. *Bundy*. UK/USA: First Look International.

Cettl, Robert. 2003. *Serial Killer Cinema: An Analytical Filmography with an Introduction*. Jefferson, NC: McFarland. 5–31.

Feifer, Michael. 2007a. *Ed Gein: The Butcher of Plainfield*. USA: Feifer Worldwide.

Feifer, Michael. 2007b. *Chicago Massacre: Richard Speck*. USA: Feifer Worldwide.

Feifer, Michael. 2008a. *Bundy: An American Icon*. USA: Feifer Worldwide.

Feifer, Michael. 2008b. *B.T.K.* USA: North American Entertainment.

Feifer, Michael. 2008c. *The Boston Strangler: The Untold Story*. USA: North American Entertainment.

Feifer, Michael. 2009a. *Drifter: Henry Lee Lucas*. USA: Feifer Worldwide/Renegade Pictures.

Feifer, Michael. 2009b. "Director's Commentary." Supplementary material on Lionsgate release of *Drifter: Henry Lee Lucas*.

Fincher, David. 2007. *Zodiac*. USA: Paramount Pictures.

Freeland, Cynthia A. 1995. "Realist horror." In: *Philosophy and Film*, edited by C. A. Freeland and T. E. Wartenberg, 126–142. London: Routledge.

Fuchs, Christian. 2002. *Bad Blood: An Illustrated Guide to Psycho Cinema Inspired by 20th Century Serial Killers and Murderers*. London: Creation Books.

Hayward, Susan. 2000. *Cinema Studies: The Key Concepts*. 2nd Edition. London: Routledge.

Hill, Annette. 1997. *Shocking Entertainment: Viewer Responses to Violent Movies*. Luton: John Libbey.

Hodges, Mike, Carlin, Paul. 2004. *Murder by Numbers*. UK: Greenhouse Productions.

Horvath, Imre. 1985. *Acts of Violence*. USA: Rainbow Broadcasting Company.

Jancovich, Mark, Lazaro Reboll, Antonio, Stringer, Julian Willis, Andrew (eds). 2003. *Defining Cult Movies: The Cultural Politics of Oppositional Taste*. Manchester: Manchester University Press.

Jenkins, Patty. 2003. *Monster*. USA/Germany: Media 8 Entertainment.

Kimber, Shaun. 2011. *Controversies: Henry: Portrait of a Serial Killer*. Basingstoke: Palgrave MacMillan.

King, Geff. 2005. *American Independent Cinema*. London: I. B. Tauris.

Kurtis, Bill. 1992. *American Justice: Myth of a Serial Killer*. Season 16. Episode 1. USA: A & E Home Video.

Landy, Marcia. 2001. *The Historical Film: History and Memory in Film*. London: The Athlone Press.

Lee, Spike. 1999. *Summer of Sam*. USA: 40 Acres & A Mule Filmworks.

McCrisken, Trevor, Pepper, Andrew. 2005. *American History and Contemporary Hollywood Film*. Edinburgh: Edinburgh University Press.

McNaughton, John. 1986. *Henry: Portrait of a Serial Killer*. USA: Maljack Productions.

Mendik, Xavier and Harper, Graeme. (eds.) 2000. *Unruly Pleasures: The Cult Film and Its Critics*. Guildford: FAB Press.

Parello, Chuck. 1996. *Henry: Portrait of a Serial Killer, Part 2*. USA: Dark Sky Films.

Parello, Chuck. 2000. *Ed Gein*. USA/Portugal: City Heat Produtions.

Parello, Chuck. 2002. "Interview with Chuck Parello" supplementary material on Dutch Film Works (DFW) special double disc release of *Henry: Portrait of a Serial Killer Parts 1 and 2*.

Parello, Chuck. 2004. *The Hillside Strangler*. USA: Tartan Films.

Rosenstone, Robert, A. 2006. *History on Film/Film on History*. Harlow: Pearson Education Limited.

Schmid, David. 2006. *Natural Born Celebrities: Serial Killers in American Culture*. Chicago: University of Chicago Press.

Seltzer, Mark. 1998. *Serial Killers: Death and Life in America's Wound Culture*. London: Routledge.

Simpson, Philip L. 2000. *Psycho Paths: Tracking the Serial Killer Through Contemporary American Film and Fiction*. Carbondale: Southern Illinois University Press.

Part 4

Celebrity Lives Reimagined

9

Fans Behaving Badly? Real Person Fic and the Blurring of the Boundaries between the Public and the Private

Bronwen Thomas
Bournemouth University, UK

In an age when we are surrounded by seemingly artificial and stage-managed celebrity stories, it might be considered refreshing that fans have taken it upon themselves to write their own stories about the actors and personalities whose onscreen and offscreen personae provide such an endless source of fascination. However, Real Person Fiction, a subgenre of fanfiction in which the protagonists are predominantly well-known figures from the media world, has proved highly controversial and contentious, not least within fan communities themselves. It has also largely been ignored by scholars of fanfiction. In this chapter I will explore some of the debates surrounding Real Person Fiction as well as setting out some of the most common variants and conventions. This will be supported by analyzing examples of Real Person Fiction (henceforward RPF) and the discussions that surround them, involving both authors and readers, as I shall argue that the latter often display a level of reflexivity and knowingness that is vital for contextualizing the fans' practices.

Precedents and definitions

Many precedents for RPF may be found in literary history, for example, the long-standing tradition of the *roman à clef* or fictionalized accounts of historical figures. The Brontë children's reimagining of the life of the Duke of Wellington in their writing as well as in their play is often cited as a precursor for the form (e.g., Stasi 2006), and is described in similar terms as a kind of "hero worship" bordering on the "obsessive." More recently, Andrew O'Hagan's novel *Personality*

(2004) took as its basis the life of Scottish child star Lena Zavaroni, offering a disturbing insight into the torment underlying the chintzy stage persona and demonstrating the potential for this kind of writing to challenge and subvert dominant images of the rich and famous. Beyond the literary sphere, authorized and unauthorized stories about film stars have been cited as precursors for the form, whereas the phenomenon of fan pilgrimages (Brooker 2007) attests to the desire of fans to gain proximity to the objects of their devotion.

However, Fanlore (www.fanlore.org/wiki/Real_Person_Fic) traces the first instance of RPF to a Star Trek fanzine published in 1968 in which cast members meet the show's creator. With the burgeoning of fandoms online, many subvariants have emerged, including actor fic, celebrity fic, bandoms (dedicated to pop bands), war fandoms, swimslash, and royalslash. As with all varieties of fanfic, the starting point is wanting "more of" as well as "more from" (Pugh 2005) the source of the fan's devotion, though the ensuing representations can range from the celebratory to the defamatory. Moreover, similar to all kinds of fanfic, RPF can take a number of different forms, from the 100-word "drabble" to long-form writing developed over several episodes or installments. Fansites provide users with menus enabling them to refine their choices in terms of character pairings, genre, and level of explicitness, and they also facilitate interaction between writers and readers of fanfic, through comments sections, forums, and the like. Meanwhile, fan art and fanvids also feature "real people," thanks to photoshopping and related technologies, though it is often difficult to deduce whether it is the real-life actors or their onscreen personae that are being depicted.

Figure 9.1 "forever mine. (Shatnoy)" by G-Skywalker. ©2012–2013. Accessed 16 May 2013 http://browse.deviantart.com/art/forever-mine-ShatNoy-310330851

Although not all RPFs have sexual content, most do, and this is predominantly based around same-sex pairings, usually male pairings, hence the interchangeability of the terms "Real Person Fic" and "Real Person Slash" in some circles. Debates about nuances of terminology, and the splintering of fans into multitudinous subgroups are far from being confined to RPF, but the amount of "fandom wank" (http://fanlore.org/wiki/Wank) generated by the ensuing border disputes perhaps reflects the passions aroused by the specific kinds of activity these terms define.

Policies and management

Many high-profile fanfiction sites ban RPF altogether. While www.fanfiction. net describes itself as having an "open system that trusts the writer's judgement," it has specifically prohibited stories featuring nonfictional characters for over 10 years, though a cursory search reveals that fans continue to find ways around this prohibition. On www.republicofpemberley.com (a community for Jane Austen fans), the advice is "We do not discuss the personal lives of actors, authors, or other celebrities," whereas on the Harry Potter site www.mugglenet. com "stories that use real living people as characters" are banned, with an explicit warning against "JK Rowling insertions." In some senses this is curious as fanfiction routinely perpetuates the strong identification of fictional characters with the actors who play them: for many Pemberleans, Colin Firth *is* Mr Darcy. Nevertheless, it seems that a boundary is crossed when the stories impinge on the "real lives" of actors or personalities in the media, particularly where this involves casting aspersions on their sexuality, making reference to their families, or broaching taboos such as incest or underage sex. Fans often refer to such stories as making them feel "squicky," and many clearly see themselves as having a duty to protect the objects of their devotion from having their reputations tarnished by others. In a particularly virulent attack prompted by an RPF based on Hugh Laurie's character from *House* in 2006, idonmatrix (http://house-wilson. livejournal.com/445654.html) accuses the writer of "depravity" and "a level of pathology that I have only seen referenced in clinical and criminal psychology journals," resulting in a "reckless disregard for the safety and wellbeing of the actors and their loved ones." This assumes rather improbably both that the actors and their loved ones are likely to come across the fic and that a fictional tale could somehow affect their "safety and wellbeing."

The strength of feeling expressed against RPF is also perhaps indicative of fans' sensitivity to enduring stereotypes and clichés about their behavior as immature, obsessive, or extreme. The term "tinhat" has been coined to refer to fans who are so convinced that a relationship exists between the celebrities they write about that they construct all sorts of conspiracies about cover-ups and media management to explain why the stars cannot be open about their mutual attraction. What this demonstrates is that fan communities are far from being the homogeneous and harmonious utopias imagined by some commentators, as fans resort to attacking and denigrating others as a means of protecting and justifying their own relationships with the objects of their devotion. Moreover, for female fans and writers of slash, it has been suggested that they "envision homoerotic relationships among male idols so as to preclude and devalue female 'rivals'" (Scodari 2007: 59), suggesting that antagonism toward other fans may also be a motivation for those writing RPF.

Although there have been some (unsuccessful) attempts to litigate against RPF, many celebrities prefer to adopt the stance of openly embracing fanfiction, whether this is based on their onscreen or offscreen personae, or indeed a combination of the two. Ralph Fiennes and Daniel Radcliffe have both read excerpts from Harry Potter slash on American television, whereas Benedict Cumberbatch and Martin Freeman have both been interviewed about slash based on *Sherlock*. In each of these instances, the actors concerned seem to go to great lengths to assure the audience that they have a sense of humor about this material, and are confident enough in their sexuality not to be perturbed by its explicit content. It is no accident, perhaps, that the fandoms in question are all highly populous and influential, and the cynics might suggest that such displays are good PR for the stars and the vehicles they promote. However, it also seems to be symptomatic of a media environment in which celebrities have come to accept some intrusion into their private lives, and to distinguish perhaps between playful and harmful, for-profit and not-for-profit examples in terms of formulating their reactions.

Key debates and contexts

Debates about RPF inevitably coalesce with debates about privacy in the media, especially virulent in the United Kingdom in 2012 with the furore surrounding the activities of the Murdoch press leading up to the Leveson inquiry. Where tabloid newspapers, gossip magazines, and confessional TV provide a steady stream of stories about celebrities' private lives, and where celebrities appear much more accessible to their fans through their websites, social media accounts, and public appearances, for many it has become increasingly difficult to know where to draw the boundaries between the private and the public. Many television shows and movies have played on the idea of celebrities performing versions of themselves, for example, *The Larry Sanders Show*, which had running gags about David Duchovny being gay, or *Extras* where Kate Winslet portrayed herself as willing to go to any lengths to get an Oscar. Even though these shows rely on the collusion of the celebrities, and frame their appearances within a context of postmodern playfulness, the humor in part at least arises from the suspicion that the individual in question does not entirely "get" the extent to which they are being sent up.

Such irreverence comes in the context of growing suspicion about the extent to which the publicity machines of celebrities control and sometimes distort the facts about their private lives, prompting a desire frequently expressed by fans to connect with the "person behind the mask" (http://naraht.dreamwidth.org/396388.html). It also comes at a time when the sheer number of masks we may be presented with across media makes it impossible to say with any certainty that they conceal the "same" person. Yet whereas spoof celebrity accounts on Facebook and Twitter are celebrated for their creativity and attract a devoted following, RPF remains largely stigmatized not simply because of the prevalence of sexual content, but for its seeming intrusion into the privacy of its subjects. Similarly, while Twitter in particular seems to validate para-social behavior (Horton and Wohl 1956) with millions "following" celebrities, addressing them on familiar terms and sharing personal anecdotes, where similar behavior is couched in the context of a work of self-declared fiction, somehow this is seen as intrusive or even pathological.

One of the reasons why people feel so outraged by RPF may therefore be that it holds a mirror up to prevailing and often highly contradictory attitudes and assumptions about celebrity. In particular, many theorists of contemporary celebrity culture point to the paradox that celebrities are viewed as simultaneously both extraordinary and ordinary, while audiences increasingly see themselves as potential stars. The impulse to expose the "real" person behind the fiction has also been linked to a wider "rhetoric of authenticity" (Dyer 1991) that defines the relationship between audience and celebrity and helps explain the success of reality TV shows such as *The Osbournes* or *Celebrity Big Brother*, where we seem to be offered access to celebrities in their more unguarded moments.

However, as Turner (2004: 122) has argued, we also have to recognize that "the pleasures of certain kinds of celebrity material are derived from their capacity to be invasive, exploitative and vengeful," and that "the desire to see what the celebrity is 'really like' obviously has a sexual dimension." Gossip magazines and tabloid newspapers certainly rely on lurid speculation about the private lives of celebrities, often resulting in a kind of frenzy to "out" the celebrity and expose their shameful secrets. This takes us back to the Foucauldian (1998) notion that the "will to knowledge" about the "truth" of sex becomes an exercise in power and a way of labeling ever-new forms of perceived "perversion."

Although fans may collude with dominant discourses about sex and sexuality, in many ways the stories they create suggest a view of sexuality and of identity that is more fluid and knowingly playful. If we accept that we must "look at the production of the meaning of stars in the terms of how audiences construct them" (Stacey 2012: 645) then we may also find that those same audiences take full advantage of the license for play and creativity this gives them. It also suggests a need to include in any analysis constructions all too often dismissed as deviant or unsavory. By focusing on fans' responses to and discussions about the stories they construct, we can begin to move away from generalizations and moral absolutes and explore instead the complex interrelations and contradictions that emerge from the various forms of engagement they have with their subjects.

The sanctimonious condemnation of RPF, often based on ignorance and sweeping assumptions about the form, also betrays a certain amount of hypocrisy, implying that somehow all other representations of celebrity are wholesome and respectable. Like the condemnation of so-called "Mary Sue" stories, where the writer is accused of inserting an idealized version of himself or herself into the narrative, fans seem quick to leap to judgment and to distance themselves from what they see as unacceptable behavior, when in fact the distinctions drawn appear far from incontestable. While we may not all indulge in fantasies about the sex lives of stars, or picture ourselves as involved in relationships with them, our readings of celebrities are surely a kind of fiction constructed around snippets of information and gossip we glean and piece together.

In addition to locating the emergence of RPF in the context of the rise of celebrity culture and growing skepticism about the credentials of the personalities held up for our adoration, it is also important to consider how far the attitudes of both writers and readers of RPF are shaped by their immersion in online environments and social networks where the idea of performing the self, and indeed of creating a "second self" (Turkle 2005), is intrinsic to the experience

of many users. Although the idea of fanfiction as a kind
been explored (Busse 2006), fanfiction studies are yet
with the wider social practices of fans online, and the deg.
activities taking place within fan communities are shaped by their exp.
of inhabiting and exploring other online spaces. Most, if not all, fans will have
their own experiences of creating avatars and profiles that may or may not bear
some resemblance to the truth of their offline selves, whereas users of online
spaces must also be hyperaware of the risks and dangers posed by those who
deliberately conceal or obscure the truth about themselves and others, such
as lurkers, groomers, frapers, and so on. In addition, online spaces and social
media facilitate and even necessitate the sharing of personal narratives and in
ways that can be both liberating and open to exploitation.

In her study of celebrity accounts on Twitter, Ruth Page (2011) draws
on Goffman's (1959) distinction between the front-stage and back-stage
presentation of the self. Page argues that in many ways Twitter is closest to
the back-stage region, offering followers the impression of going "behind the
scenes" with the celebrity to gain access to personal information. However,
she goes on to claim that the fact that this takes place in such a public context
means that in effect front- and back-stage regions collapse into one another. She
also acknowledges that Twitter is as much about self-promotion as it is about
revelation and intimacy. Nevertheless, Twitter provides in many ways a unique
insight into how "celebrity identities are discursively produced" (96), and how
they must continuously negotiate and work on their relationships with their
fans. Of course the emergence of social media has not occurred in isolation, but
one of the consequences of the sheer scale and reach of its uptake appears to be
an assumption that increased, ongoing access is both a good thing and some
kind of moral obligation on the part of those involved.

Discussions about RPF inevitably lead to a questioning of what we understand
to be real or authentic in a climate in which simulation and the hyperreal
(Baudrillard 1994) dissolve the distinction between representation and the object
being represented, and offer the illusion of increased access to information and
people hitherto kept out of bounds. In some ways, RPF might even be seen as
an expression of nostalgia for the "loss of the real" in Baudrillard's terms, as fans
try to imagine the objects of their devotion outside and beyond the distorting
gaze of the media. However, this would not do justice to the extent to which,
as I shall argue later, fans delight in meta-textual play and in teasing out the
contradictions between the image and the "reality" of the celebrities' lives.

As suggested earlier, fans frequently debate the morality and ethics of what they are doing, although it is evident that for many the sense of transgressing provides a "guilty pleasure" (bitchy grrl, http://stoney321.livejournal.com/91382. html) that is intoxicating. Jennifer McGee's (2005) study of the ethics of RPF touches on the ways in which fans try to preempt criticism, for example, by pointing to the fact that the individuals they write about are "manufactured" by the media. However, her study does not really do justice to the extent to which fans explore and reflect on the morality and ethics and of what they are doing, or to the kinds of impassioned discussions that follow. In particular, while some fans argue that RPF should be banned on the basis that the people involved might actually read it, for others this is part of the thrill ("I can't help thinking how they might feel if they read it," trepkos, http://stoney321.livejournal.com/91382. html). The need to defend what they are doing is evident, particularly in the language used to define their activities, for example, describing the sites as a "haven," or self-consciously playing up the "naughty" nature of the content found within. Occasionally, we find RPF being defended on aesthetic grounds, for example, as "a transformative, artistic form of celebrity gossip" (svollga, http://writingthewall.dreamwidth.org/4671.html). More commonly, writers of RPF assert their rights to write this kind of fiction on the grounds of artistic license and truth telling: "we recognize it as fiction, and enjoy getting as close to the truth as possible" (stoney321, http://stoney321.livejournal.com/91382. html). Meanwhile, for theorists of fanfiction, the impetus to defend RPF and slash relies on distinguishing it from pornography, for example, by referring to the supposedly "rich interior lives" of the characters depicted, or claiming that this kind of fiction is about breaking down taboos (Cumberland 2012).

Conventions, canons, and subgenres

Similar to slash fiction, RPF often comes with warnings and ratings, sometimes explicitly requiring the user to agree to terms before accessing the story. Disclaimers accompanying the stories are also often quite elaborate, stressing both their fictionality and the lack of a profit motive: "None of this happened and I'm not making any money for saying it did" (karaokegal, http://karaokegal. livejournal.com/725861.html). While some are almost apologetic about their fictions, karaokegal's profile proudly announces that she "Don't conform to fandom norms for nobody biatch," demonstrating how out of the feeling of challenging convention and resisting conformity a real sense of vindication and camaraderie can emerge.

Where fanfiction is based on some kind of preexisting text, fans can agree on what counts as "canon," construct their own "fanon," and refer back to the source text not just for inspiration, but also for validation. With RPF, the sense of an agreed canon is much more problematic, not least because, presuming the real person in question is still alive, their public persona and their private circumstances may change out of all recognition. Nevertheless, writers of RPF are keen to point out that they base many of their ideas on background research, including both extra-textual material such as interviews and "evidence" based on the close reading of scenes in which the chemistry between actors is displayed, especially those "unguarded" moments where the mask slips and the "truth" of the relationship emerges. However, they are equally concerned to distance themselves from anything that could be construed as stalking behavior, taking too much of an interest in the minutiae of their subjects' lives. In addition, the danger of having TMI (Too Much Information) is recognized: naraht claims to have to actively avoid gossip magazines for fear that this might interfere with her writing, though she goes on to say that once discovered, she would not give back any of the information gleaned (http://naraht.dreamwidth.org/396388.html).

A fascinating dilemma facing writers of RPF is that they cannot control how the story of the life of the celebrity will unfold. For example, a celebrity may behave badly, or take on a role totally at odds with their careers to date, destroying the image constructed for them by the fan: strikesoftly writes that "as soon as the RL [Real Life] actions of the people impinge on my ability to enjoy fic about them, I need to disengage" (http://writingthewall.dreamwidth.org/8806. html). Although they are not tied to the confines of a preexisting fictional world, writers of RPF share with other fanfic writers the sense that their story, and their version of the individual they write about, is one amongst many. Stoney321 (http://stoney321.livejournal.com/91382.html) articulates the contradictory impulses behind this kind of writing, on the one hand betraying a desire for control bordering on the obsessive ("when I write him somewhere, he becomes MINE") while eloquently expressing the sense of "a shadow of someone else's characterization hanging over. Like a shimmer over a hot road."

Subgenres of Real Person Fiction can involve sports stars involved in some kind of epic rivalry (Fedal = Federer/Nadal; Thorpe/Phelps); copresenters (e.g., British duo Ant and Dec), and even politicians (British Prime Minister David Cameron and his coalition partner Nick Clegg; Barack Obama and Mitt

Romney). However, the vast majority draws on celebrities identified strongly with specific fictional roles in some of the biggest media franchises, for example, actors featuring in the Harry Potter or Lord of the Rings series of films, or the leads in long-running TV shows such as *Doctor Who*. Such narratives provide fans with plenty of back-story, while the longevity of the series/show also contributes to the strong sense of identification and ownership of the character/actor. For some fans, the roles become so blurred as to be almost indistinguishable, such that we often find references to onscreen scenes including character names, in fictions purportedly about the actors in their everyday guises.

Torchwood: Getting up close

Torchwood is a British television spin-off of the *Doctor Who* series, produced by the BBC. Its origins have been attributed to fanfiction, based as it is on the character of Captain Jack Harkness who had appeared in the 2005 *Doctor Who* series, but transposing his adventures to a specific location (Cardiff), and building a team of characters around him. However, *Torchwood* distinguishes itself from *Doctor Who* by including adult themes, especially concerning the sexuality of Captain Jack, and his complex relationship with Gwen. The series featured an intense but short-lived same-sex relationship between Jack and Ianto, which soon became a major focus for writers of slash and RPF based on the show. When the character of Ianto was killed off in the third series, it prompted a huge response from disgruntled fans who set up a shrine for the character in Cardiff and bombarded the makers of the show with demands for the return of the character and even death threats.

RPF based on *Torchwood* largely centers on the actor who played Captain Jack, John Barrowman, who is openly gay and in a civil partnership, and Gareth David-Lloyd, who played Ianto, who is married with a child. Since leaving the show, David-Lloyd has kept up his connection with the fans, appearing regularly at conventions and taking part in radio dramas based on *Torchwood*. Stories involving the two also regularly feature references to Barrowman's offscreen partner, Scott Gill, and even their dogs. However, unlike female celebrity spouses such as Yoko Ono or Linda McCartney, Gill is not seen as a threat or barrier to the "true" pairing of Barrowman/David-Lloyd, but tends to be treated respectfully and with affection.

Human Nature, the *Doctor Who* Real Person Fiction archive, has a relatively modest membership (1170 as of 24 August 2012), and provides users with ratings, warnings, and disclaimers both about the sexual nature of the content and its relationship with the real world: "All stories are purely fictional, with no implication of reality intended. All the fake real people belong to themselves." Saraid, the author of "All That I Want" featured on the site (http://dwrpf. prydonian.net/viewstory.php?sid=37&ageconsent=ok&warning=4), describes herself as a "Nana" and "teacher," bearing out the research that suggests that most writers of slash are female professionals of a certain age. In Saraid's *Torchwood*-based RPF, Scott Gill and Barrowman's dog, Harris, both make an appearance, the latter being saved dramatically by Barrowman as he leaps in front of an oncoming car. The story creates a strong sense of the domestic in its treatment of Barrowman and his "husband" ("This is just like at home, right?") and refers to family members and their wider circle of friends on familiar terms. This bears out Busse's (2006) claim that RPF is frequently concerned with the supposed private life of the "extrapolated star," a fascination with the ordinary life of the supposedly extraordinary individuals who become the object of affection or devotion.

Saraid's story also explicitly refers to extra-textual affairs, drawing on gossip surrounding the actors and their interrelationships onscreen and offscreen. Thus, when Barrowman says "I can feud with Eve [Myles] if you like," the assumption is that they are involved in a kind of game whereby fuelling rumors helps boost and sustain interest in their characters and in the show. While there is quite a bit of flirtation between Barrowman and David-Lloyd in Saraid's story, the impression that we are left with is of the solidity and affection of Barrowman's relationship with Gill. In the comments posted for the story, the focus is on the depiction of this relationship and its realism ("i could feel the emotion between john and scott") with one comment explicitly linking this to extra-textual content ("it's so obvious from the photos how much Scott loves John & vice versa"). While some mention is made of the show and its creator, "Russell," the story maintains a clear distinction throughout between the fictional roles and the actors.

"Somewhere a Clock is Ticking," a Janto (Jack/Ianto) RPF published on livejournal (http://kalichan.livejournal.com/199544.html), focuses on David-Lloyd's discovery that his character is about to be killed off, and his ensuing telephone conversation with John Barrowman. It therefore fictionalizes a key moment not just for the two characters involved, but also for the fans who were traumatized by this event. The story again refers to Scott Gill and to actors from the cast, and also claims some familiarity with the offstage personalities of the leads, for example, referring to the fact that "Barrowman is fine with people taking the piss, except when he's not." However, in this story we have much more slippage between the onscreen and offscreen roles: David-Lloyd says he "can hear good old Captain Jack" in Barrowman's voice, while Barrowman knowingly says to David-Lloyd "Everyone loves you. Ianto. You know what I mean," drawing attention to the way in which "everyone" conflates the actor with this role.

While neither of these stories is particularly graphic or offensive in content—kalichan, the author of "Somewhere a Clock is Ticking," apologizes for writing "another sexless, completely fictional RPF"—as suggested earlier, many Janto (Jack/Ianto) stories are sexually explicit, focusing on the conflicts facing Barrowman as a man in a committed relationship, and David-Lloyd as a man who identifies as heterosexual. Much attention has been paid to the motivations of writers of RPF and the extent to which it may be distinguished from pornography. However, this can be a distraction from the fascinating ways in which authors and readers participate in a knowing game in which the "reality" of what is being depicted is constantly being negotiated, but where the attachment and commitment to the "paper beings" (Barthes 1977) they play with are nonetheless very powerful.

The Social Network: Reflexivity and rabbit holes

RPF based on the film *The Social Network* has prompted some particularly interesting debates within fan communities regarding how they create "rabbit holes within rabbit holes" (www.fanlore.org/wiki/The_Social_Network), resulting in often quite complex meta-textual play. *The Social Network* is a fictionalized account of the founding of Facebook by the precocious and ruthless Mark Zuckerberg. Based on Ben Mezrich's book, *The Accidental Billionaires* (2009), the film attracted controversy because of its less-than-flattering depiction of Zuckerberg and because it took some liberties with the "truth" of his rise to fame. However, it is the onscreen and offscreen chemistry between actors Jesse Eisenberg and Andrew Garfield, who played Mark Zuckerberg and Eduardo Saverin, respectively, that has attracted the interest of fans and prompted debate about how stories about stories based on real people create their own complexities and confusions.

A discussion thread opened by neoncitylight on livejournal (http://mark-eduardo.livejournal.com/28163.html) presents the dilemma that "this is a Fandom where RPF kind of inevitably intertwines with the Fiction," meaning that the author has two sources of information to draw on—material relating to the real-world Mark Zuckerberg and Eduardo Severin, and material relating to the individuals who play them, Jesse Eisenberg and Andrew Garfield. In response, it is argued that *The Social Network* is itself a kind of RPF (romancandles) or a fanfic of fanfic (forochel) while it is also suggested that the structure of the film presents the viewer with so many different points of view (crosshair) that it makes it impossible to accept any one version of events as the truth.

What such discussions often highlight is the extent to which writers of RPF wrestle with these metaphysical questions about the ontological status of the storyworlds created by fans. As has already been demonstrated, fans' attempts to articulate what they are doing as authors of these fictions, or their responses to fictions created by others, are often highly contradictory but also playful in tone. Despite constantly asserting that the characters they write about are fictional, RPF authors frequently address their real-world subjects as though to mitigate any threat to the "face" (Brown and Levinson 1978) of that individual by means of apology or flattery. Appealing to Jesse and Andrew directly ("Please don't google yourself guys"), itsanoffblue (http://mark-eduardo.livejournal.com/446716.html) goes on to say "but if u do, Andrew we love your eyebrows," drawing on real-world knowledge of the actor's physiognomy and recognizing that they could conceivably discover what is being written about them, and suggesting that this is something that is both feared and desired.

Conclusion

I hope to have demonstrated in this chapter that the issues surrounding RPF coalesce in many ways with wider debates and discussions to do with the nature of celebrity and the representation of real people in fictional contexts. I also hope to have shown that the almost universal dismissal and condemnation of RPF has been too precipitous, and that many of those engaged in this activity, both as writers and as readers, are fully prepared to explore and debate the ethics and aesthetics of what they are doing. Although my analysis of RPF has been highly selective and some might say unrepresentative in its avoidance of anything too "squicky," this was a deliberate attempt to try to steer the discussion toward approaching the fictions as part of a situated practice in which commentary, meta-textuality, and even critical reflection all play their part.

Acknowledgments

Many thanks to Bethan Jones of Cardiff University for sending me links to discussions of RPF on livejournal and elsewhere and to G-Skywalker for permission to reproduce the image "forever mine. (ShatNoy)" from the website Deviant Art (http://g-skywalker.deviantart.com/art/forever-mine-ShatNoy-310330851).

References

Barthes, Roland. 1977. "Introduction to the structural analysis of narratives." In *Image-Music-Text*, 79–124. Translated by Stephen Heath. London: Fontana.

Baudrillard, Jean. 1994. *Simulacra and Simulacrum*. Translated Sheila Feria Glaser. Ann Arbor: University of Michigan Press.

Brooker, Will. 2007. "A sort of homecoming: Fan viewing and symbolic pilgrimage." In *Fandom: Identities and Communities in a Mediated World*, edited by Jonathan Gray, Cornel Sandvoss and C. Lee Harrington, 149–164. New York: New York University Press.

Brown, Penelope and Levinson, Stephen. 1978. "Universals in language use: Politeness phenomena." In *Questions and Politeness: Strategies in Social Interaction*, edited by Esther N. Goody, 56–311. Cambridge: Cambridge University Press.

Busse, Kristina. 2006. "My life is a WIP on my LJ: Slashing the slasher and the reality of celebrity and internet performances." In *Fan Fiction and Fan Communities in the Age of the Internet*, edited by Karen Hellekson and Kristina Busse, 207–224. Jefferson: McFarland.

Cumberland, Sharon. 2012. "Private uses of cyberspace: Women, desire and fan culture." In *The Gender and Media Reader*, edited by Mary Celeste Kearney, 669–679. London: Routledge.

Dyer, Richard. 1991. "A star is born and the construction of authenticity." In *Stardom: Industry of Desire*, edited by Christine Gledhill, 132–140. London: Routledge.

Foucault, Michel. 1998 [1976]. *The History of Sexuality: The Will to Knowledge*. London: Penguin.

Goffman, Erving. 1959. *The Presentation of the Self in Everyday Life*. New York: Doubleday.

Horton, Donald and R. Richard Wohl. 1956. "Mass communication and para-social interaction: Observations on intimacy at a distance." *Psychiatry* 19, 215–229.

McGee, Jennifer. 2005. "'In the End It's All Made Up': The ethics of fan fiction and real person fiction." In *Communication Ethics, Media and Popular Culture*, edited by Phyllis M. Japp, Mark Meister, and Debra K. Japp, 161–180. New York: Peter Lang.

Page, Ruth. 2011. *Stories and Social Media: Identities and Interactions*. London: Routledge.

Pugh, Sheenagh. 2005. *The Democratic Genre: Fan Fiction in a Literary Context*. Bridgend: Seren Books.

Scodari, Christine. 2007. "Yoko in cyberspace with Beatles fans: Gender and the re-creation of popular mythology." In *Fandom: Identities and Communities in a Mediated World*, edited by Jonathan Gray, Cornel Sandvoss, and C. Lee Harrington, 48–59. New York: New York University Press.

Stacey, Jackie. 2012. "Feminine fascinations: Forms of identification in star-audience relations." In *The Gender and MediaReader*, edited by Mary Celeste Kearney, 641–654. London: Routledge.

Stasi, Mafalda. 2006. "The toy soldiers from leeds." In *Fan Fiction and Fan Communities in the Age of the Internet*, edited by Karen Hellekson and Kristina Busse, 115–133. Jefferson: McFarland.

Turkle, Sherry. 2005. *The Second Self: Computers and the Human Spirit*. Cambridge, Mass: MIT Press.

Turner, Graeme. 2004. *Understanding Celebrity*. London: Sage.

10

Remembering Frank Sinatra: Celebrity Studies Meets Memory Studies

Roberta Pearson

University of Nottingham, UK

In May 2012, on the fourteenth anniversary of Frank Sinatra's death, Nancy Sinatra remembered her father by attacking her stepmother Barbara on Twitter. Barbara, Nancy claimed, had kept her and her siblings from her father's deathbed, an act for which she would never forgive her father's widow. "He asked, 'Where are my children?' and his children didn't know [he was dying]. She is evil personified. (I wasn't allowed to visit) because then obits couldn't say, 'He died with his wife by his side'" (contactmusic.com 2012). Nancy's tweets publicized a very private trauma, implicitly contesting the account of Sinatra's relatively peaceful death recounted in her stepmother's memoir *Lady Blue Eyes*, published the previous year. Despite taking the more conventional old media form of the book, Barbara Sinatra's memoir/memorialization also publicizes the private, as the author acknowledges on the first page. "I have always been a private person, so the idea of writing a book about my life with Frank didn't come naturally to me." She was persuaded to write the book, she says, by "several of those closest to me" who said that she had "a unique perspective on what it was like to live with Frank Sinatra, a man who still commands worldwide fascination years after his death" (Barbara Sinatra 2011: ix).

Attesting to this worldwide fascination, just a month prior to Nancy's tweeted trauma, the Smithsonian Institution had issued its annual poster commemorating Jazz Appreciation Month; the 2012 version featured a portrait of a nattily dressed Sinatra (fedora, pocket handkerchief, cufflinks) holding a song sheet and singing. While Sinatra's relatives' remembrances merged the public and the private, the poster was a public and official act of remembrance originating with the arm of the US government charged with safeguarding the nation's heritage. Yet, as

Nancy and Barbara contested the "facts" of Sinatra's death, potential contestation lurked just beneath the surface of the vibrantly colored portrait originally commissioned from well-known American artist LeRoy Neiman to adorn the cover of a 1993 Sinatra album. The artist's portraits of Duke Ellington and Louis Armstrong had appeared on previous Jazz Appreciation Month posters. No controversy there, but was it now appropriate to have a white man personify an art form closely associated with African Americans, even if Sinatra was chosen precisely because of his links with the civil rights movement (Trescott 2012)?

Another public and official act of remembrance, the Sinatra stamp issued by the US Post Office on the tenth anniversary of the singer's death in May 2008, at first blush seems completely non-controversial; it bears a picture of a fedora-wearing Sinatra, his iconic blue eyes complemented by a blue background. Yet the choice of photograph privileges one representation over another; the stamp presents Sinatra as the swinging hipster of the 1950s, as opposed to the skinny boy singer of the 1940s or the pudgy, gray-haired "Chairman of the Board" who continued to perform into the 1990s. Unlike Elvis fans, who got to vote for a "young Elvis" or "old Elvis" stamp, Sinatra fans had not been consulted as to which Frank should be officially remembered. Circulating alongside these public and official texts are the myriad commodities that continue to cash in on the fascination with Sinatra; some of these present less-positive images than the official acts of remembrance originating with the US government or than the private/public remembrances of his relatives. For example, the 1938 police mug shot of Sinatra taken when he was briefly detained for breach of promise now adorns a poster, a t-shirt, and even a mug shot mug. The image undoubtedly gains its commercial appeal by resonating with the rumors of Sinatra's mob associations that dogged his career almost from the beginning.

These few examples of the posthumous remembrance of a celebrity icon raise many of the questions currently being asked in the field of memory studies. What are the connections between public and private, individual and collective memory? How does officially sanctioned public memory interact with the collective memory of the people or groups of people? How does memory represent political contestation and personal trauma? How do both public heritage and private commercial interests benefit from the exploitation of memory by privileging certain representations of the past over others? How do the media, and particularly the new digital media, represent memory? The field of media and memory studies is a rapidly growing one; see for instance the comprehensive overview provided in Joanne Garde-Hansen's (2011) *Media and*

Memory.[1] The field of celebrity studies is also thriving, now given institutional legitimacy by the launch of the journal *Celebrity Studies* in 2010. With rare exceptions, however, the two fields do not intersect; memory and media studies seem largely uninterested in celebrity and celebrity studies seem largely uninterested in memory.[2] Yet, as my Sinatra examples illustrate, the exploration of the posthumous circulation of celebrity image connects many of the debates within memory studies. This essay uses Sinatra to explore the ways in which the concerns of media and memory studies might intersect with celebrity studies, particularly in terms of sites of remembrance, the actual physical locations that remember the singer through commemorative markers and events.

Sinatra is a ubiquitous icon, although perhaps not as ubiquitous as his near contemporaries, Marilyn Monroe and Elvis Presley, whose rapid declines and tragic deaths forever secured their places at the top of the celebrity pantheon. However, it is precisely Sinatra's longevity that makes him a suitable case study. Monroe was the nation's sex symbol for a brief decade from the early 1950s until her death in 1962, while Elvis's career spanned the 1950s to the 1970s. Sinatra's career began in the late 1930s and ended shortly before his death in the late 1990s. During these 60 years, the singer/actor crossed over fields of cultural production, winning awards for his acting as well as for his singing and appearing on radio, in recordings, in films, on television, and in live performances. Elvis and Marilyn cannot equal him in this regard; Elvis made movies, mostly bad ones, whereas Marilyn's fame stemmed almost solely from the big screen. The only celebrity who can claim to rival Sinatra's success across multiple media is Bing Crosby; while he is an important figure in terms of intermedial history, changing times and mores have greatly reduced his once significant cultural resonance. Sinatra's cultural resonance remains robust; his posthumous celebrity attests to the fact that, as Gilbert B. Rodman says of Elvis, he "is an incredibly full signifier, one that is … intimately bound up with many of the most important cultural myths of our time" (1996: 40).

Sinatra, offspring of Italian immigrants in working class Hoboken, New Jersey, a small industrial city across the Hudson from New York City, was the quintessential poor boy made good, beginning his career as a radio crooner in the late 1930s. The canny Sinatra consciously and continuously adapted himself to the ever-shifting cultural and media-scape. In the 1940s, he was "The Voice," the boy singer associated both with his "hysterical" young female fans, the bobby-soxers, and with the romantic yearnings of women left behind by their military sweethearts fighting World War II. After a rapid career slide in the late 1940s and the early 1950s, his reinvention as the consummate swinging hipster in the mid-1950s and the early 1960s aligned with the post-war reconfiguration of values around sexuality and masculinity. From the 1970s on, he was an American legend to his admirers and risible symbol of an outmoded era to his detractors. Beginning in the early 1950s with his very public "tragic" romance with Ava Gardner, he was subsequently romantically linked to numerous other sex symbols, including Monroe. Rumors of his mob connections began to circulate in the late 1940s, as public sightings of him in the company of prominent Mafia bosses caused the FBI to take an interest in him. He played a prominent role in national politics, first as a Democrat, visiting Franklin D. Roosevelt in the White House and taking part in John F. Kennedy's presidential campaign, and then as a Republican, friendly with Nixon and Reagan. Sinatra articulates to multiple cultural myths concerning the American Dream, the immigrant/ hyphenated American, the Mafia, the World War II home front, showbiz glamor (both Hollywood and Las Vegas), JFK's Camelot, masculine sexuality, and, of course, jazz and the Great American songbook.[3]

This essay cannot give full consideration to all of Sinatra's posthumous manifestations. Rather it uses the Sinatra case study to investigate what might be termed "commodified public memory": memorial forms that include both the official memory (as seen in the Smithsonian poster and the stamp) and the commercial memory (as seen in the numerous manifestations of Sinatra across commercial forms such as the mug shot mug). The particular focus is upon spaces of memory, looking at the ways in which the primary places associated with Sinatra (Hoboken, New Jersey, the "hometown"; Los Angeles and Las Vegas, sites of performance; and Palm Springs, site of long-term residence) have been mobilized for heritage and for commercial purposes and, often, for both simultaneously. This investigation of the sites of Sinatra remembrance addresses the interactions of officially sanctioned public memory with the collective memory of individuals or groups of individuals as well as the ways in which public heritage and private commercial interests benefit from the exploitation of memory by privileging certain representations of the past over others.

Commodified public memory

I defined commodified public memory in a 1999 essay about the struggle between whites and Native Americans over the meaning of the battle called by the former the Little Big Horn and by the latter the Greasy Grass, the 1876 military encounter in which the Lakota and Cheyenne tribes defeated the US Cavalry led by General George Armstrong Custer. I said that

> "Commodified" refers to the economic incentives...that structure... representations [of historic events]. "Public" deliberately resonates with the concept of the public sphere, for the historical representations comprising public commodified memory usually originate from state or civic institutions. The use of "public" rather than "popular" indicates that commodified public memory emanates from above, from such central institutions...as the government and private corporations. While individuals and groups of individuals retain separate memories that often form the basis for contestation, the powerful institutions producing and circulating commodified public memory ensure that certain historical representations become both ubiquitous and dominant.
>
> Pearson 1999: 181

However, those ubiquitous and dominant representations emerge from an ongoing process of contestation. As Erll and Rigney (2009: 2) put it, "Fighting about memory is one way of keeping it alive and, as a number of recent studies has shown, the history of cultural memory is marked as much by crises and controversies running along social fault lines as it is by consensus and canon-building ... ." It is these fights that "allow certain collective memories to become hegemonic or, conversely, allow hitherto marginalized memories to gain prominence in the public arena." Since memory is an aspect of hegemony, some memories may be or become dominant, but other multiple and competing representations of historical events and figures can circulate simultaneously; different representations originate from different players, serve different purposes, and appeal to audiences differently situated within the hegemonic system by virtue of their different economic and cultural capital. Understanding the hegemonic contestation over memory entails paying attention to, as Erll and Rigney say, "the social actors and organisations which ensure that certain stories rather than others enjoy publicity and become salient; even more fundamentally, which ensure that certain topics rather than others are put on the society's commemorative agenda" (2009: 9).

Conflicting representations of Sinatra abounded during his lifetime and posthumously. Opposed to the texts that acclaim Sinatra as one of the greatest, if not the greatest, popular singer of his time are commodities alluding to his supposed Mob connections, such as the Sinatra mug shot mug. The novel *Narrows Gate* (Fusilli 2011) is a thinly fictionalized account of Sinatra's career set partly in a Hoboken under mob rule. Both the novel and the film *The Godfather*

(Francis Ford Coppola, 1972) feature singer Johnny Fontaine, a character seen by many as modeled on Sinatra while *The Sopranos* (HBO 1999-2007) abounded with references to Sinatra. The 1960s group of showbiz celebrities The Rat Pack, with Sinatra as acknowledged leader and Dean Martin, Sammy Davis, Jr., Peter Lawford, and Joey Bishop as the core members, is similarly both celebrated and vilified. Says Shawn Levy in *Rat Pack Confidential*, "It was the acme of the American Century and a venal, rancid, ugly sham" (1999: 11). However, much commodified public memory invokes heritage in the pursuit of profit and therefore tends, to quote a Sinatra standard, to "accentuate the positive and eliminate the negative." As Robert Burgoyne (2006: 211) points out in his essay on the Rock and Roll Hall of Fame and Museum, the "commercial recycling of the past [is] a form of commemoration that increasingly takes the form of an appeal to heritage." The Museum commemorates "defiantly anti-establishment figures such as Jim Morrison and Jimi Hendrix" as "national icons, exemplars of American values" and in so doing rewrites the tumultuous history of the 1960s.

My essay on the Little Big Horn/Greasy Grass argued that some representations erase the signs of contestation and temporarily halt history, "establishing a set of unquestioned, frozen, and abstracted 'facts'" (Pearson 1999: 181); this process can be seen in Sinatra heritage commodities originating with upmarket manufacturers and the government. Jack Daniel's, Sinatra's drink of choice, recently teamed up with the family-run Frank Sinatra Enterprises to launch the ultra-premium Sinatra Select whiskey (VNN Music). The taller, sleeker bottle, featuring a medallion of Sinatra's iconic fedora and highlights in the singer's favorite orange, creates a "look that is sleek and stylish, a reflection of Sinatra's timeless good taste," a phrase that literally seeks to transcend history (Cue 2012). Writing instrument manufacturer Montegrappa has an Icons series that includes a Sinatra pen; like the whiskey bottle, it incorporates the famous fedora and favored orange. And, like the whiskey, the pen makes an historical claim; Montegrappa characterizes its product as a tribute to a "performer who redefined the role of singer" (Pittilla 2011). Sinatra is also officially enshrined in the nation's heritage as seen in the poster and stamp discussed earlier. The Smithsonian poster asserts several "facts" about jazz: the terms "Spontaneous. Never Ordinary. Completely Genuine." are emblazoned above Sinatra's picture and "Born in America. Enjoyed worldwide." below. "Completely Genuine" erases the contestation around the origins of jazz as African American or European or hybrid form and legitimates the white singer as its literal poster boy. "Enjoyed worldwide" continues the exploitation of jazz as propaganda begun during the Cold War and acclaims Sinatra as an equally successful American export.

The Sinatra stamp is another example of the government's appropriation of twentieth-century popular culture for heritage purposes. During the first two decades of the century, Barry Schwartz tells us, "75.1 percent of those represented on stamps were political figures, statesmen, and men engaged in the nation's governance .... Military figures and the New World's discoverers, explorers, and settlers account together for 14.2 percent of the total; the remaining 10.7 percent consist mainly of presidents' wives" (Schwartz 2009: 148). However, in 1957 the Citizen's Stamp Advisory Committee was established to ensure "representation of as wide a spectrum of American life as possible" (Schwartz 2009: 165). From that moment, popular celebrities from the fields of sport, music, film, and so forth began to replace presidents and generals. As the letters USA in the upper left-hand corner of the Sinatra stamp attest, adorning a stamp elevates figures like Sinatra and Elvis from popular entertainers to American icons intimately connected to the nation-state; this elevation overrides past controversies over "hysterical" bobby-soxers or a gyrating pelvis. The commercial products similarly ignore the contentious aspects of Sinatra's life and career in associating him with timeless good taste or an immense contribution to American music.

The stamp, the whiskey, and the pen construct a particular memory of Sinatra while suppressing others that might be less conducive to producing revenue streams. Whether originating from public institutions or private enterprises, heritage texts are potential money-spinners; scholars and policymakers now consider heritage institutions as part of the wider constellation of creative industries. Take, for example, another source of Sinatra remembrance, *American Heritage* magazine, the title of which proclaims its ideological project. Despite its 1940s origins as a publication of the American Association for State and Local History and despite having many historians as staff members and contributing editors, the magazine is a profit-earning enterprise. Its website tells potential advertisers that, "The *American Heritage* audience consists of frequent, affluent travellers who enjoy spending their time—and money—visiting historic destinations and experiencing our national culture" (http://www.americanheritage.com/about/advertising). Judging by the 45 articles and reviews that a search for Sinatra yielded, *American Heritage* views the singer as central to the national culture it celebrates. From my perspective, the magazine's most thought-provoking Sinatra coverage is in an article not about him but about his hometown, Hoboken. The article references the city's most famous resident, saying that although Sinatra's birthplace, an apartment house at 415 Monroe Street, burned to the ground, a bronze star marks its location. Next door is the still-standing No. 417: "a former candy store where, as a boy, the singer crooned for the customers. Now it's a museum, open only on weekends, run by Ed Shirak, a fan, writer, and local politician. Shirak displays a clutter of photographs, rare records, and even one of Sinatra's silk handkerchiefs…" (Klara 2002). The magazine clearly expects that some of its frequent, affluent travelers may wish to visit Hoboken for its Sinatra connections and helpfully provides contact phone numbers for the museum (which has subsequently closed due to lack of funds).

Relatively little attention has been paid to sites commemorating entertainment celebrities although sites of commemoration are a key component of the heritage industry; they have also been a central concern of memory studies since the work of Pierre Nora and his colleagues in the 1980s (Nora 1989 and 1996–1998). However, while Nora uses the term lieux de memoire to encompass everything from the tricolor to anniversaries to cemeteries, this essay focuses specifically on physical locations and structures. Furthermore, as Erll and Rigney say, more recently there has been a "shift from 'sites' to 'dynamics' within memory studies" that "runs parallel to a larger shift of attention within cultural studies from products to processes, from a focus on discrete cultural artefacts to an interest in the way those artefacts circulate and interact with their environment" (2009: 3). The rest of this chapter explores the processes of Sinatra remembrance in four different physical locations, Hoboken, Los Angeles, Las Vegas, and Palm Springs.

Places of Sinatra memory

In his book exploring Elvis's posthumous fame, Rodman (1996) points to the surprising absence of celebrity sites of remembrance and commemoration, arguing that this absence stems from the distinction between stardom and other forms of fame. The former, argues Rodman, has a different relationship to space, determined by the mass media that "don't so much occupy space as they transcend it, and that, because it relies so heavily for the media on its own existence, stardom is typically an ethereal, non-spatial phenomenon" (Rodman 1996: 100). He continues

> the fact that the phenomenon of stardom is dependent on the media means that they can only exist *as stars* in the ethereal non-spaces of media texts and public imagination. In fact, the various connections that do exist in the public eye between stars and fixed geographic locations tend to be fairly nebulous.
>
> Rodman 1996: 101, emphasis in original

He gives as an example Los Angeles, associated with many celebrities but linked to none in particular. According to Rodman, Elvis's Graceland is the only real exception; "the longstanding connections between these two icons [work] to transform the private, domestic space of Elvis's home into a publicly visible site of pilgrimage and congregation" (1996: 102).

With the exceptions of Los Angeles and New York, similarly shared by all and specific to none, Rodman is probably right that most contemporary celebrities do not have a strong connection to a particular geographic location.[4] Contra Rodman, I think that this has more to do with the nature of stardom than with the nature of the media (after all, how do celebrities in any field become famous if not through the media?). In the United States, the traditional star trajectory is from hometown to one of the two coastal cities that bestow and confirm their celebrity status; the respective places of origin tend to blur into one undifferentiated site of pre-celebrity, marked only by the lack of the glamor and opportunities afforded by the glittering coastal metropolises. These hometowns, however, can seek to distinguish themselves through their associations with the local boy or girl who made good in the big city; the rapid growth of the heritage industry has provided powerful incentives for them to do so as it has for other locations in which celebrities lived or worked. Celebrity memory may be reported and sustained in the "ethereal non-spaces of media texts and public imagination" (Rodman 1996: 100) but acts of commemoration and associated physical markers require a geographical anchoring in specific locations. The Post Office and Sinatra's three children held the first day of sale ceremonies for the Sinatra stamp in three cities related to the singer's life and career—New York City, Las Vegas, and Hoboken (Associated Press 2008). The Jack Daniel's Sinatra Edition was launched at the Las Vegas airport, "chosen because of Sinatra's historical association with the city" (Woodard 2012). Rodman may think that celebrities are not linked to particular locations, but the Post Office and Jack Daniels believe otherwise.

Hoboken, Los Angeles, Las Vegas, and Palm Springs are all, to greater or lesser degrees, sites of Sinatra commemoration, as the cities' civic bodies, private entrepreneurs, and media seek to capitalize on the singer's memory. [5] The need for this capitalization is contingent upon the locales' other potential heritage assets, including the number of celebrities with which they are currently and historically linked. The extent and success of this capitalization are determined by each locality's Sinatra-specific and general assets: the number and type of the surviving physical markers of Sinatra's residency, together with the economic and media resources and individual energies available for their exploitation. The precise nature of the capitalization is to some extent determined by the period of Sinatra's life and career during which he was primarily associated with the locale. Lacking the resources of the more glamorous sites subsequently associated with hometown boys and girls made good, celebrity hometowns may find it difficult to fully exploit their sole heritage asset while at the same time having a greater need to do so. Locales such as Los Angeles and New York, rich in celebrity heritage assets, have a lesser need intensively to exploit each one since they do not depend on a single hometown celebrity to nurture civic pride, sustain commercial ventures, or attract tourists.

Very much in the shadow of heritage-rich New York across the Hudson, Hoboken welcomes visitors with a sign declaring itself the birthplace of baseball and of Frank Sinatra, the city's two most potentially viable heritage assets. The claim to baseball's origin is factually accurate but mythologically inaccurate. Although the first baseball game was indeed played in Hoboken's Elysian Fields in 1846, due to a muddled history too complex to recount in these pages, Cooperstown, in upstate New York, has trademarked the phrase "birthplace of baseball" and hosts the National Baseball Hall of Fame. Hoboken cannot compete with Cooperstown's well-established exploitation of baseball's history, even though the designation of the New York town as baseball's originary location shrouds the game's beginnings in myth. However, there are no rival claimants to Sinatra's origins; the singer was indubitably born in Hoboken on 12 December 1915. Just after the singer's death in 1998, the city opened the new Frank Sinatra Park (its dedication plaque proclaiming Francis Albert Sinatra "Hoboken's Gift to the World") and the adjacent Frank Sinatra Drive; it also named its main post office Frank Sinatra Station. Recently Hoboken's mayor proposed redesigning the Frank Sinatra Drive to make it "consistent with our master plan's vision for a more pedestrian friendly area with waterfront opportunities for active and passive recreation" (Moses 2012). Hoboken's master plan resembles the waterfront development and heritage exploitation seen in many post-industrial cities seeking to redevelop themselves in the age of tourism and the service economy; Sinatra's name localizes Hoboken's implementation of this strategy. Sinatra figures in Hoboken's civic infrastructure and redevelopment plans, but it is the private sector that generates the majority of the city's Sinatra memories in a "DIY" heritage driven by local fans and media. Since memory, and by extension, heritage is an aspect of hegemony, it functions in the same way, sustaining itself by enlisting many to its cause: the powerful, the would-be powerful, and the not-so powerful. Yet the not-so powerful frequently lack the resources to maintain their memories: Hoboken Historical Museum's director Robert Foster "admits Sinatra-related tourist opportunities are scant. 'It's a little dry,' said Foster. 'It's hard for people to maintain a site'" (Maurer 2010).

The Hoboken Historical Museum seems from its website (http://www. hobokenmuseum.org) to be a privately funded institution struggling to establish itself on a more secure basis. The website offers three interactive Google maps for self-guided walking tours: a Kids Tour, a Hoboken Tour, and, of course, a Frank Sinatra tour. The Google maps version of this last repeats the official PR slogan of "Hoboken's Gift to the World" found at the eponymous Park but the tour itself was "inspired" by Sinatra's fans, "with their frequent requests for information on Hoboken sites linked to the legendary entertainer." The Museum characterizes the tour more as social/cultural history than showbiz glamor, leading people to the sites of the "long-vanished social clubs, pool halls, and bars of the 30's where Frank and his contemporaries sang" in order to give tourists "a sense of what life was like here during the singer's early years—and what remains from that time." The walk begins at 415 Monroe Street, the absent birthplace, then continues to his baptismal church, homes of friends and relatives, his schools and venues where he sang as a youth. As a long-ago association with the singer elevates obscure homes and businesses to historical status, so it does the entire city. In the present, Sinatra's name presumably helps the current businesses on the tour: the bakery from which he ordered bread when in New York City and the restaurant where he ate upon his return to town. The tour takes in a commercial venue, Piccolo's Famous Cheesestake, which claims connection with the singer not through historical association but through displays of memorabilia, but also includes Lepore's Chocolates (mentioned in the *American Heritage* article), which boasts both memorabilia and a connection with the young Sinatra. The tour includes official sites of commemoration and remembrance: Hoboken City Hall, where Sinatra was presented with the key to the city in 1947, the Post Office that hosted the Sinatra stamp first-day ceremonies, the Hoboken Public Library, with its Sinatra collection, and the Frank Sinatra Memorial Park. As a whole, the tour points to the multiple and diverse goals and stakeholders invested in celebrity heritage.

Also benefitting from the Sinatra heritage are state and city media; all of the coverage of Sinatra's hometown connections discussed here originated in New Jersey and Hoboken newspapers and websites. Sinatra news fills column space and airtime and allows journalists to fulfill the civic booster role of the local press. *The Hudson Reporter* offered a Sinatra walking tour similar to that on the Hoboken Historical Museum website, claiming that "For anyone interested in finding out more about the man who became known as 'The Voice,' there's no better place to start than his former hometown" (Zinsli 2006). However, the article, like the Museum, points to the contrasts between today's Hoboken and Sinatra's Hoboken. "Sinatra grew up in a Hoboken very different from what it is today. In the 1930s, the city's residents went to work in factories or docksides on the Hudson River. By night, they frequented smoky nightspots, social clubs, pool halls and bars." While this walk similarly takes in the civic and commercial sites that constitute the city's official Sinatra heritage, offering a chance to "soak in the city's charm and history [and] grab some great food" it also promises that you will "meet some native Hobokenites who idolize the great crooner."

The voices of native Hobokenites praising their hometown boy made good are frequently heard in the local press, painting Sinatra not as official heritage icon but as a lived and individual memory. The day after Sinatra's death, *The Newark Star Ledger* ran a piece about memories of him in "old Hoboken," the "Italian immigrant enclave that lives in the barbershops, restaurants and memories of his contemporaries ... " (Braun and McGlone 1998). The reporters sought reactions from several of the native Hobokenites whose establishments feature in the walking tours and from the city's mayor, who related an anecdote about his mother's having been a domestic for Sinatra's mother. But, claimed the reporters, Sinatra lives on in the memories of all in "old Hoboken:" "Ask anyone on the street, and you'll hear about their father's cousin who was in high school with Sinatra, the time they saw Sinatra on the corner outside Kelly's Bar on Fourteenth Street." Sinatra's Hoboken fans seek to keep his memory alive in community-based celebrations of the singer and his music. Since 2010, the Sinatra Society has gathered annually at an Italian restaurant in "old Hoboken" to honor Sinatra's birthday with food, drink, and, of course, song, supplied by a Sinatra tribute singer (Kowsh 2011). In 2012, the proceeds from the event were donated to charities involved with Hurricane Sandy relief, as Hoboken's hometown hero came to his city's assistance in its hour of need (Hack 2012). The city and Sinatra fans from Hoboken and further afield team up to present an annual Frank Sinatra impersonator contest, "Sinatra Idol," in the Sinatra Park amphitheater as part of the Hoboken Department of Cultural Affairs summer events series (Skontra 2011).

Hoboken's Sinatra is not the exemplar of timeless good taste of the Jack Daniels special edition nor the American icon of the stamp and the Smithsonian poster; he is specific to a particular place and time, frozen in the history of the "old Hoboken" of the 1930s and the 1940s. As *The Newark Star Ledger* put it, he is "the young and sharply dressed Sinatra—the kid with a dark curl over his forehead and a jutting chin," "the tough, scrappy Hoboken kid," "the feisty cigarette smoker and drinker," in other words, the kid who sang in the "smoky nightspots, social clubs, pool halls and bars" of a grubbier, grittier city (Braun and McGlone 1998). However, the under-resourced city and Sinatra's aging fans struggle to perpetuate this memory that, judging by the media coverage, remains largely restricted to his hometown and his home state, unable to achieve the ubiquity or revenue of competing representations.

Hoboken gave Frank Sinatra a star; Los Angeles, the city the young singer arrived in the early 1940s to embark on his film career, has given him three. The Hollywood Walk of Fame includes stars marking Sinatra's achievements in music, film, and television. But, as *The Los Angeles Times* tells us, 2,400 other performers also have stars on the Walk. The *Times* Walk of Fame website Sinatra entry highlights Los Angeles' interconnecting web of celebrities by mentioning three related Hollywood stars on the Walk, ex-wife Ava Gardner, friend Dean Martin, and daughter Nancy. Hollywood also commemorates Sinatra with handprints in concrete in the court of Grauman's Chinese Theater, but he shares this honor with over 200 other stars (*Los Angeles Times*, Star Walk). Sinatra has to share even a more unique form of commemoration with others. La Dolce Vita, "the beloved throwback Italian restaurant in Beverly Hills" recently honored Sinatra and his "longtime studio mogul friend Guy McElwaine" by naming a booth after them. Booths are also named after George Raft and Ronald Reagan (Baum 2012).

The *LA Times* Sinatra Walk of Fame entry links to recent Sinatra articles in the *Times* archives; with a very few exceptions, such as an article about Sinatra's contributing money to the city's homeless or articles about the sale of his former residences, none of these are specific to the singer's connections with Los Angeles (*Los Angeles Times*, Keyword). As for other press coverage, there are very few Los Angeles-related Sinatra stories; two of these are from the local press. An article from *The Burbank Leader* publicizes local restaurant The Smokehouse where Sinatra often ate but also mentions seven other stars who frequented the establishment; once again Sinatra is but one celebrity among many (Bryant 2012). The spotlight shines just on Sinatra in a *Beverly Hills Courier* piece, that like its Hoboken counterpart, *The Hudson Reporter*, recommends a Sinatra walking tour, although, as might be expected the former is a bit more upmarket. Instead of Lepore's Homemade Chocolates, which failed to maintain its Sinatra Museum, we get Edelweiss Chocolates of Beverly Hills, suppliers of Sinatra's favorite Maple Creams. However, like many of Sinatra's favorite LA haunts, the shop has other celebrity customers and associations; most famously it was the location for the beloved chocolate-making episode of *I Love Lucy* (CBS, 1951–1957). Instead of Sinatra's absent birthplace, we get 882 Doheny Drive, a retro building where both Sinatra and Marilyn Monroe once rented apartments. Instead of "old Hoboken" Italian eateries, we get Ah Fong's, a Chinese restaurant owned by actor Benson Fong, which was very popular with celebrities in the 1940s and the 1950s (Hood 2010). The contrasts between the two walks sum up the different appropriations of Sinatra memory in Hoboken and Los Angeles. Star-studded Los Angeles remembers the singer/actor as but one of the myriad celebrities who have lived and worked in its environs rather than as a significant figure linked to lived memory and to a particular period in the city's history as in Hoboken or, as we shall see, in Las Vegas.

At the behest of The Las Vegas Convention and Visitors Authority and the Las Vegas News Bureau, Las Vegas casinos darkened their lights for one minute the night after Frank Sinatra died "in memory of his contribution to the Las Vegas gaming and entertainment industry" (Koch 1998). This was the second time the casinos had darkened their lights for Sinatra; the first was for the fictional robbery scene in *Ocean's 11* (William Wellman 1960) the heist film made during Rat Pack's famous early 1960 "summit at the Sands," a playful allusion to the recent summit meeting in Paris among American President Eisenhower, Russian leader Nikita Khrushchev, and French President Charles De Gaulle. Sinatra had earlier appeared in a Las Vegas film as an uncredited singer with the Tommy Dorsey Orchestra in *Las Vegas Nights* (Ralph Murphy 1941). In 1966, Sinatra's record company released "Sinatra at the Sands," an album made with the Count Basie Orchestra, which was followed 20 years later by the album "Sinatra Live in Las Vegas." These films and recordings link Sinatra more strongly to Las Vegas than to Hoboken, Los Angeles, and Palm Springs. Sinatra first played Vegas in 1951 and continued to appear there until 1994; over these four decades, the city grew from desert outpost to today's entertainment capital. In a special section "chronicling 100 people who had major impacts on Las Vegas over the city's first century," the *Las Vegas Review-Journal* (Weatherford 1999) discussed Sinatra's role in the city's rise to international prominence: "To play a game of 'What if there had been no Sinatra?' is nearly impossible, because the rise of the singer and the Strip were inseparable."

Nevada's then Lieutenant Governor Lorraine Hunt corroborated the newspaper's appraisal of the singer's importance to the city: "Prior to Sinatra, we were more of a Western-feeling town. He brought a sophistication to the Strip" (Weatherford 1999). The Online Nevada Encyclopedia confirmed Hunt's perception: Sinatra "set a new standard in defining what was 'cool,' enhancing Las Vegas's image on the national entertainment scene as the *de facto* leader of the Rat Pack in the early 1960s . . . ." (Paskevich n.d.) As the *Review-Journal* summed up, Sinatra "was a one man chamber of commerce" (Weatherford 1999).

Hoboken has a "DIY Sinatra," maintained by local residents with a little help from civic bodies such as the Department of Cultural Affairs; Las Vegas has a "Chamber of Commerce Sinatra," supported and celebrated at city and state levels and frequently endorsed by the Sinatra family. Hoboken has the Sinatra Society that honors his birthday with a gathering at an Italian restaurant; Las Vegas has city-wide Sinatra Days. In 2001, the first Sinatra day celebrated his birth. Said Mayor Oscar Goodman, "If anyone deserves his own day in Las Vegas, it's Frank Sinatra, who epitomized all the best of Las Vegas style and cool" (Associated Press 2001). In 2008 the city remembered the tenth anniversary of his death with another city-wide Sinatra day, beginning with the dedication of the Sinatra stamp with Sinatra's daughter Tina an honored guest (PR Newswire 2008). Hoboken has restaurants with Sinatra memorabilia; Las Vegas has Sinatra, the only restaurant the Sinatra family permits to use its patriarch's name, which displays the singer's Academy Award and one of his Grammy Awards (http://www.opentable.com/sinatra-encore-at-wynn-las-vegas). In Hoboken, shop owners and people on the street remember Sinatra; in Las Vegas an array of professionals have shared their memories with reporters including his longtime chef, his former personal attorney and former federal judge (Koch 1998), a retired television writer and producer, and a former Caesar's Palace dealer (Clarke 2010). Hoboken has its annual "Sinatra Idol" contest in which amateur impersonators compete for the crown; in Las Vegas proliferating Rat Pack tributes, in which professional Sinatra impersonators earn a living, led to a legal dispute over trademark. In 2009, "ruling in a lawsuit pitting competing Rat Pack tribute show producers against each other, U.S. District Court Judge Lloyd George found . . . that one of the shows 'cannot appropriate the term "The Rat Pack" for its exclusive use.'" He declared that "the phrase 'The Rat Pack,' referring to tribute shows to Frank Sinatra and his pals, is generic and isn't subject to trademark protection . . . ." (Green 2009). Rat Pack shows successfully exploit the city's heritage for commercial purposes. At the time of this writing,

The Rat Pack Tribute (http://www.ratpack.com) and The Rat Pack is Back (www.ratpackisback.com) continue to compete for the tourist trade, neither legally entitled to sole ownership of the concept but both helping to define present and past Las Vegas.

The Rat Pack era is central to the city's image, celebrated and exploited by national and international media. No account of Las Vegas history is complete without Frank Sinatra and his pals, who first acted as tour guides and boosters in *Ocean's 11*. The long-running CBS procedural, *CSI* (2000-), has also done its part for Vegas tourism and frequently invokes the Rat Pack's Vegas. Season 13 saw an entire episode devoted to the Rat Pack's legacy. In "It Was a Very Good Year" (13: 4), the title echoing a well-known Sinatra song, a female music journalist is murdered in a Rat Pack tribute venue owned by a former mobster. A rare pressing of the "Live at the Sands" album provides a vital clue to the identity of the murderer, the tribute show's Sinatra impersonator who killed the woman in a fit of jealous rage. In the BBC documentary, *The Lure of Las Vegas* (2010), presenter Alan Yentob "takes a mob tour and talks to producers and performers about the golden days when Sinatra and Dino held the stage, and the wise guys called the shots." Even New York City's Metropolitan Opera has cashed in on the lure of Las Vegas, staging the most unusual of Rat Pack tributes. The Met's 2013 production of *Rigoletto* was "set in Las Vegas in the 1960s, when the Rat Pack ruled the city, giving it a reputation for licentiousness and lawlessness." In this production, "the Duke becomes a Frank Sinatra-like performer, his palace a gaudy casino" while Rigoletto, the humpbacked jester, is "modeled on aggressive comics like Don Rickles" (Isherwood 2013).

Las Vegas's Sinatra, like Hoboken's, is specific to a particular place and time, frozen in the history of the "old Las Vegas" of the 1960s. However, unlike Hoboken's Sinatra, which remains largely restricted to his hometown and his home state, unable to achieve the ubiquity or revenue of competing representations, Las Vegas's Sinatra has recognition and commercial power that extends far beyond city and state to the Metropolitan Opera and the BBC. This Sinatra differs from the timeless exemplar of good taste of the whiskey and the pen, the American icon of the stamp and the poster and the cocky young man of old Hoboken. He is a contradictory icon, a swinging hipster who was the epitome of sophistication and cool while intimately connected with the mobsters, licentiousness, lawlessness, and exploitative sexuality seen to characterize the old "Sin City." Nevada and Las Vegas officially remember their Sinatra as cool and sophisticated, but undoubtedly benefit from the whiff of dangerous glamor associated in the past with Sinatra and his Rat Pack and in the present with the new Sin City, a liminal space where conventional rules do not apply.

And finally and briefly to Palm Springs, Sinatra's last resting place and the last stop on this chapter's tour of sites of Sinatra remembrance. Sinatra took up residence in Palm Springs in 1947, moving into the newly built mid-century modern house he dubbed Twin Palms. In 1957 he moved to The Compound in the nearby town of Rancho Mirage where he lived until shortly before his death and burial in Palm Springs' Desert Memorial Park. With its many former and current resident film stars, Palm Springs almost level pegs with Los Angeles in the celebrity stakes. The Palm Springs Visitor Center (http://www.visitpalmsprings. com/page/hollywood's-playground/8183) terms the city in the California desert "Hollywood's Playground," explaining that stars flocked to the city because of the film studios' "Two Hour Rule," which mandated that actors could go no further than 2 hours away in case of last minute retakes. The website lists some of the celebrities who "purchased hideaway homes," including Sinatra, Dean Martin, Sammy Davis Jr., Bob Hope, Bing Crosby, Kirk Douglas, Cary Grant, and Jack Benny. Like Los Angeles, Palm Springs has a walk of stars; Sinatra's was dedicated in 1994 but as in Los Angeles he shares this honor with numerous others. Like Hoboken, Palm Springs has a Frank Sinatra Drive, but there is also a Dinah Shore Drive, a Bob Hope Drive, and several other streets named after former celebrity residents. Palm Springs has a celebrity golf tournament named after Sinatra but similar tournaments remember Hope and Shore. The Visitor Center's website 5-day Palm Springs tour includes a day devoted to "Hollywood's Favorite Playground." Visitors can "discover the secluded retreats and exclusive estates of Frank Sinatra, Marilyn Monroe or Elvis Presley by taking a celebrity tour, or staying overnight in one of the celebrity hideaways." They can also "Follow Palm Springs' own Walk of Stars throughout downtown Palm Springs featuring more than 300 stars of celebrities, humanitarians, professional athletes, civic leaders and other influencers" (http://www.visitpalmsprings.com/page/ itinerary-ideas/14241).

Palm Springs' Sinatra was prominent but not unique, one of the many famous names the locale employed to lure tourists and power its economy. However, the economic downturn of 2008 seems to have affected even the Palm Springs economy to such an extent as to encourage greater exploitation of the city's Sinatra assets. In a 2010 article, *The San Francisco Chronicle* noted that Sinatra is something of a going concern. Perhaps because the recession affects even tony places such as Palm Springs, the official city visitors bureau is now rather brazenly offering a list of favorite Sinatra haunts. The idea is for Sinatra fans to drive around the desert and check out bars, restaurants and fancy houses associated with him.

Rubenstein 2010

The most famous of these haunts is Sinatra's first Palm Springs residence, Twin Palms, a building of some architectural note designed by then up-and-coming architect E. Stewart Williams. A year earlier, The Palm Springs City Council had designated the house a Palm Springs Class 1 Historic Site, gifting its entrepreneurial new owner a public relations bonanza. The owner rents the house out for two thousand dollars a night and also makes it available, at a cost of course, for photo shoots, weddings, and the like. Whether due to him or the Palm Springs City Council, the house attracts a wealth of publicity; features in/on *Vogue* and CBS in 2011 and the Travel Channel, *Vanity Fair, The Telegraph*, and the German *Elle Magazine*, media outlets considerably more international and upmarket than the *Hudson Reporter* or *Newark Star Ledger* that publicize Hoboken's Sinatra and comparable in reach to those that publicize the Las Vegas Sinatra (http://www.sinatrahouse.com/category/media-and-press/).

Sinatra fans staying at Twin Palms can get a close-up view of the crack in the bathroom sink that, according to varied accounts, resulted from Sinatra throwing a champagne bottle at then-wife Ava Gardner or vice versa. Less well-heeled fans must content themselves with the other stops on the Palm Springs Sinatra heritage trail: his second residence, The Compound, marked by a brass plaque; Melvyn's Restaurant, where the singer used to scatter twenty dollar bills on the floor for the janitor to find in the morning; the Sinatra talking rock in Wolfson Park (Frank greets you at the push of a button); two churches where he and family members attended mass and finally his tombstone in Desert Memorial Park, inscribed "The best is yet to come" and frequently surrounded by fan tributes of miniature Jack Daniel's bottles. The *San Francisco Chronicle* detailed the stops on the tour but so did *The Los Angeles Times* (Nunes 2012), UK travel site, Travelbite (www.travelbite.co.uk), and UK newspaper *The Daily Mail* (Oswell 2010), attesting to the Palm Springs Sinatra's international appeal. Similar to the Las Vegas Sinatra, the Palm Springs Sinatra has global resonance but as a somewhat more salubrious figure associated with architectural good taste and generosity to the less fortunate, a church-going pillar of the community who serves as spokesman for a city amenity. Given that his Palm Springs residence spanned more than half a century, this Sinatra is not frozen in a particular period of the city's history. Nonetheless, the foregrounding of specific memories serves the interests of the Palm Springs Visitor Center, the Palm Springs City Council, and local businessmen such as the current owner of Twin Palms.

Earlier I argued that since memory is an aspect of hegemony, multiple and competing representations of historical figures circulate simultaneously: different representations originate from different players, serve different purposes, and appeal to audiences differently situated within the hegemonic system by virtue of their different economic and cultural capital. Following Erll and Rigney's (2009) advice to pay attention to social actors and organizations, this chapter has shown that each of the four locations discussed constructs a distinctive Sinatra. These distinctive Sinatras emerge first from the location's motivation to exploit this particular celebrity asset and second from the Sinatra-specific and general resources available for exploitation. Lacking heritage assets, Hoboken has most need of Sinatra but has the resources to construct only a "DIY" Sinatra that appeals primarily to local residents and the occasional visiting Sinatra fan. Los Angeles has both the necessary Sinatra-specific and general resources for exploitation, but with its abundance of celebrity resources lacks the motivation for intensive exploitation. Los Angeles's Sinatra, like Hoboken's, remains localized, although it may attract many more tourists. Las Vegas and Palm Springs both have the motivation to exploit their Sinatra assets and both have "Chamber of Commerce" Sinatras whose fame extends far beyond the city boundaries. It is Las Vegas, however, that like Hoboken enshrines the singer at the very heart of its history.

Notes

1 Garde-Hansen (2011) provides a useful guide to the memory studies literature. See also Erll and Rigney (2009).
2 Among these rare exceptions are Garde-Hansen's (2011) chapter on Madonna, Annette Kuhn's (2002) chapter on the Fred Astaire/Ginger Rogers' films, and Robert Burgoyne's (2006) essay on the Rock and Roll Hall of Fame and Museum. See also Baty (1995) and Rodman (1996) although neither of these authors engages with the memory studies literature.
3 For an excellent analysis of the multiple meanings of Sinatra and his films, see McNally (2008). For a somewhat acerbic take on Sinatra's cultural significance, see Rojek (2004).

4   Although most celebrity people may not have strong connections to particular geographic locations, celebrity texts do. This gives rise to the phenomenon of fan pilgrimage that has been investigated by several scholars. See Hills (2002), Brooker (2007a, 2007b), Couldry (2007), and Cunningham (2012). In addition to Sinatra, there may also be a few other celebrities with strong connections to places, as with Bruce Springsteen and New Jersey.

5   For a discussion of Sinatra's relationship to place focusing specifically on his music see Milburn (2012).

References

Note: All websites cited below were accessed 25/4/2013

Associated Press. 2001. "Vegas to Honor Frank Sinatra." *Billboard*. http://www.billboard.com/news/vegas-to-honor-frank-sinatra-1177682.story#/news/vegas-to-honor-frank-sinatra-1177682.story

Associated Press. 2008. "Frank Sinatra Stamp Goes on Sale." 13 May, http://today.msnbc.msn.com/id/24506692/ns/today-entertainment/t/frank-sinatra-stamp-goes-sale-may/#.UHvnBLT3Adk http://www.americanheritage.com/about/advertising

Baty, S. Paige. 1995. *American Monroe: The Making of a Body Politic*. Berkeley: University of California Press.

Baum, Gary. 2012. "Frank Sinatra's daughter on his newly dedicated booth at Beverly Hills Italian Restaurant La Dolce Vita." *The Hollywood Reporter*. 10 July, www.hollywoodreporter.com/news/frank-sinatra-la-dolce-vita-346687

Braun, Jenifer D. and McGlone, Peggy. 1998. "In Hoboken, Frank lives on—in midnight tales and memories." *Newark Star Ledger*. 15 May, http://www.nj.com/sinatra/ledger/index.ssf?/sinatra/stories/0515x.html

Brooker, Will. 2007a. "A sort of homecoming: Fan viewing and symbolic pilgrimage". In *Fandom: Identities and Communities in a Mediated World*, edited by Jonathan Gray, Cornel Sandvoss, and C. Lee Harrington. 139–148. New York: New York University Press, 149–164.

Brooker, Will. December 2007b. "Everywhere and nowhere: Vancouver, Fan pilgrimage and the urban imaginary." *International Journal of Cultural Studies 10*, no. 4, 423–444.

Bryant, Rebecca. 2012. "Dining review: A taste of old Hollywood." *Burbank Leader*. 21 July, http://www.burbankleader.com/entertainment/tn-blr-0722-dining-review-a-taste-of-old-hollywood,0,7753962.story

Burgoyne, Robert. 2006. "The rock and roll hall of fame and museum". In *Memory, history, nation: Contested pasts*, edited by Katharine Hodgkin and Susannah Radstone. 208–220. New Brunswick: Transaction Publishers.

Clarke, Norm. 2010. "You can still find Sinatra hangouts." *Las Vegas Review-Journal*. 12 December, http://www.lvrj.com/news/you-can-still-find-sinatra-hangouts-111745814.html

Contactmusic.com. 2012. "Nancy Sinatra rages at stepmother on dad Frank's death anniversary." 15 May, http://www.contactmusic.com/news/nancy-sinatra-rages-at-stepmother-on-dad-franks-death-anniversary_1328279

Couldry, Nick. 2007. "On the set of the sopranos: 'Inside' a fan's construction of nearness". In *Fandom: Identities and Communities in a Mediated World*, edited by Jonathan Gray, Cornel Sandvoss, and C. Lee Harrington. 139–148. New York: New York University Press.

Cue. 2012. "Jack Daniel's Sinatra select." http://www.thedieline.com/blog/2012/11/7/jack-daniels-sinatra-select.html

Cunningham, Douglas A. Ed. 2012. *The San Francisco of Alfred Hitchcock's Vertigo: Place, Pilgrimage and Commemoration*. Lanham, MD: The Scarecrow Press, Inc.

Erll, Astrid and Rigney, Ann. 2009. "Introduction". In *Media and Cultural Memory/Medien und kulturelle Erinnerung: Mediation, Remediation, and the Dynamics of Cultural Memory*, edited by Astrid Erll and Ann Rigney 1-11. Berlin: Walter de Gruyter.

Fusilli, Jim. 2011. *Narrows Gate*. Las Vegas, NV: Amazon Encore.

Garde-Hansen, Joanne. 2011. *Media and Memory*. Edinburgh: Edinburgh University Press.

Green, Steve. 2009. "Judge says phrase 'The Rat Pack' can't be trademarked." *Las Vegas Sun*. 2 October, http://www.lasvegassun.com/news/2009/oct/02/judge-says-phrase-rat-pack-cant-be-trademarked

Hack, Charles. 2012. "Frank Sinatra fan club to celebrate birthday, raise money for Sandy victims." *Jersey Journal*. 6 December, http://www.nj.com/hobokennow/index.ssf/2012/12/frank_sinatra_fan_club_to_cele.html

Hills, Matt. 2002. *Fan Cultures*. London: Routledge.

Hoboken Historical Museum. Frank Sinatra Tour. https://maps.google.com/maps/ms?ie=UTF8&oe=UTF8&msa=0&msid=112931872226853044970.00048f60399a6fe58e4a6

Hood, Abbey. 2010. "Frank Sinatra's Beverly Hills: A tour of His Favorite Haunts." *Beverly Hills Courier*. 4 June, http://www.bhcourier.com/article/Local_News/Local_News/Frank_Sinatras_Beverly_Hills_A_Tour_of_His_Favorite_Haunts/68202

Isherwood, Charles. 2013. "To heighten the art? Take it to Vegas". *The New York Times* 23 January.

Klara, Robert. April/May 2002. "The city at the nation's front door." *American Heritage* 53.

Koch, Ed. 1998. "Frank Sinatra dies at 82." *Las Vegas Sun*. 15 May, http://www.lasvegassun.com/news/1998/may/15/frank-sinatra-dies-at-82/

Kowsh, Kate. 2011. "Sinatra birthday bask held in Hoboken eatery." *The Jersey Journal*. 12 December, http://www.nj.com/journalnews/index.ssf/2011/12/sinatra_birthday_bash_held_in.html:2.

Kuhn, Annette. 2002. *Dreaming of Fred and Ginger: Cinema and Cultural Memory*. New York: New York University Press.

Levy, Shawn. 1999. *Rat Pack Confidential*. London: Fourth Estate Limited.

Los Angeles Times. "Keyword." http://articles.latimes.com/keyword/frank-sinatra/recent/5

Los Angeles Times. "Star Walk." http://projects.latimes.com/hollywood/star-walk/frank-sinatra/ *The Lure of Las Vegas*. http://www.bbc.co.uk/programmes/b00rf10t

Maurer, Mark. 2010. "Frank Sinatra's dwindling tourist turf in Hoboken." *The Jersey Journal*. 31 March. http://www.nj.com/hobokennow/index.ssf/2010/03/frank_sinatra_for_hoboken

McNally, Karen. 2008. *When Frankie Went to Hollywood: Frank Sinatra and American Male Identity*. Urbana and Chicago: University of Illinois Press.

Milburn, Kevin. 2012. *Geographies of Metropolitanism and Mobility in the Music of Frank Sinatra and The Blue Nile*. University of Nottingham: Unpublished PhD thesis.

Moses, Claire. 2012. "Mayor Proposes Plan to Redesign Frank Sinatra Drive." *The Hoboken Patch*. 16 October, http://hoboken.patch.com/articles/mayor-proposes-plan-to-redesign-frank-sinatra-drive

Nora, Pierre. Spring, 1989. "Between Memory and History: Les Lieux de Memoire." *Representations* 26, 7–24 Translated by Marc Roudebush.

Nora, Pierre. 1996–1998. *Realms of Memory: Rethinking the French Past*. 3 Volumes. Edited Lawrence Krtizman, translated by Arthur Goldhammer. New York: Columbia University Press.

Nunes, Maxine. 2012. "Palm Springs, His Way." *Los Angeles Times*. 12 October. http://articles.latimes.com/2012/oct/12/news/lat-palm-springs-his-way-20121012

Oswell, Paul. 2010. "Ol' Blue Eyes, architectural marvels and searing heat in the Palm Springs desert." *The Daily Mail*. 14 November. http://www.dailymail.co.uk/travel/article-1328789/Palm-Springs-Where-Frank-Sinatra-Marylin-Monroe-spent-weekends.html

Paskevich, Michael. No date. "Frank Sinatra." *Online Nevada Encyclopedia*. http://www.onlinenevada.org/frank_sinatra

Pearson, Roberta. 1999. "Custer loses again: The contestation over commodified public memory." *In Cultural Memory and the Construction of Identity*. edited by Dan Ben-Amos and Liliana Weissberg, 176–201. Detroit: Wayne State University Press.

Pittilla, Jane. 2011. "Montegrappa Icons series pays homage to Frank Sinatra." 26 October, http://www.moodiereport.com/document.php?c_id=1115&doc_id=29009

PR Newswire. 2008. "Frank Sinatra Back on Las Vegas Marquees." 14 May 2008, http://www.prnewswire.com/news-releases/frank-sinatra-back-on-las-vegas-marquees-may-14-57237827.html

Rodman, Gilbert B. 1996. *Elvis After Elvis: The Posthumous Career of a Living Legend*. London and New York: Routledge.

Rojek, Chris (2004). *Frank Sinatra*. Cambridge: Polity.

Rubenstein, Steve. 2010. "Doing Palm Springs Sinatra's way." *San Francisco Chronicle*. cit 17 January, http://www.sfgate.com/cgi-bin/article.cgi?f=/c/a/2010/01/15/TRUQ1B6DVU.DTL

Schwartz, Barry. 2009. *Abraham Lincoln in the Post-Heroic Era: History and Memory in Late Twentieth-Century America*. Chicago: University of Chicago Press.

Sinatra, Barbara. 2011. *Lady Blue Eyes*. London: Hutchison Sinatra House. http://www.sinatrahouse.com/category/media-and-press/

Skontra, Alan. 2011. "Sinatra idol contest crowns new crooner." *Hoboken Patch*. 17 June, http://hoboken.patch.com/articles/sinatra-idol-contest-crowns-new-crooner

The Rat Pack is Back, http://www.ratpackisback.com

The Rat Pack Tribute, http://www.ratpack.com

Travelbite, http://www.travelbite.co.uk/travel-partners/articles/adventure-holiday/visit-the-home-of-frank-sinatra-with-palm-springs-holidays-$1378797$1377632.htm

Trescott, Jacqueline. 2012. "The Smithsonian's Jazz Appreciation Month underscores activism and music." *The Washington Post* 2 April.

Visit Palm Springs. "Hollywood's playground." http://www.visitpalmsprings.com/page/hollywood's-playground/8183

Visit Palm Springs. Itinerary Ideas. http://www.visitpalmsprings.com/page/itinerary-ideas/14241

VNN Music. 2012. "Frank Sinatra Commemorated by Jack Daniels [*sic*] Whiskey." 25 October, http://www.music-news.com/shownews.asp?H=Frank-Sinatra-commemorated-by-Jack-Daniels-Whiskey&nItemID=58535

Weatherford, Mike. 1999. "Frank Sinatra: The swinger and the strip." *Las Vegas Review-Journal*. 7 February, http://www.lvrj.com/1st100/part2/sinatra.html

Woodard, Richard. 2012. "Jack Daniel's Releases Frank Sinatra Edition." 23 October, http://www.thespiritsbusiness.com/2012/10/jack-daniels-releases-frank-sinatra-edition/

Zinsli, Christopher. 2006. "Frank Sinatra's Hoboken: See the haunts of Ol' Blue Eyes on a self-guided walking tour of his hometown." *The Hudson Reporter*. 11 March, http://hudsonreporter.com/view/full_story/2407890/article-Frank-Sinatra-s-Hoboken-See-the-haunts-of-Ol--Blue-Eyes-on-a-self-guided-walking-tour-of-his-hometown00

Notes on Contributors

Craig Batty is Senior Lecturer in Creative and Professional Writing at RMIT University, Australia. He is a screenwriter, script consultant, and script editor, with experience in short film, feature film, television, and online drama. He is author of the books *Screenplays: How to Write and Sell Them* (Kamera Books, 2012) and *Movies That Move Us: Screenwriting and the Power of the Protagonist's Journey* (Palgrave Macmillan, 2011), and co-author of the books *The Creative Screenwriter: Exercises to Expand Your Craft* (Methuen, 2012), *Media Writing: A Practical Introduction* (Palgrave Macmillan, 2010), and *Writing for the Screen: Creative and Critical Approaches* (Palgrave Macmillan, 2008).

Peri Bradley is Lecturer in Media Theory at Bournemouth University. She has interests and publications in horror, reality TV, 1970s cinema and television, and LGBT culture. At present, she is working on an edited collection on Food on Screen and a monograph looking at makeover TV and the Carnivalesque—specifically UK TV personality Gok Wan.

Simon Grennan, who has been part of the transatlantic collaborative team Grennan and Sperandio since 1990, is acknowledged as a pioneer of interventionist, New Genre, and post-relational arts practice, in publishing, television, and social action projects. His partners have included Museum of Modern Art New York, Channel 4 Television, Museum of Fine Arts Boston, Sculpture Chicago, and MTV. Simon has been Director of Viewpoint Photography Gallery, Salford, and Director of Public Art Forum (now IXIA). He is Research Fellow in Fine Art at Chester University.

Shaun Kimber is Senior Lecturer in Media Theory in the Media School at Bournemouth University. He is the author of the book *Controversies: Henry: Portrait of a Serial Killer* (2011) published by Palgrave Macmillan. Recent book chapters include 'Zombies Are Us: The Living Dead as a Tool for Pedagogical Reflection' In: A. Whelan, C. Moore & R. Walker (2013) (eds) *Zombies in the Academy: Living Death in Higher Education* (Bristol: Intellect Press).

Marina Lambrou is Principal Lecturer in English Language and Communication at Kingston University, London. Her research interests include narratology;

stylistics, with a specialism in personal narratives, including narratives of trauma; pedagogical stylistics in an ELT context; language and media; and intercultural communication and ethnographic approaches to data collection. Marina is the co-author of *Language and Media* (Routledge, 2009) and joint-editor of *Contemporary Stylistics* (Continuum, 2007), which includes her chapter "Oral Accounts of Personal Experiences: When is a Narrative a Recount?" She is also editor of the "Narrative" Special Edition of *Language and Literature* (Sage, 2014).

Darren G. Lilleker is Director of the Centre for Public Communication and Senior Lecturer in the Media School, Bournemouth University. Dr Lilleker's expertise is in the professionalization and marketization of politics, in which he has published widely, including the textbooks *Key Concepts in Political Communication* (Sage, 2006) and *Political Campaigning, Elections and the Internet* (Routledge, 2011). He has co-edited *The Marketing of Political Parties* (MUP, 2006), *Voters or Consumers* (CSP, 2008), and *Political Marketing in Comparative Perspective* (MUP, 2005).

Roberta Pearson is Professor of Film and Television Studies at the University of Nottingham. She is the author, co-author, editor, and co-editor of numerous volumes, book chapters, and journal articles. She has a long-standing interest in the meanings of cultural icons ranging from Batman to Shakespeare, and Sinatra is the latest on the list.

Julia Round is Senior Lecturer in Communication in the Media School at Bournemouth University, and edits the academic journal *Studies in Comics* (Intellect Books). She has published and presented work internationally on cross-media adaptation, television and discourse analysis, the application of literary terminology to comics, the "graphic novel" redefinition, and the presence of gothic and fantastic motifs and themes in this medium. She is currently completing a monograph on comics and the literary gothic (provisionally entitled *The Gothic in Comics and Graphic Novels: A Critical Approach*, McFarland 2014). For further details, please visit www.juliaround.com.

Bronwen Thomas is Associate Professor and Convenor of the Narrative Research Group at Bournemouth University's Media School. She is the author of *Fictional Dialogue: Speech and Conversation in the Modern and Postmodern Novel* (University of Nebraska Press, 2012) and co-editor (with Ruth Page) of

New Narratives: Stories and Storytelling in the Digital Age (University of Nebraska Press, 2011). She has published widely on fanfiction and online communities, and is the author of *Narrative: The Basics* (Routledge, forthcoming).

Sue Thomas is an independent researcher and digital pioneer. In 1995 she founded the trAce Online Writing Centre, an early global online community, which ran for 10 years. From 2005 to 2013 she was Professor of New Media in the Institute of Creative Technologies at De Montfort University, where she researched biophilia, social media, transliteracy, transdisciplinarity, and future foresight. Her books include *Technobiophilia: nature and cyberspace* (2013); *Correspondence* (1992), short-listed for the Arthur C. Clarke Award for Best Science Fiction Novel; and *Hello World: travels in virtuality* (2004), a travelogue/memoir of life online. She lives in Bournemouth, Dorset, and maintains a virtual presence at www.suethomas.net.

Index